# JANE WYMAN

## The Actress and the Woman

LAWRENCE J. QUIRK

# JANE WYMAN

## The Actress and the Woman

### AN ILLUSTRATED BIOGRAPHY

DEMBNER BOOKS · NEW YORK

Dembner Books
Published by Red Dembner Enterprises Corp., 80 Eighth Avenue, New
York, N.Y. 10011
Distributed by W. W. Norton & Company, Inc., 500 Fifth Avenue, New
York, N.Y. 10110

Library of Congress Cataloging in Publication Data

Quirk, Lawrence J.
    Jane Wyman, the actress and the woman.

    Includes index.
    1.  Wyman, Jane, 1914–     .     2.  Moving-picture
actors and actresses—United States—Biography.
I.  Title.
PN2287.W8Q57      1986          791.43′028′0924   [B]          85-25284
ISBN 0-934878-68-4

All photographs in this book are from private collections.

For Doug McClelland

# Books by Lawrence J. Quirk

THE FILMS OF JOAN CRAWFORD
ROBERT FRANCIS KENNEDY
THE FILMS OF INGRID BERGMAN
THE FILMS OF PAUL NEWMAN
THE FILMS OF FREDRIC MARCH
*PHOTOPLAY MAGAZINE* ANTHOLOGY (wrote Foreword)
THE FILMS OF WILLIAM HOLDEN
THE GREAT ROMANTIC FILMS
THE FILMS OF ROBERT TAYLOR
SOME LOVELY IMAGE (a novel)
THE FILMS OF RONALD COLMAN
THE FILMS OF WARREN BEATTY
THE FILMS OF MYRNA LOY
THE FILMS OF GLORIA SWANSON
CLAUDETTE COLBERT: AN ILLUSTRATED BIOGRAPHY
LAUREN BACALL: HER FILMS AND CAREER
BETTE DAVIS: HER FILMS AND CAREER (update 1965–1985)

C O N T E N T S

ACKNOWLEDGMENTS

With deep appreciation to my editor, Therese Eiben, and my publisher, S. Arthur Dembner. And with thanks to those living and dead, those named throughout this book and those who declined to be named, who shared their memories of Miss Jane Wyman with me over the many years I collected material on her, in New York, Hollywood, and abroad.

My special thanks to Doug McClelland, to whom this book is dedicated, who lent me many valuable photographs, clippings, and other material on Jane Wyman. Also to Douglas Whitney, who lent me many handsome Wyman photographs.

Also thanks to Ernest D. Burns of Cinemabilia, New York; Mark Ricci and The Memory Shop, New York; Dorothy Swerdlove and Dr. Rod Bladel of the Billy Rose Theatre and Film Collection, New York Public Library at Lincoln Center, and their able assistants; Mary Corliss of the Museum of Modern Art Photo Archives; Jerry Ohlinger's Movie Material Store, New York; the staff of the Margaret Herrick Library of the Academy of Motion Picture Arts and Sciences, Hollywood; and the James R. Quirk Memorial Film Symposium and Research Center, New York.

And DeWitt Bodeen, Sam Gill, Ben Carbonetto, Lou Valentino, Bill Chapman, Andy Achsen; The British Film Institute, London; Bob Board, Robert Cosenza, Peter Thompson, Bob Harman, Philip Kendall, Kirk Crivello, John Cocchi, and Romano Tozzi.

Also thanks to James E. Runyan, William Schoell, Michael Ritzer, Arthur Tower, Don Koll, John A. Guzman, Jim McGowan, George Geltzer, and Albert B. Manski. And with appreciation also to Warner Bros., MGM-UA, Universal, RKO-General, Paramount, Columbia, Twentieth Century-Fox, Walt Disney Productions, NBC-TV, CBS-TV, and ABC-TV, the companies that control them, and their personnel.

# 1

## Very Much Her Own Woman

Jane Wyman learned the harsh lessons of self-sufficiency—and became very much her own woman over seventy-two years—the hard way. In the year that I first met her—1948—she had just undergone two testings of her mettle, one personal and one professional, and had survived both—one resiliently and one triumphantly. That fall she had come to Boston on a personal appearance tour to promote *Johnny Belinda*. She was a beautiful young star of thirty-four, and I was a young Boston reporter of twenty-five sent to interview her. Even now, thirty-eight years later, I can vividly recall the energy, the vibrancy, the sheer strength of personality that she generated that day.

She was enormously proud of the picture that had just opened and infinitely pleased that she had, in her honestly humble opinion, tried to summon her truest instincts and strongest powers to, hopefully, do justice to what she described to me at our first meeting as "the role of my career." And so it proved to be, winning her an Academy Award and a secure and permanent place among Hollywood's great starring legends. But 1948 was also the year that her marriage to Ronald Reagan broke up. She may have felt like the Catholic devotee who had prayed to the quixotic Saint Rita, famous in legend for taking something away for anything she granted. Jane Wyman had reached the peak of stardom—and had lost her husband.

"[*Johnny Belinda*] was the most difficult assignment I ever had, but the most rewarding," she told me. "I knew when I read the script that it would be the role of a lifetime, and I felt humble—and deeply honored—to be taking on so richly conceived and technically demanding a characterization—as a deaf mute who learns the fullness of womanhood the hard way."

Her eyes grew meditative. "There were so few parts along the way that I could really get my teeth into, prior to this. *The Yearling*, for one. And to be honest, I hadn't felt that real stardom might ever come—and now so many people have been kind enough to tell me that it has." She added, "Of course, so much depends on the pictures I get from now on. There have been false starts—and false hopes—before. This new 'stardom' may be—for all I know—a flash in the pan, a quick cometlike thing—but this picture, *Johnny Belinda*, will, I feel, endure. . . ."

And so has her stardom endured—through seventy-odd films and numerous television shows—over a career that runs fifty-four years, from the day in 1932 when she found herself, age eighteen, in the chorus of the Eddie Cantor film musical *The Kid From Spain* until now.

The acclaimed star of the long-running television series *Falcon Crest*, Jane Wyman can look back on a varied, buoyant career in which she has demonstrated sterling dramatic talents, sharp comedy skills, and a singing-and-dancing expertise that in later years came as a happy surprise to audiences and co-workers who did not know of her early thorough musical training. Over the years there have been other Academy nominations following the Oscar she won for *Johnny Belinda*. But her private life was to be a synthesis of sadness and joy. There were five marriages, two children, a fair share of abortive, sometimes heartbreaking love affairs, and a host of friends, well-wishers, admiring career associates, and just-plain fans who have never ceased to dote on her.

That day in 1948 I noted a certain haunted sadness in her eyes. At times, for all her warmth and cordiality, there was a distracted, harried look about her. She seemed tense and nervous, and when I broached personal issues, such as her home and her two small children, she came close to tears. But whatever her private tensions and sorrows on that occasion, she was kind, witty, down-to-earth, and invited me to look her up when I next came to Hollywood. "This tour keeps me exhausted and keyed-up at the same time," she said. "I do hope I'm giving you what you want. Whatever's missing, I'll make up at our next interview, be sure."

Actually she gave me quite a lot that day. I heard about small Maureen, then seven, and Michael, then three, and how she missed them and couldn't wait to get back to them. I heard about her film plans, her ideas on screen acting, her meticulous preparation before she went on tours. She talked about fashion ("dress for yourself, as an individual"), art ("it has to excite *me*; I am not concerned with how it affects others"), and music ("I was lucky to be born with a good ear, a good sense of rhythm").

But there was one subject on which she remained adamantly silent: Ronald Reagan. I felt that she was consciously side-stepping any mention of him, and I did not press it, especially after I witnessed her psychic withdrawal whenever our talk touched even peripherally on him. Even in later years, long after both had remarried, I always found her references to him respectfully terse, admiringly impersonal, strangely vague. She would imply, to me as to so many other reporters, that she thought in-depth, personalized discussion of a former mate was in poor taste. I respected and admired her all the more for that.

On her career, however, I found her always voluble. She had had one of the slowest and most tortuous ascents to stardom on record. From 1932 to 1936, ages eighteen to twenty-two, she had languished as a practically invisible chorus girl in one film musical after another. Occasionally she won a bit part, but even that sometimes landed uncere-

moniously on the cutting-room floor. From 1936 to 1939, as a Warner Bros. contract player, she plodded along with whatever valiant good grace she could summon, as a distinctly also-ran wisecracking blonde and second lead in numerous B films. This type of character was there to console the heroine or provide needed comic relief when the romantic situations got too heavy. When she achieved a lead in a second-rate film, she found herself the hapless gal-along-for-the-ride who told Joe E. Brown he had said a mouthful or convinced pudgy fudge-face Frank McHugh that he was attractive, at least to her. The B movies in which she languished were popular staples of the 1930s, thrown in to round out a three-hour program, along with the main feature, newsreels, and shorts. They left the customer feeling that the twenty-five or fifty cents he carefully dispensed in that Depression era was well-spent, for quantity if not quality. And the B's also provided a fine training ground for young actors who were still unsure of themselves.

During the boom War Years—1940 to 1945—when it seemed that everyone went to the movies for escape from brutal real-life tensions and defense-plant work schedules, Wyman wangled increasingly larger parts. But they did not amount to anything she could really get her teeth into. In this period she served as a pretty, well-dressed, vivacious, reliable, but only cursorily noted, leading lady to such as Edward G. Robinson, Jack Carson, and Kay Kyser. In these she would get fatherly advice from Robinson, tell Jack Carson what a wonderful guy he was, or take the audience's attention off the fact that Kyser was a swinging musician but a lame actor.

And then at age thirty-one in 1945 she demonstrated, to the surprise of many, startlingly dramatic expertise as Ray Milland's girlfriend in the harrowing study of an alcoholic, *The Lost Weekend*. The next year she electrified audiences as the drably authoritative mother in *The Yearling*, played without makeup as a realistic depiction of a Florida backwoods woman. For this she got her first Academy Award nomination. Then, after co-starring with Dennis Morgan in a blah Western, *Cheyenne*, and with James Stewart in a near-miss study of a small community in crisis, *Magic Town*, she blossomed at last, at age thirty-four, into the moving, eloquent, major-star-calibre actress so compellingly on display in *Johnny Belinda*.

In 1949 a couple of so-so comedies followed for Warner Bros.—*A Kiss in the Dark* and *The Lady*

As a chorus girl, right, in *King of Burlesque* (1935).

Jane Wyman, 1940.

*Takes a Sailor.* Then the quality of her films improved dramatically. She played for Alfred Hitchcock a woman of some ambivalence in *Stage Fright* and went on to portray one of Tennessee Williams's most unforgettable characters, the sensitive Laura who was sliding inexorably into madness, in *The Glass Menagerie.* By 1951, age thirty-seven, she had truly metamorphosed into a First Lady of the screen as the selfless governess who devoted her entire life to children. For this she won yet another Academy Award nomination for *The Blue Veil.*

During the early and middle 1950s, Jane Wyman, a star in full bloom, alternated sparkling comedy performances such as in *Let's Do It Again* with moving dramatic portrayals such as in *So Big, Magnificent Obsession,* and *All That Heaven Allows.* By 1955 she was shifting her activities to television, where she won a whole new order of success with *Jane Wyman's Fireside Theatre* and other shows that she hosted and in which she often appeared.

Alternating movies with television appearances, she continued into the 1960s and 1970s as a graciously maturing character star whom viewers always welcomed. Now in the mid-1980s, two years past the Biblical three-score-and-ten average lifetime, she continues in *Falcon Crest* as one of television's major personalities.

As I interviewed her over the years, on movie and television sets in Hollywood, I noted her philosophical and cultural growth. "I play my life day by day," she told me in 1960. "What's important is the present. I know it's some kind of cliché, but the past is gone and can never be recovered, and the future will come when it will come—and maybe it will never come. How you feel inwardly, about yourself, life, other people, is what counts. I am grateful for each day, and assume its burdens and its joys with

Jane Wyman, 1945.

Author Lawrence J. Quirk interviews Jane Wyman in Boston during her national *Johnny Belinda* tour, 1948.

equal readiness—for the burdens toughen, challenge, and mature one and the joys give the spirit rest and refreshment."

In 1966 she told me, "Too many people hate to see the wrinkles and bulges come, and they make a big hassle out of the loss of youth. Each time has its own rewards and its own problems. I am happy with myself just now [she was then fifty-two] and in some ways I am happier than I was in youth. Youth isn't all it's cracked up to be—too much uncertainty, struggle, competitiveness, all kinds of tensions and insecurities. I've worked toward balance and serenity, relatively anyway, for I'm human and have my mood swings like anyone else."

She has always been generous and supportive toward fellow-performers, helping to assure that

they are shown to maximum advantage in their scenes with her. One example was the young Rock Hudson, who at twenty-eight was insecure about his acting abilities. Rock told me years later that during the shooting on their first picture together, *Magnificent Obsession* in 1954, she pumped into him the needed adrenalin of self-confidence, pointed out his plusses as a performer, and helped him minimize his minuses. From that picture he emerged a star.

"I know what it is to struggle and pray for recognition or some kind of appreciation," she told me, "and in my own small way I like to help other people to get it. Why? Because it gives me a good feeling, that's why. So I guess it's actually a kind of selfishness."

People who worked with her swore by her, all the

8

way from venerable character actor Donald Crisp and co-star Van Johnson to supporting players like Anne Seymour, who recalled her concern and her thoughtfulness. Wyman worked over the years with the biggest male stars: Cary Grant, Jimmy Stewart, Ray Milland, Gregory Peck, David Niven, Kirk Douglas, Charlton Heston, Bing Crosby, Fred MacMurray, and Bob Hope, among others. All of them spoke of her with admiration, respect, and genuine fondness. The many people I have interviewed over the years who had known her as friend and co-worker were overwhelmingly pro-Jane. She seems to have achieved, over those fifty-four years in show business, a popularity with associates that rivals that of her good friend, Barbara Stanwyck, always one of the most beloved of stars.

Jane Wyman, as the fullness of time has revealed, has shown herself a major artist in her chosen field. But her deepest triumph has been as a human being—one of the finest and truest.

# 2

## "Essentially Alone . . ."
### 1914–1936

Jane Wyman once said, "I have always felt that I was essentially alone at the beginning of my life—and that I will be essentially alone at the end of it." Her loner status until she was twenty-two is certainly accentuated by everything she did and by everything she thought. She became an individual, uncompromised by the actions and beliefs of her peers. Her unique professional and personal life attests to an inner strength that evolved long before she arrived in Hollywood.

She was born in Saint Joseph, Missouri, on January 4, 1914. For some reason known only to herself, she would insist in later years that the date was January 5. (The record indicates January 4.) She was christened Sarah Jane Fulks. Born when her parents were well into their middle years, she had a much older brother and sister, who were teenagers when she was born. Very little is known of them, except that they were both college-educated. Her sister, Elsie, and her brother, Richard, Jr., later moved to Los Angeles and became a doctor. Both siblings were living in the Hollywood area by the time Sarah Jane reached her teens.

A veil of mystery hangs over her entire family. Richard D. Fulks, her father, was prominent in the affairs of Saint Joseph, having held such offices as County Collector and Chief of Detectives. (Later, Warner Bros. publicity department inflated his post to that of Saint Joseph's mayor, which Wyman was later to deny.) Her German-born mother, Emma Reise, had come to America from Saarbrücken as a young girl. Her parents, especially her father, seem to

have been remote figures in her early life, and because of their tremendous age difference, and the fact that they left Missouri so early in her life, the same seems true of her brother and sister.

At times, so isolated and alone did she feel, she wondered if she were not perhaps adopted. The record indicates that she was not. She did feel that her parents did not particularly welcome her advent, and that her conception might have been an accident.

A continued reticence about her family, throughout her young adulthood, combined with the overly inventive releases put out by the Warner Bros. publicity department, has thrown a veil over her early life that has persisted to this day. On rare occasions, and then only when pressed, she has admitted her childhood was quite unhappy, recalling her parents as extremely strict, humorless, and inflexible. Her father seems to have been a man of a balefully compulsive and conformist nature. His relentless self-drive eventually undermined his health. When he became semi-invalided and housebound, the home atmosphere became even more grim.

Despite the chilly, withdrawn approach her parents adopted toward her, they insisted on high standards, and she remembers the sense of keen inferiority it gave her, as she did not feel she could ever meet their expectations. But the tyranically hard-riding style her parents took toward their December child undoubtedly inspired her initial determination to make the most of her abilities, just to

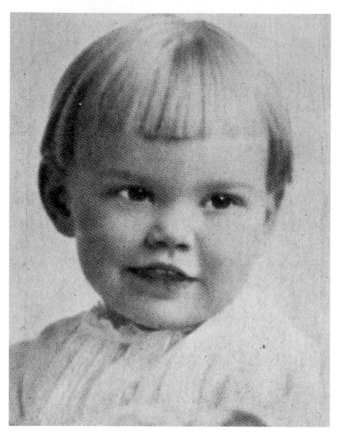

Jane Wyman at age 3, 1917.

show them. Jane Wyman's memories of that early life in Saint Joseph, which became public in reticently doled out bits and pieces after she became famous, seem tinged with bitterness, ruefulness, and sad regrets—"either because I never felt it was humanly possible to please them completely or because I resented their unrealistic demands."

Wyman always was to remember her extreme shyness as a child. She told Norman Vincent Peale's *Guidepost Magazine* in 1964, "Shyness is not a small problem; it can cripple the whole personality. It crippled mine for many years. As a child, my only solution to the problem of shyness was to hide, to make myself as small and insignificant as possible. All through grade school I was a well-mannered little shadow who never spoke above a whisper."

She later recalled one incident that hurt her deeply as a child of eight. She overheard a neighbor woman comment: "With that turned-up nose and those bug-eyes, no one will ever take that child seriously." Nor did her parents prove helpful. They dressed her in drab, utilitarian clothes, devoid of any

suggestion of personality, style, or color. Her hair was kept straight. Her stockings were drab cotton. Bows or furbelows of any kind were *verboten*.

The Fulks house was a Victorian gingerbread horror, its furnishings lank and forlorn. Sarah Jane's longing for pretty dresses, attractive hairdos, sleek grooming, and bright, cheerful surroundings became a prevailing childhood obsession. The streets of Saint Joseph weren't any more cheerful. Everything was stolid, Germanic, functional; the pursuits of commerce, Midwest-style, reigned. There was little culture; indeed, culture was held in suspicion.

One bright spot in this welter of drab mediocrity was Dad Prinz's dancing school. The sounds of merriment and busy feet that emanated from his establishment made many townspeople glower. But, Sarah Jane was attracted to those sounds. It cost fifty cents to enter a class (which was a lot of money in those days). Shy as she was, she knew, deep down, that she needed room to *breathe*, somewhere, somehow. She would breathe or she would die.

When she first broached the subject of dancing school to her mother, the outwardly stolid Emma resisted. Then, because of the child's extreme withdrawal, socially, she reluctantly agreed, feeling that it might cure her "sick bashfulness" and bring her out of her shell. Wyman idolized "Dad" Prinz, as the children called him, on sight. "He was the most understanding man I had ever met, and I longed to tell him so. I never did," she later recalled. In ballet class, to which she was at first assigned, she "haunted the corners of the room" at first, hoping no one would see her. The very thought of performing in front of others made her wilt with fear.

But "Dad" Prinz, who understood "loner" children and the creativity that their shyness often concealed, gradually brought her out of her shell. He held a theory that introspective people were often artistic people, and that if they directed their energies aggressively outward, they were setting a psychological pattern for later success. Warmed by his interest, Sarah Jane began to bloom.

At home the gloomy father had taken to his bed. The sadness rarely left her mother's face. "Dancing is foolishness" was her usual answer to nosy neighbor's inquiries about her girl's new interest. Then Sarah Jane, emboldened by her growing dancing skills, tried another tack. She appealed to Emma's maternal pride. Emma, the authoress of Sarah Jane's very being, saw her daughter as a permanent furtherance of Emma's physical self. She consented to visit the dancing school.

Here Emma, to her surprise, found another Sarah Jane, happy, laughing, lithe, responsive to "Dad" Prinz's every suggestion, turning outward toward the other youngsters. This contrasted dramatically with what had gone before—the lack of company in the grim family home, the outlawing of lively young playmates (had Sarah Jane been able to find any) because of fears they would irritate the ailing father. She had been so set apart from her peers. She was to tell a writer years later of the wonder she felt when she happened to come upon another child's mother in the neighborhood, a young woman so different from the dour townspeople about her, gaily skipping rope with her daughter.

Whatever the young Jane Wyman's love-hate feelings for Saint Joseph, she was not to forget it. When she began to paint, in adulthood, she did one of her best canvasses with her childhood church as a subject, an old-fashioned church with tall steeples, swathed in winter snows. At "Dad" Prinz's dancing school, Emma Reise discovered that her child could momentarily displace all the restrictions imposed on Jane by their harsh, puritanical community.

Emma was impressed. As Prinz had earlier, she sensed talent in Sarah Jane, something, perhaps, out of the ordinary. Thawing memories of long-ago Germany, richly melodious music, gay waltzes, human variety, atmospheric color, came back to this mother who had grown so frozen in Philistine Saint Joseph. It seemed that there was more to Emma Reise Fulks than at first met the eye. Outwardly a woman of stolid Germanicisms and a forbidding harshness that amounted to the puritanical, Emma, it appears, had inwardly nurtured a yen for the glamour and excitement of show business. Her prosaic marriage to a dull, unimaginative man, now sliding inexorably into psychosomatically induced disease, and the demanding tasks of a motherhood extended over decades, had stifled any creative urges in herself; she seems to have suddenly shifted gears and begun to project those youthful dreams, with growing obsessiveness, onto little Sarah Jane.

The surprised "Dad" Prinz shortly found himself being urged by Emma to polish up Sarah Jane's singing and dancing skills. He gave her his special attention. Her steps grew ever more graceful, her ways with a song ever more winning in a childish way. It was 1922 then and she was eight years old.

Emma made a decision. Her grown son and daughter were now making new lives for themselves in the booming movie capital of Los Angeles. They had "had it" with the starchy stultifications of Saint Joe long since. She had been promising to visit them, and one day the surprised little eight-year-old—recaparisoned in crisp white dresses and childishly becoming hairdos replete with curls and bows—found herself plunked down in 1922 Hollywood as an aspiring child performer.

Old Fulks, languishing in his bed, was told that Emma and Jane needed a change. Emma's new-found resolve to make her daughter a movie actress surprised the prosaic-minded son and daughter. The former ugly-duckling, now-swannish Jane was taken around to an endless succession of movie people—agents, producers, casting directors, anyone who could be inveigled into watching the child "for just five minutes."

"I vividly remember the Hollywood of the early 1920s," Wyman later said. "By the time I landed there, I had blossomed into being a blonde-cute type of the kind they placed a premium on in 1922, with big eyes and curly hair, and Jackie Coogan was the child star all kids emulated and wanted to outshine—at least all kids who wanted show business careers. I know my mother wanted that for me—probably to partially compensate for what she considered decades of drabness in her own life—but I was just a kid, and I wasn't sure what I wanted."

"Emma even in 1922 sensed that Sarah Jane would make a movie star," one of Wyman's intimates later commented wryly, "and considering she was only eight, that woman must have had a serviceable crystal ball among her effects."

But soon mother and daughter ran out of money, and brother and sister couldn't afford to keep them in Hollywood. The studios had proven thoroughly unresponsive to Sarah Jane's childish charms; their casting offices were awash in a sea of pretty, big-eyed, blondish kids. So it was back to Saint Joe, and the semi-invalid father whose bleak silences proceeded to convey his suspicions and disapproval.

Seven years passed in Saint Joseph, during which Sarah Jane, growing ever prettier and more confident, entered her teen years. In high school she began attracting boys, but she found them stodgy, cloddish types, destined for gas stations and bank-teller posts. Each year saw old R.D. growing more ill, Emma more frustrated and restless, and Sarah Jane more eager for the great outside world, of which, at eight, she had had but a mere taste. She remembered that as of 1928, age fourteen, "[My mother and I] were both bored to death with that town—it was oppressive, straight-laced, hypocritical."

Then in 1929, when Sarah Jane was fifteen, her father died. She does not seem to have grieved. "We were never close," was her later cryptic reaction to the fact of his decease. Mother and daughter agreed that there was now nothing to keep them in a place they had come to despise. Again they joined the older children in Hollywood.

It was no longer the Hollywood of the silent days. The talkie boom had hit full-force, and stars with poor speech found themselves on the street, while a whole new crop of pear-shaped-tone stage actors and actresses invaded the studios. The movies now attracted, as well, such comedians as the Marx Brothers, fresh from Broadway, who proceeded to make their stage hits into movies. There was a new spirit in the air. Emma Fulks' hopes for her daughter were renewed. This time the mother was patient— and systematic. She rationed their savings carefully, enrolled Jane in Los Angeles High School, bought her clothes as becoming as their careful budget allowed, kept her at the singing and dancing lessons, and bombarded the studios with pictures of her. But it was slow going.

The Jane of 1930 and 1931 began to retreat into the shell of her earlier years. She found Los Angeles big and frightening; the boys seemed more predatory, the pace bewilderingly fast, the atmosphere cold-hearted. Years later she recalled her seventeen-year-old high-school self circa 1931: "Now a new and more threatening dimension had been added to life outside the big city high school walls. Dating. It seemed to me that on some prearranged signal, every boy and girl in school paired off. Every girl, that is, except me. I don't know whether I could have had dates or not; it simply never occurred to me to try. Hadn't I been told many times that I was not pretty? I lugged home piles of books every night and disappeared into them."

However in 1931 it appeared that seventeen-year-old Jane fell in love. The shadowy, much-debated, much-denied, much-covered-up young Eugene Wyman entered her life. From what is speculated about him, he was a fellow student in high school who took a special interest in her and brought her out of her shell. He was about her own age. The first person

to confirm this story of Eugene Wyman was Ruth Waterbury, an old associate of mine who had started as a feature writer in the 1920s for my uncle James R. Quirk's then eminent *Photoplay Magazine*. Whatever there was to know about the stars' pasts, Ruth knew it, and when Wyman later began to be better known, she did the first fan magazine pieces on her. As late as 1957, Nell Blythe in *Movie Life* described the Wyman encounter in these terms: "Still in her teens, she impulsively entered marriage. Jane never talks about that first heartbreak, but in less than a month she knew it was a terrible mistake and the marriage was dissolved."

There has been much speculation over the years about Eugene Wyman. Had that actually been his name? Had he ever existed? Ruth Waterbury always insisted to me that he had indeed, and that that had been his name. Wyman herself adamantly dismissed mention of him. Her friends were always to wonder why she simply didn't acknowledge him as an early mistake and casually leave him on the record. Had the circumstances surrounding her love for, and brief marriage to, him been too painful to recall? The Eugene Wyman legend baffled Jane-watchers in the fan press as late as 1939, when the death of an Ernest Wyman was reported, and he was called Jane's stepfather. Had Emma ever remarried? Was *Ernest* Wyman actually young *Eugene* Wyman? Like so much that is speculative about Jane's early life, complicated as it was by overly imaginative publicity releases from the studio, the matter remains in limbo. People who knew her well in later years, like actress Joy Hodges, have been willing to talk rather freely about the young Jane Wyman they knew, but clam up at mention of Eugene Wyman. Yet when she finally adopted a permanent stage name, the name Sarah Jane Fulks chose was Jane Wyman.

In 1932, when Wyman was eighteen, she made her film debut. Hollywood was reaching the peak of its talkie period, with the techniques of sound showing a new fluidity. Pretty girls were all over town, pushing and shoving for the breaks. It wasn't enough to be good-looking; Hollywood was full of good-looking people. To get one's head above the crowd, one had to have something extra, talent, drive, charisma. If you had a combination of these, you were on your way; if you didn't, you ended up a party girl, or a waitress.

There was one other element that played a crucial role in success: a good connection. If you knew someone you used him for a break; if you didn't know that right someone, you were behind the proverbial eight ball. Emma and Jane did know someone: Leroy Prinz, the son of Wyman's old dancing teacher. And they went to see him.

Jane had left high school and was taking whatever jobs she could find. For reasons never fully explicated, her siblings and her mother had become totally impoverished and could not help her. The Prinz connection was her only hope.

Prinz was impressed with what he saw. He was then the choreographer for various films in progress, including Eddie Cantor's Samuel Goldwyn film, *The Kid from Spain*, a lavish musical. Prinz discovered that Jane had a good rhythm sense. As long as she had that, he told her, he could teach her the rest. He also saw other qualities in Wyman that arrested his attention and soon was coaching her in dancing and singing. LeRoy Prinz got Wyman her first job in the chorus of *The Kid from Spain*.

Also in the chorus were Betty Grable and Paulette Goddard. They were spunky, ambitious girls, and their own rises were to be slow but sure. Prinz personally supervised Wyman's debut, made sure she was made up and dressed becomingly, and spotted her favorably in the chorus. The musicals of the time were elaborate affairs, and the dance numbers were soon to be brought to their peak by the inventive Busby Berkeley, who arranged the girls in geometrical patterns, with the camera spotted above. While primarily a dance coach, LeRoy Prinz also had a good sense of composition, which he used to telling effect in the pictures to which he was assigned.

Wyman, who had been laboring under a return of her original shyness, faced as she was by so much peer pulchritude and talent, later told *Guidepost Magazine* about her burgeoning chorus girl career: "It was work when the family badly needed the money, but for a girl who had grown up in terror of being looked at, it was also agony. Then I made a discovery: a good shield for shyness is a bold exterior. Did my heart turn over when the man with the megaphone bellowed out my name? Were all the other dancers prettier? Never mind. I covered up by becoming the cockiest of all, by talking the loudest, laughing the longest, and wearing the curliest, most blatantly false eyelashes in Hollywood."

A fellow chorus girl had advised her to wash her face to get rid of the fancy makeup that she had adopted. She came to realize that in her anxiety to get ahead, to look striking, she had made herself up to look garish, artificial—even cheap. Encouraged to rely on her natural beauty, she relished, as she later recalled, the congratulations of a stranger who complimented her on her new, wholesomely pretty appearance. "For me, it was the heavens parting. Could he have meant that I looked great? It was the first hint that I had that I could be myself without the sky falling in. But the insight went only skin-deep."

Why and how did a girl so intrinsically shy and self-conscious make her way in the competitive chorus lines of 1932 and 1933? Her mother, of course, was still pushing her; there were money pressures; she found part-time jobs unendurable in their drabness; she had an instinctive feel for the escapist romance of show business—and in time, she was to find that she could *escape* from the intolerable world about her by immersing herself in a dream of romance and beauty that the lavish surroundings and beautiful costumes on sets encouraged. Later she would find, in acting, that escape many shy people have found: *they could become someone else*, at last, if only for the duration of a dance or a role; someone other than the self they despised or deprecated.

The "tough, smart little shell" also helped in the escape from reality, a reality that had included a disillusioning real-life marriage. It felt good to live a harmless, glamorous "sham existence" for a while.

In later years the publicity department at Warners threw out many contradictory signals as to just what happened to Wyman in the 1932 through 1935 period. There were many false reports. Such publications as *Current Biography* and *Films in Review*, when they got around to doing her life story, had her going back and forth between Missouri and California. There were stories that she had studied music briefly at the University of Missouri, but failed to last the semester.

Other reports had her taking the name Jane Durrell while she sang on radio. An even more outlandish report had her touring the Midwest and South as a "blues singer," no less, and knocking around in tank towns north, south, east, and west.

All of these tales are now considered more or less apocryphal, and it is now believed that in that entire 1932 through 1935 thirty-six–month span she stayed put in Hollywood making do as best she could, gradually freeing herself from her impoverished, but

Jane Wyman (bottom right) at age 18 in the chorus of *The Kid From Spain* (1932). Paulette Goddard is fourth from the bottom. Lucille Ball is second from top.

still strictly supervisory, family and striking out on her own.

An intimate was to say of her later: "That time when she was nineteen, twenty, or so—well, I think she got badly kicked around; she was initially quite romantic and trusting about men, and her looks and personality attracted some wrong-o types who left her rather disillusioned. It toughened her, no doubt about that. By her twenty-first birthday she was a hardboiled show girl who took no nonsense from anyone and who had earned a college degree in *men* and *life*."

During this period, she made the casting rounds persistently, rebuffing dozens of men who sought to exploit her sexually. She worked as a model, a switchboard operator, a waitress, a manicurist, a secretary—anything she could scare up. "I wasn't going the primrose route," she later said. "I had had enough of being manipulated and exploited by men for the wrong reasons; that kind of life led nowhere but *down*, and I wasn't having anymore of it."

She was to tell a friend, "At twenty all I wanted was to earn my own rent and food, come home at night, put up my feet, and know I was beholden to no one and could come and go as I pleased." The exact role played by the remaining members of her fam-

18

ily—the ever-more-shadowy mother and siblings—in this hard-luck period remains as speculative as is so much else about that time in her life. According to Jerry Asher, a friend, she had become estranged from them.

Asher, a fan magazine writer, told me many years later: "That period, 1932 through 1935, was very rough for her. There was the memory of a love that had led—briefly—to marriage and that had gone sour in weeks—but had left her with a memory, however brief, of what a man and a woman could conceivably mean to one another in a relationship surpassing the merely physical. The physical was pushed on her by one insensitive man after another, but being an artist . . . Janie always had a place reserved in her heart for something *better*—and even though that 'something better,' sadly enough, was not to come for years yet, when it *did* come, Janie was ready for it—long since ready. . . ."

Meanwhile she continued to do bits and chorus-girl stints in various movies, such as the Joe E. Brown starrer *Elmer the Great* in 1933. Her friend LeRoy Prinz got her into the chorus of a 1934 Paramount film directed by Norman Taurog, *College Rhythm*. She had continued to work hard on her dancing and singing, and Prinz took note of her steady improvement. One time she asked him about her possibilities as an actress. Prinz was frank with her. "Your speaking voice is poorly pitched and unsteady," he told her, "and it doesn't match your face." Wyman began studying diction and stage comportment at once. She worked hard. Around the sets, her distinctive face, uniquely heart-shaped, earned her the name of "Dog-Puss," which she took good-naturedly—or anyway, pretended to.

Eventually a friend introduced her to actor William Demarest, who was then moonlighting as an agent. Demarest was later to recall: "There was something about that girl—I couldn't put my finger on it—that made me want her to make it. But was she a jumpy one! She couldn't stand any man even touching her! Help her down the steps—just a light touch on her arm—and she'd jump sky-high! I guess she got some rough treatment before I met her." Demarest, a fatherly type who was popular with his female clients because he did not put the make on them, proceeded to busy himself in her behalf.

In 1935 Wyman had fleeting appearances in three Paramount films, *Rumba*, *All the King's Horses*, and *Stolen Harmony*. She closely studied the techniques of the stars with whom she worked, including Carole Lombard and Mary Ellis. In the first two films she was still in the chorus, but in the third, *Stolen Harmony*, she appeared briefly as a dancer. At Fox she had an unbilled part in *King of Burlesque* (1935), and she has recalled admiringly watching Alice Faye and Warner Baxter but cannot remember anything about the bit she was assigned.

At times during her bouts of recurrent despair in 1935 she had toyed with the idea of returning to her Missouri roots. She said years later, "For a time I deluded myself that my home area held answers for personal roots, personal happiness. I guess I thought the right man would be more likely to show up there than in the predatory, artificial Hollywood environment. Then I came to realize that people are people everywhere."

She told a *Guidepost Magazine* interviewer: "One day on the set [I heard] something that shone another bit of light through the defense I had set up." A co-worker had told her that she had discovered that Hollywood held two kinds of people, the closed, careful types who didn't take risks, hence never got hurt, and the open people who gave life all they had. Sure they made mistakes and got hurt, but they also got in return much joy and fulfillment. Wyman there and then recognized herself as one of the closed people and saw that her bright personality was merely the shell for a clam. She decided, "I began to want very much to open the shell. I began to loathe the brassy blonde I played in the movies. Suddenly I longed to play real people, to move the hearts of real people." She added, "Today I would call this quality of deep yearning 'prayer.'"

Wyman would need that prayer to sustain her through all the years of work and life experience she would yet have to weather before she could play truly and move hearts truly. Hers was to be one of the most painfully slow and tortuous rises in the annals of Hollywood stardom.

# 3

## The Slow But Sure Emergence
## 1936–1942

In 1936 the beginnings of an acting career came at last. For reasons she has never figured out—perhaps some sympathetic friend spoke up for her—Wyman was picked out of a Universal chorus line for a bit part in the William Powell-Carole Lombard screwball starrer, *My Man Godfrey.*

As Wyman remembered it, "I was twenty-two; that was damned late to be starting at the bottom in youth-crazy Hollywood; other girls had made it at sixteen or seventeen; the camera loved fresh faces—but that bit in *Godfrey* raised my spirits nonetheless." There was a party sequence in the picture and she was given a few lines to speak to Carole Lombard. "She was such a big star then, and my knees shook, and I thought my voice would fail me," she recalled. "But she was awfully nice, and I guess I got by."

Her spirits plummeted when the picture came out and her bit had been left on the proverbial cutting-room floor. However, soon thereafter an executive at Warner Bros., who had heard of her from William Demarest (always her fatherly standby), called her in and offered her a stock contract at that studio. That was in May 1936.

At this point she adopted the name Jane Wyman—thus immortalizing the surname of the shadowy Eugene. Though in later years she had wanted only to forget him, and refused to let her intimate friends even mention him, in 1936 he still must have meant something to her because she took his name as her own.

A series of bit parts followed, and somewhere along the line she picked up the nickname "The Hey-Hey Girl." "Perhaps she got tabbed with that because she was so damned *lively,*" William Demarest remembered. "And she couldn't keep still for a second, loved nightclubs, dancing, singing with her friends. 'There's a lot of living to be done, and I'm going to do it!' she'd say."

Her first official Warner's film was *Stage Struck.* In that year, her hair was still dark. She did an unbilled chorus-girl stint. Next in *Polo Joe,* starring Joe E. Brown as a would-be polo player, she was just one of the girl entourage circling the star. "She has *something,*" the Warner casting director said of her. "Now let's find out what the hell it is!" She was sent to coaches to train her still unsteady voice; she was groomed for hair and dress styles; she was given intensive instruction in acting.

Toward the end of 1936 she found herself playing a hatcheck girl in one of Glenda Farrell's Torchy Blane pictures *Smart Blonde.* In *Gold Diggers of 1937* she was a chorus girl. Then, in her early 1937 release, *Ready, Willing and Able,* a less-than-memorable Ruby Keeler musical, she barely made the billing as a dumb bunny. *The King and the Chorus Girl* (1937) found her billed fifth as a floozie, and in *Slim,* a Pat O'Brien-Henry Fonda co-starrer, she was Stuart Erwin's girlfriend.

Directors like Busby Berkeley, Ray Enright, Mervyn LeRoy, and Lloyd Bacon, who had observed her promise in these films, began talking her up in the

*Smart Blonde* (1936), with Barton MacLane and Glenda Farrell.

With Stuart Erwin in *Slim* (1937).

front office. She fit perfectly (at the time) a type that was common in films of the thirties—the tough blonde with a vulnerable heart; the wisecracker laughing on the outside, crying on the inside; the crude but valorous semi-call girl who usually chooses to love an attractive heel and who often opts for masochistic hurt over boredom and loneliness. Such girls were products of the Depression displacements; their frequent migrations and expeditious alliances were often desperate acts for survival.

With her hair now lightened, Wyman was hailed as successor to Joan Blondell and Glenda Farrell, whose days at the studio were numbered. She remembers doing everything to put herself over: "I did all the starlet things—went to exhibitor's conventions and palled-around with people whose looks and manners I didn't particularly care for." Soon she was assigned for publicity purposes to attend premieres of new Warner Bros. films with dates arranged by the studio. They were either promising male personalities who needed exposure in the fan magazines via being rumored to "being her new romance" or with full stars temporarily unattached in whose reflected news-camera glory she might bask—"some of whom tried to make me after the show, some of whom left me mercifully alone."

Her attitude became, of necessity: "If you don't toot your own horn, nobody else will." "What is your long-range ambition?" one 1937 studio questionnaire put to her. "To be not just *an* actress but *the* actress at the studio," she wrote. Some who read that statement snickered, little dreaming that twelve years later it would come true. Of her 1937 self she later said: "I had been through five years of hard times" (meaning, of course, joblessness, uncongenial work when she got it, watching others get ahead, de-

A pouty still shot, 1937.

termination to keep up a sometimes faltering confidence, coping with Hollywood wolves, etc.), adding, "I had twenty-three years of energy, thank goodness, but sixty-three or seventy-three years of life experience, and all the disillusion of them, too! Was I ready to take over from Glenda and Joan as Resident Tough Blonde? Heck, I'd been living the part for years!"

She later recalled Warner Bros. as "really more like a big family than a studio." She carefully studied the manners and technique of such Warner luminaries as Kay Francis, Bette Davis, James Cagney, and Pat O'Brien. "Pat was like an older brother," she recalled. "He taught me many tricks of the acting trade. Such a nice guy—happily married—never tried to make me." Bette Davis, who had weathered some tough times herself, called all the newcomers "the kids"; Wyman remembered her, circa 1937, as kind and encouraging. Kay Francis had Wyman to her home, cued her in on many performing devices, as did James Cagney, whom she recalls as "a stickler for discipline." But first and foremost she learned by doing, in picture after picture.

After another small part in *The Singing Marine*, a Dick Powell starrer whose title tells its story, Wyman got her first leading role opposite Kenny Baker in *Mr. Dodd Takes the Air* (1937), which was based on a Clarence Budington Kelland story involving a small town electrician with a fine singing voice (Baker) who goes to New York for a chance at the big-time. Wyman was on hand to lend romantic moral support. The story was built primarily around Baker but, as she recalls, "I was a leading lady, a co-star, if you will, at last!"

Next came a film called *Public Wedding*, and she and William Hopper (actor son of Hedda) were the leads. The plot was some silliness about a group of down-on-their-luck show-folk who hit on the zany idea of staging a public wedding inside a stuffed whale's mouth to make a hit at a sideshow. Wyman and Hopper brave the stuffed whale's mouth, but due to a fluke they find they are actually husband and wife by the end of the proceedings.

On loan-out to Universal for her first 1938 release, *The Spy Ring*, Wyman, again in a lead, opposite William Hall, found herself on an army base where espionage suddenly runs riot. Back at Warners she had a small part with Carole Lombard and Fernand Gravet in *Fools for Scandal*, then took the lead opposite Frank McHugh in *He Couldn't Say No*, in which she was the "dream" girl of a timid clerk (McHugh) who develops the manhood to conquer all, due to the unlikely and rather convolutedly explicated inspirations of a statue called Courage. Wyman turns out to be the prize worth winning.

Next, on loan to Columbia, she played the light o'love of timid soda-jerk Joe E. Brown, who finds himself involved with the underworld but manages to blunder through in the usual hilarious Brown

Singing up a storm in *Ready, Willing and Able* (1937).

*The Singing Marine* (1937), with
Dick Powell and Veda Ann Borg.

*Mr. Dodd Takes the Air* (1937),
with Kenny Baker.

The Spy Ring (1938), with William Hall.

He Couldn't Say No (1938), with Frank McHugh.

*Wide Open Faces* (1938), with Joe E. Brown.

style. Wyman later recalled that she had learned much about comedic timing from closely observing the antics of McHugh and Brown. She had already come some distance, from being a nameless member of Brown's feminine entourage in the 1936 *Polo Joe*. She was his 1938 leading lady. The title of the picture was *Wide Open Faces*.

About this time her personal life began to deepen and expand beyond her wildest expectations. She met a young actor named Ronald Reagan. A number of conflicting stories have arisen as to the first meeting of Jane Wyman and Ronald Reagan on the Warner Bros. lot, where Reagan had been taken on as a contract player in 1937 after a stint as a radio announcer in the Midwest.

Some reports have them meeting in the commissary soon after his arrival at the studio in 1937.

Others suggest they met in the publicity department while shooting photos. While insiders claim that they began dating, discreetly, in late 1937 or early 1938, Reagan also took pains to be seen around with other young actresses, including a stunner named Ila Rhodes. A fling with Susan Hayward was publicist inspired, mostly.

Wyman has recalled that when she first laid eyes on Reagan, twenty-six, handsome, muscular, unmarried, forthrightly naive, and replete, even at that relatively tender age, with a reputation for conservatism in conduct and outlook along with a charmingly old-fashioned, chivalrous stance toward the opposite sex, she told herself: "That's for me!" "The knight on the white charger had finally showed up," William Demarest later said. "Ronnie was the dream of true, perfect manhood personified that this little girl had always held in her heart through thick and thin." Demarest added, "She was the aggressor, the intent pursuer, from the start. She was far more worldly and experienced than he was, though she was three years his junior. I think Ronnie at first was somewhat bewildered by her fast come-on; then he started to like it, then her, and then he fell in love."

But there was a complication. A big one. Wyman was a married woman.

She had met Myron Futterman, a wealthy, middle-aged clothing manufacturer from New Orleans, in 1936 when, rumor had it, she party-girled at the studio's behest to entertain visiting entrepreneurs from the hinterlands who sought to ease the fatigue

In 1938, age 24.

of deals with feminine companionship. Reportedly Wyman, unlike some of the other starlets, had refused her favors as a matter of policy, and this had intrigued Futterman. In January 1937 Wyman married him, going to New Orleans for the ceremony.

Nearly twice Wyman's age, conservative, and businesslike, Futterman seems to have represented—for a time—safety and stability to a twenty-three-year-old whose own father, cold and withdrawn, had denied what Futterman seemed to offer—a protective father image. Soon, however, it became apparent that Futterman was neither fatherly nor even particularly affectionate.

"We all wondered *why* she married Futterman," said a friend from the period. "The only explanation I can think of is that she was tired of young guys with busy hands and felt an older, more settled man might give her more security and permanence." Others reiterated that she had seen in Futterman the fatherly understanding and closeness that the reserved father back in Missouri had, lamentably, failed to accord her.

Futterman shortly proved himself to be the wrong man for her. Their interests diverged crucially. He, too, had been disillusioned by an earlier marriage that had not worked out, and he tended to place unrealistic expectations on his second. A little over a year after their elopement, they separated—later to divorce. One friend suggested that they had mistaken need for love. In her divorce proceedings Wyman declared that Futterman refused to have a child by her because he already had a teenage daughter by his first wife—an inexplicable reason on the surface. She also stated that he had compared Wyman, to her face, with his first wife, and told her that, by comparison, the first wife had been superior to her, despite the fact that he had often knocked his first wife to her. He also accused her of being flighty and flirtatious at parties.

But the recurring rumor that clean-cut, conservative young Ronald Reagan had been the true cause of the marriage breakup would not die. Futterman—not a man to create issues when his basic desire was to be done with it all—quickly faded from Wyman's life and from the Hollywood scene, unmourned and unremembered.

For many years thereafter both Wyman and Reagan insisted to all comers that they had not begun dating or getting serious about each other until 1939. The reason for this was Reagan's embarrassment at courting a woman who had been technically still another man's wife. At any rate both did all they could to keep the actual courting dates mixed up.

In the middle of her divorce proceedings, distracting and nerveracking as they were, Wyman found herself unaccountably kicked over to Metro-Goldwyn-Mayer in mid-1938 for a small part in a Robert Taylor prizefight melodrama *The Crowd Roars*. In this she plays Maureen O'Sullivan's best pal. Both are products of finishing school in the plot, which Wyman privately felt was a horselaugh given her hardboiled image and early years knocking-around.

This was one of MGM's chronic 1938 through 1939 attempts to toughen up Robert Taylor, who was regarded as "too dangerously pretty" around the lot and whose masculinity was being questioned by some of the more macho (though that wasn't the popular 1938 term) fans. First MGM had sent him to England to play an intrepid American athlete in *A Yank at Oxford*—after that, in such melodramas as *The Crowd Roars* and *Stand up and Fight*, the "toughening of Taylor" continued with reasonably successful results.

The plot of *The Crowd Roars* has to do with fighter Taylor in the toils of racketeer Edward Arnold, whose gently reared daughter, O'Sullivan, doesn't know her father is a crooked fight promoter. Wyman, as the heroine's sidekick, has only a few scenes, but she makes them count. In one humorous exchange with O'Sullivan, when they are driving by Taylor's training farm, she begins primping up, bubbling: "If he's a gangster, he might get fresh with me." When O'Sullivan tells her not to be "so silly," Wyman rejoins, "Well, if I fix myself up, he might."

Wyman scores again in another scene. Having maneuvered Taylor to her school dance where he twirls her briefly around the floor, she has to surrender him to a moonlight stroll with his true-love O'Sullivan, whom he marries after finally, in disillusion after considerable melodrama, putting away his gloves for keeps. In 1964 Wyman came up during a conversation with Robert Taylor, who recalled that even in 1938 she was a sparkling, charismatic little lady who stood out in a scene, even when neglected, as she then was, by director and cameraman.

*Brother Rat*, Wyman's sixth and last film of 1938, a year in which she was handed pedestrian and thankless parts but proved, nonetheless, a vital presence, is the film in which she really got to know—and fell in love with—Ronald Reagan. Though their parts in it were essentially supporting, they teamed for the

With Maureen O'Sullivan during shooting *The Crowd Roars*, 1938.

*Brother Rat* (1938), with Ronald Reagan.

first time romantically. And their dawning attraction for each other vividly shows on the screen on any and all reviewings.

Originating as a hit Broadway farce (the stage original was written by John Monk, Jr., and Fred F. Finklehoffe), *Brother Rat* made the screen courtesy of writers Richard Macaulay and Jerry Wald, with William Keighley directing at a professionally frantic pace that milked laughs at every turn. The film inaugurated the appearance of the juvenile Warners stock company, which included Wayne Morris, Priscilla Lane, Jane Bryan, Eddie Albert, Wyman, and Reagan, and such lesser lights as Johnnie Davis, Gordon Oliver, and William Tracy.

*Brother Rat* (meaning new cadet) covered the final hectic semester at Virginia Military Institute (the VMI of legend) and front and center were three particularly obstreperous cadets and their girlfriends. Monk and Finklehoffe, incidentally, well

knew their material, as they themselves were graduates of VMI, which over the decades had come to be known as the West Point of the south. Wayne Morris and Priscilla Lane were the ostensible leads, but Eddie Albert managed to steal much of the show as the illicitly married, baseball playing, relentlessly sad-sack cadet. This started Albert off as a prominent Warners leading man. Later he was to win considerable fame as a dependable character actor in numerous films.

As Lane's college roomate Wyman plays a pert I'll-take-care-of-it type, her confidence and gall reinforced by her position as daughter to VMI top banana Henry O'Neill. Also present is Jane Bryan as Eddie Albert's wife who complicates the plot by announcing a Blessed Event (a plot twist that comes to fruition in the 1940 *Brother Rat and a Baby*). Morris is Albert's brash, mischief-making roommate whose high spirits keep the plot percolating, and Reagan is the conservative roomie who grudgingly goes along with Morris' harebrained shenanigans.

As Doug McClelland recalled in *Cinema Notes*: "Reagan played a good-looking foil for the others. In light of future events the humor is aggrandized today in the scene where Morris, hoping to get Priscilla Lane alone, had to cajole Reagan into blind dating the intellectual Wyman with the words, 'This girl's a great little number.' On their date Wyman—a rangy blonde with immense brown eyes that were barely contained by the large dark-rimmed glasses she wore here—revealed she was a chemistry major who always wanted to be a bacteriologist and was hoping for a fellowship from the Rockefeller Foundation. Reagan's awed whistle at this made her quickly add: 'Oh—oh—but I like men, too!'"

When Morris and Reagan get caught after being out after taps with the girls, Wyman pulls her weight with her commandant father, who lets the boys off easy with penalty tours. Graduation is coming, and the boys, aware that Albert's impending fatherhood has made him more than slightly pixilated, commandeer Wyman to sneak into the barracks and coach him for his chemistry exam. Reagan kisses her during this, and she asks (having just removed her spectacles), "Does this happen all the time when a girl doesn't wear glasses?"

William Tracy, who had been in *Brother Rat's* West Coast company, livened the action considerably as the often hazed, squirrel-nerved, squeaky-voiced flunky. Johnnie Davis is a cadet of the hayseed variety and the other cast members, especially Louise Beavers and Henry O'Neill, acquit themselves in lively fashion.

Keighley directed *Brother Rat* at a fast clip, cleverly disguising the inconsequential sophomorisms implicit in the situations. But to today's viewers Wyman—fresh, pretty, lively eyed, and twenty-four—and Reagan—composed, manly, and sexually charismatic at twenty-seven—are the main interest as they play out, for all to see, the beginnings of one of Hollywood's most legendary relationships.

*Brother Rat* (1938), with Ronald Reagan and Wayne Morris.

A glamour shot circa 1939.

*Variety's* review commented: "Essential elements of the stage play were retained in toto in transmutation to films. Production guidance was skillful in keeping picture close to line of the original, and only sidelight material was inserted in the screenplay to round out proper production footage. None of the factors that made the play a success has been lost. Same authentic feeling of military college life holds in the film as with the play. The adventures, loves, and headaches of three cadets during their last ten weeks at the school are finely interwoven to present plenty of laughs and suspense."

*Variety*, as did other reviewing sheets, tended to shortchange Wyman and Reagan in their notices, and while the secondary nature of their roles is granted, they do seem, in retrospect, to have deserved more attention. After calling Eddie Albert "splendid" and commenting on Wayne Morris's "good characterization," *Variety* finally gets around to 1938's most retrospectively famous lovebirds, calling Reagan "fine" and Wyman "nicely cast."

Priscilla Lane later recalled, "Everyone could see that Janie and Ronnie were falling in love. It was all over their faces. It was rather touching to see. . . ." Wayne Morris later said, "You got the feeling those two couldn't wait to get to the love scenes—and they were annoyed that the scriptwriter had given them so few of them!"

For her first 1939 release (shot in late 1938) Wyman found herself loaned out to Twentieth Century-Fox to do *Tail Spin*, where, under Roy Del Ruth's direction, she found herself lost in a considerable crowd of players, some of them, like Constance Bennett and Charles Farrell, on the way down. Also rounding out the cast were Joan Davis, Kane Richmond, Wally Vernon, Harry Davenport, and Mary Gordon.

The star was Alice Faye, and there was divided

All dolled up for *The Kid from Kokomo*, 1939.

opinion in the press as to whether she was tendered this film as some kind of studio punishment or whether it was some misguided attempt to enhance her image and demonstrate her ability as a performer. The best that could be said for Del Ruth's direction was that he managed to keep the action moving fairly well and choreographed all the personality turns with some agility. Frank Wead's screenplay didn't help much, covering more twists and turns of plot than an eighty-four-minute film could comfortably handle.

In *Tail Spin* Faye is an energetic flying devotee who injects herself into a cross-country aerial derby. Her arch rival is society dilettante Constance Bennett, who also has ace flying ambitions. There are love affairs, flying meets, brittle feminine competi-tiveness, assorted wisecracks from comic Joan Davis, and appeals to team spirit as the flying buffs get together to save the day after Faye cracks up in a competitive flight.

Wyman lends some bright wit and amusing cama-raderie to her scenes as one of the girls involved in the proceedings, and considering the attractive com-petition, does *not* get lost in the entourage. Screen-writer Wead even lets her toss off a few wisecracks. Her attitude while doing the film was that she was there to study the radically different styles of her co-players and give herself a refresher course in reacting individually to each. Attitudes like this made her thankless assignments in this period bearable, she found.

After his success in *Kid Galahad* (1937) in which

Playing an Easter-Greeting Bunny during shooting of *The Kid from Kokomo*, 1939.

*Torchy Plays with Dynamite* (1939).

he played off the likes of Bette Davis and Edward G. Robinson as a handsome fighter on the side of the angels, Wayne Morris seemed to the Warner higher-ups a natural for more kid-stripe fare. Wyman's second 1939 release found her in *The Kid from Kokomo*, in which Morris was again—you guessed it—a nice guy with innocently dreamy leanings and with manly virtue intact. With what grace she could muster, Wyman, the love interest for handsome Wayne, let him have center stage throughout. The director Lewis Seiler gave her no opportunities to shine, nor did the Jerry Wald-Richard Macaulay script (from a story by Dalton Trumbo).

Film commentator Clive Hirschhorn dismissed this effort: "With the word *kid* in the title, *The Kid from Kokomo* (released in Britain as *Orphan of the Ring*) *had* to be a boxing film. And indeed it was, though a pretty wretched one as it turned out. The farcical tale of a fighter who believes that he and Whistler had the same mother, and that her living counterpart is a booze-sodden kleptomaniac in the shape of May Robson, it starred (surprise) Pat O'Brien as the brainless fighter, with Wayne Morris, Joan Blondell, Jane Wyman, Stanley Fields, and

Sidney Toler on hand to share the punishment meted out by the writers."

Morris is given some precious farm boy stuff, such as, on sabbatical from heavier duty, feeding calves with bottles. Blondell and O'Brien make with the fast patter and wry observations. Wyman is on hand for a few tepidly romantic scenes with Morris. Grand old trouper May Robson steals the show.

Since making a solid hit in Frank Capra's *Lady for a Day* (1933), in which she played a 1933-style bag-lady dressed up by kindly gangsters to bluff through her daughter's society wedding, Robson was on top of the Hollywood character-actress heap throughout the 1930s. Wyman said that studying the technique and playing off the kinetic personality of this stage veteran had been her chief benefit from the film.

In her third 1939 film Wyman got a crack at the Torchy Blane character that Glenda Farrell had standardized since 1937 under such titles as *Smart Blonde*, *Fly-Away Baby*, *The Adventurous Blonde*, *Blondes at Work*, followed in 1938 and 1939 by such items as *Torchy Blane in Chinatown*, *Torchy Gets Her Man*, and *Torchy Runs for Mayor*. Wyman's version was *Torchy Plays with Dynamite*. The features were always on the second half of a double bill, and usually ran about an hour.

Torchy was a fast-talking, tough-acting, wisecracking ace reporter forever in hot water with a sidekick homicide detective who was not too bright and made a comic foil for her lightning machinations against gangsters, kidnappers, crooked politicians, and other enemies of the law. He was also her boyfriend.

Barton MacLane had made the role of Steve, the dumb cop friend of Torchy's, his own, but for one picture Paul Kelly was substituted, and Lola Lane of the Lane sisters was given one crack at Torchy. After a brief reinstatement of the Farrell-MacLane combine in 1938, Wyman and Allen Jenkins were deputized for the roles. It turned out to be the last—and weakest—of the series, not due to any deficiencies in Wyman's or Jenkins's interpretation, but because the direction was slight and the writers had run out of gas.

*Variety* liked Wyman in the final run of the series, with its reporter writing: "Jane Wyman is new to the title role of the newspaper scribbler and is a happy choice. She clicks nicely. Allen Jenkins as her detective sweetheart also promises much." The review also stated: "Torchy, the demon femme reporter goes through another exciting experience with mobsters. . . . In an effort to land a good yarn and help her detective sweetheart win a reward, Torchy gets herself jailed for eleven months to win the confidence of a [bank-robber's] moll. Scheme works, the pair slip out of the workhouse, and [the mobster] is inveigled by his unsuspecting sweetie into visiting her."

*Variety* added about Wyman: "[She] circumvents any temptations to overact and makes her romance with the detective lieutenant realistic."

Wyman later said of cheapjack billers like *Torchy Plays with Dynamite*: "The writing, direction, and overall production values may not have been much, but they did have to move fast to get it all packed into one hour, and I found that the pace and shortcuts sharpened my timing and gave a razor-edge

*Private Detective* (1939), with John Eldridge, left.

*Kid Nightingale* (1939), with John Payne.

to my style. They may not have been much, pictures like this, but they were part of my ongoing apprenticeship, and I'm not sorry I did them."

Movie-mag writers of the time enjoyed comparing the respective styles of Glenda Farrell, Lane, and Wyman. Farrell was the hard, tough, wisecracking Torchy. Lane (for only one film) was softer, more genial, less sure of herself. Wyman, not as brassy as Farrell, not as tepid as Lane, was very much herself, in control, sure of where she was going, and, as fellow actor Allen Jenkins later said of her, "very much her own woman." Certainly, in purely physical terms, Wyman was the most attractive of the three.

Jenkins remembered the Warner potboilers of this time: "Boy, did we go fast—those hour-long pictures were sometimes wrapped up in a week or two. Three weeks was considered overhead extravagance, and the front office would accuse us all of goofing-off. But the result was a hell of a lot of good pacing, compressed action with not a second wasted, and an overall root-a-toot-toot effect that, I'm afraid, action films tended to lose when they got too long and 'careful.'"

Wyman co-workers remember that while she was always neat, professionally made up, and attractively dressed, she was far from being a mirror watcher or difficult with the cameramen. "She did her job," actor John Ridgely remembers, "and pitched in with the rest of us and was an all-around cooperative and nontemperamental person. But boy, was she good-looking; the crew used to stare at her like lovesick pups. She'd kid with them, but she didn't fool around."

After some hesitation about continuing Wyman in the *Torchy Blane* series, Warner executives decided to give her one more go with the theme and character. Soon thereafter a decision came from on high that the Torchy series had grown stale, and there would have to be a new twist. The result was *Private Detective*.

Running just fifty-seven minutes, it was seen on the bottom half of double bills all through the end of 1939 and the beginning of 1940, and contributed little to the stature of its principals. Screenwriters Earle Snell and Raymond Schrock, working from a story by Kay Krause, created a new occupation for Wyman—female private detective.

On hand in the old Barton MacLane–Paul Kelly–Allen Jenkins incarnation of a dumb cop-sweetheart was Dick Foran. *Variety* commented: "Warners put the Torchy Blane series into the garage for an overhauling and repaint job. *Private Detective* has a new finish, but underneath it's plainly the Torchy formula, with wider cruising range apparent than was the case in the girl reporter series."

In love and forever planning marriage, with one interference or another causing them to postpone the ceremony, Foran and Wyman find themselves rivals in the crime-solution game. When she beats him out in cracking the malfeasances, he grumbles and grouches, then like a good sport has to admit his private-detective girlfriend is more hip on these matters than he is. They get involved in the murder of a blackguard type who is killed while trying to get custody of his child from his long-suffering wife. At first the wife is top suspect, but of course the trail leads elsewhere, specifically to a trust fund for the child being manipulated by a crooked lawyer.

*Photoplay* called *Private Detective* "Merely routine stuff," while *Variety* said: "Miss Wyman and Foran team nicely in the top spots."

Foran spoke of Wyman as "a real trouper, a good sport, a go-through gal—no temperament, always a pleasure to play with."

To round out a lacklustre 1939 Wyman found herself in yet another kid picture, only this time the title was *Kid Nightingale* and the kid was handsome John Payne, who got a chance to show off his super-wide shoulders and rocklike muscles as an opera tenor who aspires to be a pugilist.

*The New York Times* yawned, "By the skin of the teeth of Walter Catlett, Harry Burns, and Porky Ed Brophy and by virtue of their low-comedy mugging, a spindling prizefight picture called *Kid Nightingale*, now at the Palace, manages with fair consistency to tickle the risibilities even if it never gets across a fast one to the midriff. Sure, it's all B-grade farce—something pointless about an aspiring operatic tenor rather handy with his dukes, who falls in with a shady fight promoter and becomes a dupe (not to mention a dope, which he already was) until saved by 'the little girl' (Wyman—who else?). But with Catlett as a flibbertigibbet pug scout, Burns as a fake singing teacher, and Porky Ed as a dyspeptic mana-

ger, it builds up enough points on giggles to qualify for the prelims."

*Variety* snickered: "Its producer must certainly have had his tongue-in-cheek. It's a combination in one film of every form of pap, hokum, and comedy business that Hollywood has used since Mark Sennett's Keystone Kops. It's so absolutely silly it's almost good."

Payne and Wyman got to sing a bit, professionally chirping a ballad duet called "Who Told You I Cared?" among other numbers. One reviewer commented, "They warble fairly well, but MacDonald and Eddy they're not—nor does singing belong in this foolish farce."

Wyman and Payne worked well together, but Payne recalled in later years that she was so in love with Ronald Reagan that she couldn't wait to wind up the scenes so she could rush to meet him. (Wyman and Reagan were married a month later.)

A lot of people wondered how long the Reagan-Wyman combo would last, given the evident disparity in their temperaments and backgrounds. Jerry Asher remembered, "Jane and Ronnie really made a strange combination. She was so experienced, hardboiled, intense, and passionate, and he was so pragmatic, down-to-earth, not overly imaginative. Sure, everyone respected, in spite of themselves, his clean-living ways and solid character but he was—well, rather a square. Serious, respectful of women, steady of mind and manners. In short, predictable and a little dull. He was a very sexy looking man, of course—looked wonderful in swimming trunks, great body and all that, but he was a little earthbound for someone like Jane."

Jerry continued: "Oddly enough, Reagan, a graduate of Eureka College in Illinois who was well-read and even at that youthful age kept up faithfully with current events, was probably better educated and more articulate by far than Jane was at the time. She never pretended to be an egghead, used slang terms like 'sang up a storm,' and was altogether unassuming in her ways; her words usually came out one syllable to his five or six!"

Wayne Morris, who had seen Wyman and Reagan's love blossom during *Brother Rat*, was one of those who felt that their mutual attraction was sexual, primarily, and another friend said that "they were hot numbers physically, though Ronnie was of the save-himself-for-marriage school."

In an article from a 1946 *Motion Picture*, co-written with Alice Craig Greene, Wyman recounted aspects of the Reagan-Wyman courtship and marriage proposal. She said, "I still remember our first date. We had a dinner date and went to a Sonja Henie opening afterward. We had a wonderful time and it seemed to me we made a pretty good team off screen as well as on. Neither of us was going with anyone special at the time [Reagan's brief fling with Susan Hayward had ended] so we decided on each other. Our favorite night spot was Grace Hayes Lodge. We used to go there for dinner and sit and listen to our 'theme song,' *Deep Purple*, and hold hands under the table. A very romantic courtship? Yes, but the proposal was about as unromantic as any that ever happened. We were both working on a picture and were about to be called for a take. Ronnie simply turned to me as if the idea were brand new and had just hit him and said, 'Jane, why don't we get married?' I couldn't think of any reason why we shouldn't. I'd been wondering for a whole year—since I first saw him—why he hadn't asked me. I was just about to say a definite yes when we were called before the cameras. In trying to step down off my own personal cloud, I managed to muff a few lines and toss in a whispered 'yes' afer the director said 'cut.'"

Circumstances enabled the pair to put aside the constant B roles in B films for a time. By 1939 Wyman and Reagan were two of many male and female starlets on a cross-country promotional tour with Louella Parsons, who was to announce their engagement onstage to a theater audience. They were known after that as "Louella's Favorite Love Birds" and indeed were to find the formidable columnist a den mother they could not shake before or after their marriage. On January 27, 1940, at the Wee Kirk o' the Heather Church at Forest Lawn, they were married.

With Ronald Reagan during their engagement, 1940.

Reagan and Wyman on their wedding day, 1940.

The Reagans talk it over at breakfast, 1940.

With her new baby girl, Maureen, 1941.

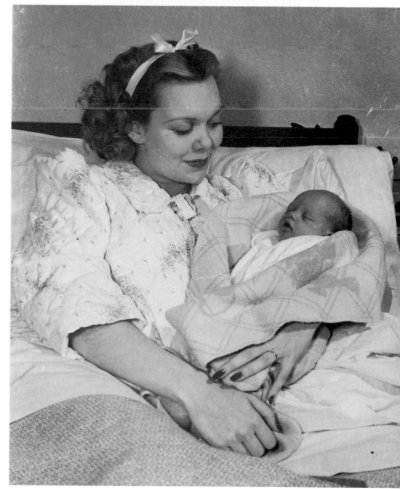

Wyman later recalled it as "a very small wedding, with Louella Parsons giving us a lovely reception afterward." "Theirs is the perfect marriage," Louella rhapsodized in column after column, but her gushes were interspersed with such juicy (for the time) items as "Jane always seemed so nervous and tense before she found Ronnie. She was a girl on the make—for life, for love. I think she wanted—well, *everything*. But steady, solid, decent young Ronnie has slowed down her pace, and it is all for the best.

"Yes," Louella continued, "It was an 'opposites-attract' thing, but I'm predicting here and now that these opposites will celebrate their twenty-fifth *and* fiftieth wedding anniversaries—together." Soon Louella and arch-rival Hedda Hopper were billing and cooing, in their columns and in person, over the Reagan's first baby, Maureen Elizabeth. "And you can bet she arrived *a solid year* later," Bill Demarest chuckled. "Ronnie was the last thing from a five-month daddy type."

June Allyson in her autobiography recalled aspects of Wyman and Reagan as husband and wife that were illuminating. Her husband, Dick Powell, had worked with Jane in *Gold Diggers of 1937* and *The Singing Marine*. He called Wyman "Button Nose," a nickname she loved—or pretended to.

According to June Allyson, "[During a session at my house,] Ronnie, a staunch Democrat (then), tried to convert Richard while Richard argued just as hard to turn Ronnie into a Republican. I figured the only way to get into this conversation was to pop some basic questions at Ronnie.

"He answered me carefully, methodically. When Ronnie got through explaining something to me, Jane Wyman leaned over and said, 'Don't ask Ronnie what time it is because he will tell you how a watch is made.'"

Joy Hodges Schiess, an actress who accompanied the Reagans on a tour, recalled in a long private letter, "Jane was always *strong*, very, very intelligent, and 'hep' about everything—except politics, and that was part of the boredom she felt being married to Ronnie because it was always an important subject in his life. Jane was almost overly generous; money seemed to be meant for one thing: spending it on others. I remember when we went shopping she wanted to buy two of everything, one for herself and one for me.

"Jane loved to sing, and finally did a pretty good job at New York's Strand Theatre for which I loaned her some orchestration. That was after our Louella Parsons vaudeville tour in 1939, which we did with Ronnie, Susan Hayward, Arleen Whelan, June Preisser and, of course, Louella. During the tour Jane and 'Dutch' (as Ronnie was called) were very circumspect and fitted themselves in as single persons, though they were going together—no intimate hanging-out. I always thought that was pretty nice of them. In other words she shared Dutch—ha!"

Joy Hodges, who had been with them at the beginning, also witnessed the end. "[Jane] said one prophetic thing to me one night in the powder room of the Sonny Werblins a short time before the announcement of their breakup. I said I was aware that she and Dutch did not seem too happy during their last trip to New York, and she replied, 'Well, if he is going to be President, he is going to get there without me.' I have never told that to anyone else, but I was shocked. I am almost sure this was 1946.

"We went back to California by train—Jane, my husband at the time, Paul Dudley, and I. We sat with her and played gin all the way across the United States. I would go into her compartment now and

then and her eyes would be red. She truly loved Dutch, and the real reason—the very most intimate reason—for their breakup has been known only to them—at least not to me.

"Jane was fun-loving. She worked like a demon, but when fun time came, she went all the way. Dutch was not all that serious a person, but he never seemed to enjoy frivolity as much as some others. His sense of humor comes through now, when he is President, much, much more than it did in those early years. Jane wanted to laugh. Jane gave beautiful parties—again, always wanting to give out."

Regardless of how it ended, her first years of marriage to Ronald Reagan were a dream-come-true to Wyman, graduate of the school of hard knocks. And although she made no earth-shattering films during that time, she did continue to work very hard.

In 1940, the year of her marriage, Wyman ground out six forgettable films, all of them for Warners, three of them with Reagan. "What a cute pair of newlyweds," Louella Parsons gushed over and over, and Hedda Hopper said that they were "an adorable twosome." The Warners publicity department continued to play them up as "romantic young marrieds" accompanied by a slew of smoochy pictures and such copy as "Marriage has not dimmed the glory and wonder of their young love. Every day is a romantic refreshment and renewal. These kids love being together; they have eyes only for each other."

After Wyman became pregnant with Maureen the following April, the copy grew even more lush. "A baby is coming to put the seal on a union that Hollywood predicts will last forever and ever," one fan magazine, heavily sponsored *and* influenced by the Warners publicity department, read. "Will it be a blue blanket or a pink? Be it boy or girl, he or she will share in the perpetual honeymoon bliss of Hollywood's Most-in-Love couple."

In that same year another Hollywood couple, Lana Turner and John Shelton were being cast in films like *We Who Are Young* (young romance *par excellence*). But when called upon to appear together at Warners, Wyman and Reagan were relegated to silly, trivial fare that failed to zero-in on the evident on-screen physical and emotional attraction for each other that they were "shooting off like hot sparks," as fan-mag writer Jim Reid put it.

Ruth Waterbury had learned her screen journalism as a protegee of famed editor-publisher Jimmy Quirk of *Photoplay* in the 1920s and later, after his death, edited *Photoplay* herself for a time before returning to feature writing and interviewing. She told me years later, "In the midst of all this sickeningly saccharine condescension it seemed never to occur to the Warners to find a nice romantic love story for them, one in which Ronnie and Jane could have seriously established themselves as Hollywood's Young Married Lovers: 1940 style." Waterbury felt that the Wyman-Reagan on-screen chemistry and warm appeal was being frivolously wasted. In 1965 Ruth told me, "In the 1940 period the Warner people were patronizing them almost contemptuously and treating them as if they were a couple of young bubblehead pretty-types long on muscles (his) and curves (hers) but short on brains or real talent. What a surprise *those* two turned out to be later!"

The first of the 1940 film instances where this off-hand condescension visited the hapless pair was *Brother Rat and a Baby,* a weak sequel to the *Brother Rat* of 1938, in which Wyman and Reagan had first discovered each other, on screen *and* off. Most of the original crew were on board for this, including Wayne Morris, Eddie Albert, Jane Bryan, and Priscilla Lane—"a sort of Warner Bros. Stock Company,

Junior-League–style," as Adela Rogers St. Johns called them.

Retrospective critic Clive Hirschhorn has sniffed at it as "not nearly as successful as [the original] with its mindless screenplay . . . it involves its star Wayne Morris in such inflammatory escapades as arson as well as stealing a Stradivarius, which he pawns for petty cash. The cast . . . brought a degree of effervescence to Ray Enright's flat direction." Other reviews, contemporary and retrospective, have gone along the lines of "Good performances don't help this weak script," and "Sassy followup to *Brother Rat* is not the same success but still fun with three comrades graduating from military school."

Eddie Albert was the cadet who fathered the baby, and while Wayne Morris and Priscilla Lane got in some bright lines, Wyman and Reagan mostly stood around reacting, smiling, laughing, frowning—with decent dialogue for them at a minimum. It was obvious, from the tired situations dreamed up by writers Fred Finkelhoffe and John Monk, Jr., that *Brother Rat*—baby or no—did *not* lend itself to sequels.

*Brother Rat and a Baby* (1940), with Wayne Morris, Priscilla Lane, Eddie Albert, Jane Bryan, and Ronald Reagan.

Wyman and Reagan were on hand together yet again for *An Angel From Texas*, the first film to be released after their marriage, and again they were teamed with Wayne Morris, Eddie Albert and Jane Bryan—with sister Rosemary subbing for Priscilla Lane. Again the Wyman and Reagan roles were badly written and prevented them from developing characterizations. Since Reagan was by then twenty-nine and Wyman twenty-six, one critic expressed alarm at their plight, commenting: "Ronnie and Jane are grown people now, so why make them so juvenile and empty headed all the time? These two are capable of delivering far better work *if* they are given the proper directing and writing to back up their efforts."

*An Angel From Texas*, a remake of a George S. Kaufman stage vehicle *The Butter and Egg Man*, elicited from *Variety*: "[It] wasn't made with the hope of knocking the critics for a loop or lining up standees at the boxoffice, but it serves its purpose as a good little audience picture with a fair share of laughs, once the patrons are in."

As *Variety* synopsized the plot, "Eddie Albert, of the befogged cranial machinery, sees his high school Bernhardt girlfriend, Rosemary Lane, off to New York and a career in the theater after they've grown up in Lone Star, Texas. In following her there with his mother's life savings ($20,000), with which he hopes to buy a hotel, he runs into her bosses, a couple of shoestringing producers, Wayne Morris and Ronald Reagan.

"They verbal Jesse James him into buying a piece of the show, instead of the hotel, for which he insists he shall have the right to star Rosemary. Show finally goes on as a refined version of *Hellzapoppin'* after being intended as a serious period story and is a hit."

Wyman found herself with a little more coverage than was usual for her in this period with *Variety* noting: "Of the four *Brother Rat* repeats, only Jane Wyman slips out of gear, and instead of the mousey type that was, she has a throttle on the pursestrings of the money belonging to her and her husband, Ronald Reagan—he having made the grave error of buying a winning sweepstakes ticket in her name."

Morris's character was brassy, big with the talk and promises, while Reagan was more conservative. Albert's character was described as "a babe in the timber and an easy goad into an unsound investment." Director Ray Enright kept the pace fast and the action as bright as the Fred Niblo Jr.–Bertram Milhauser retread of Kaufman's old play allowed.

*The New York Times* dismissed *An Angel From*

*An Angel from Texas*, (1940), with Ronald Reagan.

*Flight Angels* (1940), with Wayne Morris, Virginia Bruce, and Dennis Morgan.

*Texas*—which shared the second half of a double bill at the Palace—in one long paragraph, calling it "a bright little farce about a couple of yokels from Texas who outwit a pair of Broadway theatrical sharps. The story is neither new nor exciting, and, except for the addition of some modern slang, is pretty much the same as when George S. Kaufman told it in 1925," adding, as some consolation for the hard-working cast, "It has been smartly acted by a pleasant company. . . . Ray Enright has directed in a breezy, farcical manner."

Jane Bryan, whose name was so similar to Wyman's that they were sometimes confused in both the fan-mail department and the commissary, was later to marry Justin Dart, a millionaire Californian who would help stake Ronald Reagan to a White House run forty years later.

*An Angel from Texas* was one of a number of transcriptions of Kaufman's play. The original film, called *The Butter and Egg Man*, was released by First National in 1928. Warners remade it in 1932 as *The Tenderfoot*; in 1935 as *Hello Sweetheart*; in 1937 as *Dance, Charlie Dance*, and as late as 1953 it was showing up on movie marquees as *Three Sailors and a Girl*. "It should never have been made after the first time out in 1928," was one critic's dismissive verdict.

For *Flight Angels*, her next 1940 effort, Wyman was given a sabbatical from the perennial Reagan presence onscreen, this time in a rather dull tale of the assorted adventures and romancings of airline stewardesses. One critic called it "as obvious as the nose on your face and typical Grade B second-feature fare."

Dennis Morgan, Wayne Morris, Ralph Bellamy, and Virginia Bruce (already on the stellar downgrade after her promising MGM years), joined Wyman for this, under the direction of Lewis Seiler. Critic Clive Hirschhorn's retrospective verdict on this was "The corn was as high as an elephant's eye (8,000 feet to be precise) in a soap-opera of the air which zeroed in on the private lives and public duties of air stewardesses and the men who pilot the planes in which they serve. Romance, drama, and excitement cohabited shamelessly in Maurice Leo's familiar screenplay."

Wyman's firm friendships with Wayne Morris and Dennis Morgan were fortified by their regular ap-

Gambling on the High Seas, 1940.

My Love Came Back (1940), with Eddie Albert.

pearances together. Morris in later years referred to their early days of camaraderie (along with Eddie Albert, Reagan, the Lane sisters, and Jane Bryan) as "The One-for-All and All-for-One Society-of-Busy-Bees" (B for B-pictures).

Wyman was to remember this picture primarily as one in which her uniforms were well-tailored and her hats perky—but as for the rest, forget it! Virginia Bruce later said of *Flight Angels*: "God, when you start to slip, the slipping is steep and the pictures [are] putrid."

Picture number four for Wyman in that grind-'em-out-like-sausage year of 1940 (again without new-hubby Reagan) was a pleasantly romantic little item called *My Love Came Back* (a title guaranteed to magnetize the matinee afternoon ladies). In it she was the violinist friend of Olivia De Havilland, who was technically starred opposite Jeffrey Lynn; Wyman, in a one-step-backward foray, was in support along with Eddie Albert. Originally titled *Episode*, then redubbed *Two Loves Have I*, it was called by *Screen Life* "the best comedy of the month. Amusing from start to finish, it owes its success to the fine direction of Kurt [later Curtis] Bernhardt, who handles the situations with a liveliness that should be an inspiration to other better-known directors. [Note:

Bernhardt was indeed to become a "better-known" director himself before the decade was out.] The laughs are gentle but there are plenty of them. And the music (they swing the classics) in good through-out." The *Screen Life* reviewer continued, "Let me suggest this movie for that hot summer evening when the Dodgers have lost, the neighbor's kid is howling, and Hitler has just swallowed another country. It's guaranteed to snap you out of your gloom."

*My Love Came Back*, with a plot, according to *Screen Life*, that "was much too complicated to be told in a small space," was roughly eighty-five percent De Havilland and fifteen percent Wyman, and even that fifteen percent she had to divide up with Eddie Albert and Charles Winninger. "Frothy" and "delightful" were the superficially dismissive comments of typical reviewers. The plot had to do with violin student De Havilland looking for love and studying on a scholarship at an academy. Winninger owns a phonograph factory and is secretly sponsoring De Havilland, whose pursuit of the right violin tone and the right man is predictably success-ful. Wyman called her part "a nothing."

Wyman (without Reagan) next appeared in a film called *Gambling on the High Seas*, with the billing

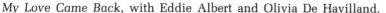

*My Love Came Back*, with Eddie Albert and Olivia De Havilland.

*Tugboat Annie Sails Again* (1940), with Ronald Reagan.

On the set of *Tugboat Annie Sails Again* (1940).

starring Wayne Morris and featuring her. Running only fifty-six minutes, it was strictly a B offering hardly justifying Morris's "stardom," let alone Wyman's appearance. *Variety*'s reviewer commented, "Could the newspapers of the country but hire the see-all, know-all, tell-all reporters trained in the B-picture corner of the Warner lot, there'd doubtlessly be not even space on page one for news from the war in Europe. They would be too full of underworld inside and cracking wide open of crooked gambling joints through the smart work of newspapermen who look like the Boy Scouts of America personified."

Morris here is the intrepid reporter—white knight duelling with crime out to nail gambling-ship owner Gilbert Roland for a murder. Wyman is Roland's secretary, but soon she is siding with Morris and District Attorney John Litel in their efforts to get the goods on the wily and viciously manipulative Roland.

*Variety* summed up this item: "To the credit of Warners and writer John E. Kent, they recognize a fifty-six-minute B when they see it. They tell the story simply and directly and without the addition of complicating facets, a highly successful formula which several other makers of secondary fare can't seem to get hep to. George Amy has directed it in the same manner."

Wyman in later years was to remember how disproportionately grateful she was when she got singled out in these reviews for any attention whatsoever, and she glowed (reportedly) at *Variety's* throwaway but nonetheless well-meant words in that same review about (surprise!) *her*. In this case the encomium in-passing stated: "Miss Wyman makes a very aesthetic vis-a-vis to American Boy Morris."

During an extended talk with handsome actor Gilbert Roland in 1964, I asked him about the Jane Wyman of 1940. This ace appreciator of womankind—and talent—glowed as he spoke of her. "There was *talent* written all over her, but she was a late bloomer—a lot of people are, you know. I think marriage and motherhood—she had a child shortly after this film was made—were the important things to her, *then*. And I don't think, for all her surface bravado, that she was the most confident person in the world about her talent—not *then*. But like so many others, I was in no way surprised when she bloomed into a great star later. I think confidence and concentration did it for her. One has to recognize that certain flame within and fan it—eventually she did."

Wyman's friends felt that she was much too accommodating to the studio's casting whims where she was concerned during the first year or so of her marriage to Reagan. "But her husband came first—she really wanted to see him succeed big as an actor, though she was too perceptive not to know that his creative talents did not match his intellectual ones," Ruth Waterbury of *Photoplay* told me in 1966. "But in those years she was the most supportive, boosting-type wife any man could ask for. She really worked at the marriage, really tried to build Ronnie's ego and confidence. I think when he started to get interested in union organizing and when he stopped *talking* politics and began to *live* it—that's when he began to lose her."

Waterbury added, "The Janie I knew in the early 1940s really did put wifehood and motherhood first. She was really in love with Ronnie then, thanked her stars for landing him, worshipped the ground he walked on. The cooling off came later, sadly. . . ."

Wyman was reunited with Reagan for their third and last 1940 effort together, *Tugboat Annie Sails Again*, a sequel to the famed 1933 *Tugboat Annie*, which Marie Dressler and Wallace Beery had made memorable over at MGM. This time the fine character actress Marjorie Rambeau was on hand to essay *Annie*, and while she lacked the larger-than-life, beautiful, homely humanity of Marie Dressler, then six years dead, she was most creditable in her own right.

Wyman and Reagan fool around on the *Tugboat Annie Sails Again* location.

During the shooting Wyman was some months into her pregnancy and starting to show it, with the result that the cameramen managed to keep her prettily hidden behind various items of furniture and assorted cast members. Her dresses, too, were cannily designed to keep her looking slim. But the photographer made sure to catch the special glow in her eyes that came from impending motherhood, and while the romantic opportunities with soon-to-be-father Reagan were on the sparse side, as usual, there *did* seem to be something extra in the onscreen romancing of this pair on the verge of parenthood.

From a screenplay by Walter De Leon, based, as was the earlier film, on characters created by Norman Reilly Raine, the plot deals with Tugboat Annie's life as a widow and her problems with rival tugboat captains who want to drive her off the waves. Reagan is the knight in white armor who wins the day for her, and Wyman backs him all the way.

Both Wyman and Reagan remembered Marjorie Rambeau with special fondness for this fine old character actress, who in youth had known the glories of top stardom on the Broadway stage, was a fount of wisdom and tolerant understanding of human foibles. According to a 1940 Warners publicity release, Wyman said of Rambeau: "Her seasoned talent and enormous thespic self-assurance awed me at first, and then I discovered the big heart and wonderfully supportive nature of this fine woman." These sentiments, if not verbiage, seemed to run true enough to Wyman, though an overly zealous publicity writer might have inserted such words as *thespic* which, according to fan-mag writer Jerry Asher, were distinctly *not* typical of Wyman's highly colloquial and slangy speech as of that time.

"She was always an extremely intelligent woman," Jerry Asher said, "but I don't think Jane began seriously *studying* and *thinking* until some years later. She had had a difficult life and was full of street smarts with a razor-sharp ability to size up people and situations, but she was not the *reader* Ronnie was—not then. But even in that early period, I always knew instinctively that when it came to genuine artistry, Jane's was the greater inherent talent. Ronnie was *bright*, but Jane was *creative*."

In *Tugboat Annie Sails Again* Wyman's role was hardly more than reactive—meaning she reacted in turn to Reagan's romancings and Rambeau's rough-hewn but kindly maternalizings. She was on hand to look prettily sympathetic to the old woman's travails and pertly receptive to her leading man—and noth-

Jane Wyman, 1941.

ing more, as she later commented. She did add that she tried to study the assorted techniques of such experienced character actors as Alan Hale, grand old man Clarence Kolb (about whom she was later to say had forgotten more about acting than she would ever learn), Chill Wills, and Paul Hurst.

Director Lewis Seiler later said of Wyman, "I always sensed an excellent natural intelligence and instinctive creativity in Jane. In spite of the nothing assignments she was given, she seemed to me to be always trying to give the banal lines and situations something extra. And she watched and observed talents around her that she considered worthy of emulation."

Of 1941, when Wyman played four highly forgettable roles in four highly forgettable films, she later recalled: "I was twenty-seven years old, had been in films for nine years, and felt like a total beginner—not in my inner training but in the outward treatment given me. It seemed forever like *one* step forward, five steps backward—and there were *years* of that."

She added, "People think everyone—but anyone—who is in the movies is automatically rich, but I can remember getting a lousy sixty-eight dollars a week after taxes and being scared each time my contract came up for renewal that I'd be dropped." But she added, "I didn't blame anybody but myself for my slow progress. I thank Bryan Foy, who was in charge of the Warner Bros. B unit, for keeping me busy."

In 1941 she was quoted as saying, "I've been the Queen of the Sub-Plots. I've been the star's adviser, confidante, chum, sister, and severest critic. These were indeed the paper doll years of my career."

In 1941, *nine* years after first showing her face in the movies, the *Motion Picture Herald* and *Fame* poll taken by Quigley Publications selected Wyman as a Star of Tomorrow. But there was only a slight improvement in the films—and roles—given her.

The so-so year led off with a slight farce *Honeymoon for Three*, a remake of the 1933 Warner film *Goodbye Again*, which had featured Warren William as a famed novelist who rekindles an affair with married Genevieve Tobin. Meanwhile, his secretary, Joan Blondell, who is secretly in love with him, kibitzes disapprovingly. Michael Curtiz directed this bit of froufrou that in 1933 came and went with little or no notice taken of it.

The 1941 remake, also based on the Allan Scott–George Haight play, had George Brent in the lead, and Brent's lack of farcical expertise was depressingly evident. One retrospective commentary on this read: "*Honeymoon for Three* had the temerity to cast George Brent as a literary Don Juan at whose feet a profusion of ladies unconvincingly throw themselves."

Osa Massen was the girl who was second time around on Brent's romantic merry-go-round, and Ann Sheridan was the love-bemused secretary. Charlie Ruggles provided the picture's few bright moments as Massen's long suffering husband, and lost in the crowd surrounding Brent, Massen and Sheridan were William T. Orr, Lee Patrick, Walter Catlett—and Wyman in a nothing part. She stood around observing the action and commenting with wry weakness on it in *one* outfit—an unattractive wide-brimmed hat and a foulard dress, complete with messy ribbon, that would have worked superbly for Bette Davis in her ugly-duckling scenes a year later in *Now, Voyager*.

One reviewer proceeded to nail it all down with

*Honeymoon for Three* (1941), with Osa Massen, William T. Orr, and George Brent.

Sporting the latest in 1941 hat fashions.

the words: "This comedy falls flat on its face with the help of mediocre acting, writing, and production." When one co-actor reportedly kidded Wyman in the Warners commissary with the words: "The critics said we were all just awful in it!" Wyman wittily riposted that she might have been terrible if she had had a chance to be—then on the other hand, Wyman said, she might have been sensational—but her sparse dialogue and the slight attention paid to her by the camera left the verdict indeterminate.

Lloyd Bacon directed this in his usual hurried, pedestrian style, and the only bright note in the film, according to a retrospective commentator, came with: "Walter Catlett as a waiter—whose confusion during a restaurant scene—in which Brent is simultaneously entertaining two parties, neither being aware of the other's presence—was the brightest spot in an otherwise pallid comedy."

Noticeable in reruns of the film is cameraman indifference to Wyman and the almost nothing lines given her by screenwriter Earl Baldwin—"a hello-how-are-you, good-bye" role as Charlie Ruggles later phrased it.

On a number of occasions in later years Wyman characterized her second film of 1941, *Bad Men of Missouri*, as her all-time worst, but a viewing shows it to be a not bad action film—no world beater or Oscar candidate, but competently directed (by Ray Enright) and acted. Wyman was starred with Dennis Morgan, Wayne Morris, and Arthur Kennedy, and awash in such males as Victor Jory, Alan Baxter, and funnyman Walter Catlett. Possibly Wyman resented the film because it afforded her little attention or footage. Despite being technically starred (after Morgan), she felt "I was playing second fiddle to a bunch of men, outnumbering me a thousand to one and now and then, amidst the noisy gunfire, I was permitted a meow or two."

A 1941 glamour shot.

*Bad Men of Missouri* (1941), with Wayne Morris and Dennis Morgan.

As Kennedy's girlfriend she does little but peer through rainy windows, show up at climaxes, nod approvingly or disapprovingly depending on what the situation calls for, and look pliant and susceptible in "romantic" confrontations—*romantic* being placed in quotation marks because there is little time for smooching and hand-holding with all the shootem up action going on.

As *Variety* put it: "This is another cinematic glorification of the exploits of a daring band of desperadoes operating in Missouri during the postCivil War years. . . . It's strictly a shoot-em-up action meller with plenty of excitement injected along the way, making for a programmer that will find tough riding."

The Younger brothers—Morgan, Morris, and Kennedy—find themselves and their families and friends victimized by a land-grab to assure a railroad right of way, and set out to finish off their carpetbagger enemies forthwith. When villain Victor Jory kills

their father (Russell Simpson), it's hell to pay, and for a while they team up with equally ruthless Jesse James (Alan Baxter) to rid the land of the varmints. Wounded in a fracas, they wind up in a hospital—a *prison* hospital—but there get the heartening news that pals are maneuvering for pardons.

*Variety* thought little of all this, sniffing: "Picture makes little pretext of providing anything more than plenty of riding, holdups, and chases. Script and story both fail to establish credulity and use technique of a quarter century ago." In 1941 that would have meant 1916. Some critics found the outlandish, occasionally non sequitur situations downright laughable. In one sequence, when Wayne Morris is wounded in the chest, he emerges from the physician's office with his arm in a sling. Wyman is given such dialogue toward the finish as: "They're sayin' you did a lot of bad things—but a lot of good things, too."

Wyman was described by one critic as "in evidence now and then, pretty and spirited, with a pensive moment or two indicative of things to come." Clad in a snood (fashionable both in the 1860s and in the World War II 1940s; it kept the women's hair out of the machinery in the defense plants), replete with gingham dresses (cut rather close to the bust but otherwise quite dowdy, in that or any era), and a succession of decorously drab bonnets and cloaks, but with her hair defiantly, gloriously garish-blonde throughout, Wyman now and then found herself handed a "livelier" snatch of dialogue, calling one heavy a "no-good, low-down carpetbagger," and kicking a protesting bookkeeper (comic Walter Catlett) in the shins.

Some critics complained of the undue comic intrusions, chiefly courtesy of Catlett, a super-busy comic of the period. He held up the picture time after time with a series of stand-up and fall-down gags great for a vaudeville act, but inappropriate to the progressions of an action film so bloody and brutal as this one.

Not all critics and show reviewers agreed with *Variety* on *Bad Men of Missouri*. One exhibitor reported to his showbiz journal: "This makes the third time I've played this feature and it still did average business. For you that are playing it first or second run to people who love westerns, give it *A* time by all means. It's an action-packed western filled with well-known stars in every role, and the trailer is an attention getter. Reviewer's Rating: 3 stars; Good." And from another exhibitor: "If your customers like action and plenty of it, show this. It ought to satisfy them for a spell. I never saw so much shooting in my life. Some of the bad men from Missouri in this picture, I never heard of. I guess it was before my time."

The two exhibitor reviews quoted above were respectively from Ralph Raspa of the State Theatre,

*The Body Disappears* (1941), with Edward Everett Horton.

Rivesville, West Virginia, and Dorothy Hickok Lewis of the Dream Theatre in Effingham, Kansas. Told of favorable exhibitor reaction to her "starring" picture, Wyman replied tartly: *"They* didn't have to act in it—I *did!"*

Several of the men connected with the film, director Ray Enright, actors Arthur Kennedy and Wayne Morris, and screenwriter Charles Grayson, held Wyman's potential in high esteem. Arthur Kennedy told me years later that he "felt they could have built up Jane's role more," adding, "she was supposed to be one of the stars." The late Wayne Morris said he had always greatly admired her and learned something from merely being in the same scene with her. "She was always natural and spontaneous," Ray Enright told me. "I don't think she was very happy in the picture—let's face it, the men got all the action, the footage, and the camera angles. There was nothing in it for a woman—but she gave her conscientious best, within the limits of a skimpy role."

Wyman was again "starred"—this time right after Jeffrey Lynn—in *The Body Disappears.* Of this critic Clive Hirschhorn wrote in a retrospective summation: "[In this film], a farce which relied more on trick photography for its effects than on Scott Darling and Erna Lazarus's screenplay, leading man Jeffrey Lynn turned invisible after being injected with a serum invented by Edward Everett Horton. Horton followed suit; so did leading lady Jane Wyman. The only thing not injected with the stuff was the film itself—which, in the circumstances, was an oversight not easily forgiven."

D. Ross Lederman, of whom not much was heard thereafter, directed, and he didn't have all that much to do, what with that champion comic mugger and screen stealer Edward Everett Horton operating under his own power throughout, and with Wyman and the rest of the cast walking through their roles with the weary aplomb of people who had been that trite, foolish way many times before. *The Body Disappears* soon was languishing as the top half of a third-rate double-bill in small towns in the Midwest, with second honors going to an item called *The Gorilla Man,* which was accompanied by the audience-enticing legend "He's LOOSE! With a KILL-LUST!" It played great in Emporia, Kansas, and Peoria, Illinois.

One plus for Wyman in *The Body Disappears* was being able to work with one of the great comedic stylists of all time Edward Everett Horton, who played her mad-scientist father. She recalled in later years that she had learned much from observing and reacting to Horton's sallies, which came from his own experienced (and inspired) instincts, with no credit to hapless director Lederman. Horton later told associates that Wyman made a wonderful straight woman, that she had an authentic comedic talent all her own, and that he held her in high esteem.

Wyman's always shy and self-deprecating leading man Jeffrey Lynn, of whom it was said, "He was too much of a gentleman to fight his way to major stardom," was not as skilled in comedic nuances, but some of Horton rubbed off on him, too. He later declared: "Janie and Eddie Horton were really supportive co-workers."

*You're In The Army Now,* which according to Clive Hirschhorn was the last Warners release of the year 1941, got dismissed (along with a "Morally Suitable For All" tag) by *Harrison's Reports* with the words: "A farily good program Army camp comedy. The fact that most of the gags are pretty old does not detract from their amusing quality; this is due to the expert clowning by Jimmy Durante. He is ably assisted in these comedy bits by Phil Silvers. And some of the new gags are fairly comical." About Jane Wyman, this time reduced to a hapless, smaller-type third lead in the ads, *Harrison's Reports* says nothing.

The silly, inconsequential plot has Durante and Silvers as unsuccessful vacuum-cleaner salesmen who join the army by mistake. Then they find that their colonel, Donald McBride, has chased them from his home after they made an unholy mess of their vacuum-selling session.

Colonel's daughter Wyman takes pity on them. Meanwhile Durante is forever landing in the brig for one mishap after another. Soon, out of gratitude to Wyman for her kindnesses to them, the boys are trying to salvage her situation with her father, who disapproves of her love alliance with tank officer Regis Toomey, who to Colonel McBride's rage, is trying to mechanize his outfit. All ends well, with Durante and Silvers engineering the success of the romance and a reconciliation between Wyman's father and suitor.

As one critic pointed out: "The draft was big news in 1941, and any number of films got on the war wagon. A simple-minded vehicle for the roughhouse antics of Jimmy Durante and Phil Silvers, it had much in common with at least three other current

You're in the Army Now (1941), with Phil Silvers and Jimmy Durante.

pictures, Bob Hope and Eddie Bracken's *Caught in the Draft*, Laurel and Hardy's *Great Guns*, and, especially, Abbott and Costello's *Buck Privates*."

Wyman found herself pushed aside through most of the Durante-Silvers action, allowing for a few weak-tea romantic episodes with Regis Toomey, but she finally came into her own when she got to sing "I'm Glad Your Number Was Called" in a patriotic, garishly caparisoned U.S.O. show number. Clad in a fetching beaded white Army "uniform" with her pretty legs peeking out provocatively below the skirt, her cap fetchingly askew, Wyman—for the brief time allotted her—came through with all colors flying. Her admirers of 1941—and they were growing— were left to wish there had been more of her in musical action.

As one critic mentioned: "*You're In The Army Now* was no classic, but there was a scattered yok or two. Jane Wyman was a piquant, saucer-eyed good sport, and looked to be having fun. In fact, in a couple of the would-be serious moments she seemed on the verge of breaking up at the inanity of it all."

Both Jimmy Durante and Phil Silvers held her in high regard, Jimmy's words for her being "a real pretty woman—and a good trouper" and Silvers' comment: "Wonderful eyes—and great gams." Regis Toomey, then on his way down as a lead (he later did well in the character-acting contingent), remembered that on her way up however slowly Wyman was "sparkling, on top of things, and very funny on the set." He added, "I think she knew it was all a lot of hooey, but she seemed to want to enjoy herself, and in that musical number they gave her, she looked and sang like a million!"

*Variety*, however, had deflating words for the Toomey-Wyman combine with the brief and dismissive paragraph: "Regis Toomey and Jane Wyman carry the romantic interest, which necessarily is played away down." And on the movie itself: "A bit corny in spots and lays the slapstick on heavily."

61

MODERN SCREEN

JANUARY

Still **10** CENTS

JANE WYMAN
RONALD REAGAN

**"MY SOLDIER" BY JANE WYMAN**

The January 1943 cover of
*Modern Screen.*

In early 1942 Ronald Reagan, married and the father of a year-old daughter, found himself in the service. William Demarest knew the stateside Army captain. "I don't think Ronnie minded World War II anywhere near as much as some of the guys who were pulled from their promising acting careers into uniform. He had never really gotten decent roles in pictures of any consequence, knew he wasn't taken seriously as an actor, for all his charm and affability, and with a nowhere Warner Bros. contract where he was only technically a star, he didn't feel he was leaving much for a uniform. Of course he missed his family," Demarest said.

It was true that Reagan had had few solid roles in films. He had been in Bette Davis's famed *Dark Victory* (1939), but only in a small supporting role as a drunken playboy. He had had a small but telling role as George Gipp (a star football player) in the Pat O'Brien starrer, *Knute Rockne: All American* (1940). His best break had come in *King's Row* (1942) in which he was town sport Drake McHugh, who got his legs deliberately amputated by a fiendish doctor, Charles Coburn, who had disapproved of Drake's attentions to his daughter. (This inspired the title of Reagan's later autobiography, *Where's The Rest Of Me?*) Under Sam Wood's sensitive direction Reagan turned in a fine performance in this excellent picture, which dealt with small-town life in the Midwest at the turn of the century. *King's Row* had a baroquely morbid ambience that was strangely powerful and romantic, along with a haunting sense of the unseen and unspoken spiritually all the more potent for being indefinable. Along with sincere acting performances from an all-star cast and one of Erich Wolfgang Korngold's loveliest scores, *King's Row* reached, over the years, the status of a classic.

*King's Row* was always to be Reagan's all-time favorite of his movies, and he often screened it during the years of his marriage to Wyman, to her increasing boredom and annoyance. Many years later, fan-mag writer Jerry Asher said that he felt that "Jane had a violent aversion to her then husband Ronald Reagan's film *King's Row* because the whole ambience of the picture, located in the general area of her childhood, evoked horrible spectres of the repressed rigidity and sanctimonious hypocrisy of her beginnings. It wasn't that she envied Ronnie his one serious success in films," Jerry told me. "It was just that the morbid, repressed, baleful ambience of the picture brought back her Missouri past much too vividly. Jane as a prescient artist knew the picture itself to be a fine one, but Ronnie's compulsive efforts to foist continued screenings on his guests to underline his pride in one of the few pictures he thought had showcased him decently, drove her wild, and depressed her."

Jerry continued: "Ronnie was a hell of a bright guy, but he lacked, I'm afraid, the sensitivity to discern that he was opening old wounds in Jane by rubbing that picture into her." The pictures he did after that one were disappointing. He was often given star billing, technically, but he was assigned pedestrian fare. He romanced Ann Sheridan for dullishly tawdry results in a farrago called *Juke Girl*. He palled around with Errol Flynn in a knockabout World War II opus called *Desperate Journey*.

After these thankless chores, with more threatening to come, Reagan, his cronies felt, welcomed U.S. Army service as a refreshing new adventure. He spent his first service months undergoing basic training at Fort Mason in the San Francisco area. After eight weeks he was back in the film capital. Here he was assigned to the Special Services unit as an Army Air Force officer, his rank lieutenant. He worked on training films in various capacities, sometimes acting, sometimes directing or narrating. Off and on, he was able to live at home with Wyman and

his daughter, and as a sideline did much work for the Screen Actors Guild.

The fan magazines made much of Reagan's uniform, featuring him on their covers along with his wife and creating much hoopla about his being the perfect American officer who had gone to war despite the responsibility of a wife and daughter. He told friends that he felt guilty not to be overseas, where other men were fighting and dying, but his weak eyes had precluded combat service. When fan-mag mavens, of both sexes, did interviews with Reagan during 1943 and 1944 he was known to say, "Why write about *me*? Write about those guys out there doing the *real* work of the war!"

"I am positive that he didn't particularly miss the Warner lot or the parts they had been giving him," Jerry Asher told me. "He said to me more than once, 'I'm afraid a *King's Row* will come along only once in my life.' And he certainly must have had a private crystal ball around, because he turned out to be dead right. Even after he went back to Warners when he got out of service, they continued to hand him nothing roles in nothing pictures. Obviously Fate had not designed him to be a movie star."

Wyman was supportive while her husband was in service. When he was home, she strove to make him comfortable. When he was away, she kept in regular touch with letters, and, when possible, phone calls. Meanwhile she pursued a film career of her own that in the 1942 through 1944 period was certainly no great shakes, and she lavished Maureen with maternal devotion.

In early 1942 Wyman found herself in a lead opposite Edward G. Robinson, whom she was always to recall as "stimulating and inspirational." Robinson returned the compliment with his words to me years later about his appearance with Wyman in *Larceny, Inc.*:

"The talent stood out in her for all to see, and I was not at all surprised when a few years later she became Warners' most important star." Robinson added, "The only mystery to me was why it took them so long to get on to her potential. I always felt it was most patient and steady of her to take all those undemanding, silly roles they handed her. In *Larceny, Inc.* I saw her make a lot out of very little. She was very flamboyantly handsome in her looks, but, surprisingly, understood the value of underplaying, and I found her most professional, and good company on the set, with a great sense of humor."

The film dealt with a gang of outlaws who take

With army officer husband Reagan, holding Maureen, 1943.

*Larceny, Inc.* (1942), with Broderick Crawford, Edward Brophy, Jack Carson, and Edward G. Robinson.

over a New York luggage store with the intention of tunneling into the bank next door. They are interrupted by unwelcome intruders, including neighborhood shop owners, all innocents trying to be friendly. Wyman, who plays Robinson's daughter, has a romance with a luggage salesman played by Jack Carson. Due to constant screwups among Robinson's henchman, the robbery plan goes to pot. Wyman is bright and witty as the daughter, and tries to generate some romantic steam with Carson, despite dialogue that would have taxed the resources of the cleverest performer.

This was the first of Wyman's several teamings with Jack Carson, who said of her: "That was a natural talent if ever there was one. And she got herself across quietly, spontaneously, nothing forced about her. And what a scene stealer! She kept me on my toes every second." On hand in *Larceny, Inc.* for one of his early screen appearances was Jackie Gleason. Then twenty-six he played an eavesdropping soda jerk.

On a loanout to RKO Radio in 1942 Wyman found herself playing with Kay Kyser. Kyser, then about forty-five, was a bandleader who had found himself, fleetingly, in the movies after making something of a splash on radio as the quizmaster of "Kay Kyser's Kollege of Musical Knowledge." Among his few films were *That's Right, You're Wrong* (1939); *You'll Find Out* (1940); *Playmates* (1942), the ill-starred John Barrymore's last picture; and *Swing Fever* (1943). A pleasant, humorously relaxed fellow, Kyser never pretended to be much of an actor and his films were distinctly light-weight fare.

*My Favorite Spy*, for which Wyman was loaned to co-star with Kyser and Ellen Drew (Wyman had third billing), was best described by a lavish ad with legends like: DON'T SHOOT, MEN! KAY'S A THOUSAND LAUGHS AHEAD OF YOU—AND WITH MUSIC, TOO! The ad went on: "What a show for fun and gags! Spies spy on spies, and a sultry blonde takes the plot . . . with Kay in a whirl of dizzy intrigue that merry-go-rounds the axis . . . plus a photo finish of action that keeps you howling as you thrill!" In the ad was Wyman looking provocatively bosomy in what appeared to be a filmy black lace negligee. Ellen Drew in a larger photo shared the "woo-action" with star Kyser. In the supporting cast was Wyman's earlier mentor, William Demarest.

*Screenland* Magazine nailed down the proceedings as follows: "A spy comedy with Kay Kyser playing a not-too-bright bandleader who is called to Army Service on his wedding day, later released, and made a counterespionage agent. His efforts become amusingly complicated when he can't explain his doings to his unkissed bride. Sure Kay bags the spies, Ellen Drew, the bride, and Jane Wyman, his blonde secret operator-partner. Good, but we missed Ginny Simms [who often appeared with Kyser] and didn't get enough of Kay's band. It's not our favorite Kyser film."

*TV Movies* retrospectively gave it two stars with the brief dismissal: "How did we win WW2 with bandleader Kay as spy? Nonsensical musicomedy tries to explain."

From Chapel Hill, North Carolina, in December 1973, Kay Kyser wrote of *My Favorite Spy*: "Jane Wyman has a great sense of humor, a keen sense of loyalty, and a heart as big as all outdoors. She's big on soul, too, sings a pretty darn good song (another band singer turned actress), and has discerning taste in music—which proved to be profitable to me.

"A recording date came up during the filming of *My Favorite Spy*. At a time when we were not needed on the set, my arranger, George Duning, and I met to select from many, four songs for recording. Jane eagerly accepted our invitation to help us. Her number one pick was 'Who Wouldn't Love You.' We concurred. It was one of our biggest hits!

*My Favorite Spy* (1942), with Gail Russell, Kay Kyser, and Una O'Connor.

*Footlight Serenade* (1942), with Phil Silvers, John Payne, Betty Grable, and Victor Mature.

"Jane gave me many tips on acting, all the while modestly claiming that she couldn't act, that she only knew the tricks of the trade. Some movies later, she won the Oscar for *Johnny Belinda*. I sent her this wire: 'If there's anything I can't stand, It's a liar.' Later, when we met in Romanoff's, she asked with tears in her eyes what she'd done to deserve the wire. To which I replied, 'You once told me you couldn't act.'"

The director of *My Favorite Spy*, Tay Garnett, wrote from Hollywood in the same year: "[I feel I should mention] the unusual rapport—the atmosphere of warmth and harmony that prevailed on our set. It was felt and commented on by every member of our cast and crew. It was a fun set—unique in my experience. All my sets have been pleasant, but this one was truly a standout. Too bad the picture couldn't have reflected a bit more of this."

Wyman enjoyed working with Tay and Kay, as members of their devoted crew dubbed them, and while conceding that the picture might have turned out better than it did, with no one being particularly to blame, always spoke well of her associates on it,

and kept up her friendship with them through the years.

For *Footlight Serenade*, her third 1942 picture, Wyman was borrowed, for reasons which to date remain inexplicable, by Twentieth Century-Fox for one of her typical roles—the heroine's sidekick.

Here she found herself in a musical with a show-business background, starring—who else?—Betty Grable, with John Payne, and Victor Mature. The ridiculous story had a heavy-weight champ, Mature, deciding he'd like to do a Broadway show. Here he encounters dancer Grable, who is secretly married to Payne, but doesn't want it known for career reasons.

Payne naturally resents Mature's brash advances to his wife and gets his chance at revenge when he plays the champ's partner in a simulated fight and gives Mature the old one-two on-stage. Wyman? Deputized to console the star at any and all times, she patiently plays solitaire while the star dallies on the phone, and rubs her ankles after a tough dance practice—Wyman even spars with Grable in *their own* simulated boxing match on stage.

Aside from getting sore wrists from soothing the

A "boxing" number with Betty Grable and chorines in *Footlight Serenade* (1942).

Grable ankles and the threat of a dislodged tooth or swollen jaw from her sparrings with the lady, Wyman emerged from *Footlight Serenade* unscathed—but somewhat enervated by the same console-the-lead-gal stuff.

Wyman took what comfort she could from pleasant conversations with Grable, whom she found down-to-earth, and from friendly joshings with he-men Mature and Payne. She also got some laughs out of the malapropisms, wild Russian accent, and quirky temperament of director Gregory Ratoff, a gifted but eccentric man.

Many Wyman students in later years have wondered why she tolerated the drek in which she found herself for so long. They ask why her talents weren't recognized sooner by the studio. One answer lies in the fact that, for all her bravado and surface pushiness, she was fundamentally accommodating, grateful to a studio that had groomed and sustained her, and honestly analytical about her chances to protest and push successfully. She had noted that established stars had tried to buck the studio, and had

failed. She knew that tough blondes of the kind she played so well remained in vogue for longer than expected, and felt that it was not wise to abandon a good thing until its possibilities had been exhausted. And she had the security of a contract (no matter how small the pay). Outside the studio gates there were girls who were envious of that security and would have sold their souls to have a chance at it—and the upwardly mobile hope it represented.

Certainly her climb over those six years had been impressive. Slow—tortously slow—but sure. She had started in 1936 as an absolute nothing, barely a bit player, and by 1942 she had become a leading lady to such as Edward G. Robinson and Kay Kyser. Those years had brought marriage and motherhood and a slowly growing self-esteem. She had made many friends and had solidly established herself in Hollywood. But the goal of stardom in the true sense still remained elusive. More hard work, more trials, and disappointments loomed ahead before that stardom was to be finally attained.

# 4

## Things Start Looking Up
## 1943–1947

From 1943 through 1947 Hollywood and its followers witnessed the emergence of the Jane Wyman of cinematic legend. In early 1943—age twenty-nine—she was still known primarily as that cute blonde vixen who was married to soldier boy Ronnie Reagan and had borne a daughter, two years old by then, who was a miniature edition of her mother. She seemed to be without particular ambition, and was regarded as a nice steady contractee on the Warner lot who never gave anybody any trouble. She took whatever roles were thrown at her, never kicked up a fuss, and rarely, if ever, generated copy, either for the publicity flacks or for the eager but frustrated fan-mag mavens.

A good mother to Maureen, a patient, keep-the-home-fires-burning wife, Janie was in 1943 the best little girl in all the world. Some friends felt that too much of Ronnie's stodginess and seriousness had rubbed off on the former hey-hey girl, that the spontaneity and sparkle that had characterized her in 1939 had degenerated into a good-homemaker, good-second-lead image.

Warner Brothers was no help. In 1942 they had not employed her in any of their releases for that year other than the Robinson film. The lead opposite Kyser at RKO had been innocuous and forgettable enough, and the girlfriend spot next to star Betty Grable in *Footlight Serenade* was an even more deadly and repetitious play on her long-standing image—or rather, lack of it.

Of course, the war years had caused some significant changes at the studio. A number of pictures made at the time were held up for release, often shown first to the servicemen in camps and overseas (not only for the sake of their morale, but also as novel testing grounds for the product). Fewer pictures were being made at Warners to save on costs, what with materials being diverted to defense purposes and so many workers, many of them skilled craftsmen, taking off for either defense plants or the service. The ones who remained did double duty. As a result, the planning and execution of scheduled films became tighter, more carefully executed.

During this time Wyman was busier with off-screen duties than with her roles before the camera. She entertained soldiers at the Hollywood canteen and elsewhere and helped out with fund drives. Two-year-old Maureen filled up much of the time she spent waiting for Ronnie to come home on leave. The infrequent roles she was assigned were uninspired.

Warners, to keep their contractees from flagging, and to promote the fewer films they were releasing in 1943, sent a number of players around the country on publicity tours, either for their own films or for whatever product was opening around the circuit. Wyman travelled on one of these tours, which was gruelling, often two nights in one town and one day in the next. However, it was during this tour that her luck significantly changed.

Wyman had completed a picture with Olivia De Havilland and Robert Cummings called *Princess O'Rourke* just prior to her tour. Luckily for her the picture was released fairly soon after production had

*Princess O'Rourke* (1943), with Robert Cummings, Jack Carson, and Olivia De Havilland.

been completed. (A number of Warner films made in 1942 and 1943 did not see national release until 1946 when the war was over and the studio took advantage of the boom in attendance, a result of the emotional release after the war.) Producer Charles Brackett, over at Paramount, happened to see an advance print of *Princess O'Rourke*, and was struck by a scene involving Wyman. The picture is a slight affair about a princess (De Havilland), incognito in New York from a mythical European country, who romances an airline pilot (her country has been overrrun in World War II), and Wyman plays the WAC officer wife of Jack Carson, co-pilot buddy of De Havilland's love interest, Robert Cummings. Played for laughs, it seemes forced and arch today. However the film contained a restaurant sequence that gave Wyman a chance to strut her stuff.

On the town with De Havilland, Cummings, and Carson on the eve of the boys' joining up with the air force, Wyman reveals that she married Carson a week or so after their meeting on a bus (her dress had caught on his buttons). During this restaurant scene that arrested producer Brackett's attention, Carson and Wyman get up to dance. There was a certain bittersweet poignancy in the way she played the scene. They had recently wed, he was off to war, and she soon would be at loose ends again. She was bewildered and hurt by it, yet still tried to keep up a brave front for his sake. In this scene Jane Wyman showed depths of feeling no one at Warners or anywhere else had noted in her before. That scene was to have important consequences for her.

*Princess O'Rourke*, inexplicably to me, won the Best Original Screenplay Academy Award for 1943. Seen in the 1980s, it is slight, coy, rather carelessly strung together, with forced humor. The situations date badly, and the romancing is unbelievable, given the basic backgrounds (on screen) of principals Cummings and De Havilland. But the qualities in Wyman that Charles Brackett saw and reacted to in that fateful restaurant scene are still very marked, and presage the Wyman who was to burst upon the world as a full-fledged star later.

Brackett went to the Paramount brass, showed them the scene, and suggested she be given a screen test for the role of alcoholic Ray Milland's long-suffering fiancee in *The Lost Weekend*. He learned she was in New York on that particular leg of her publicity tour, and phoned her and asked her to read the book. She read it straight through, but couldn't imagine what part in the screen version Brackett could possibly want her for.

As she recalled it later, "I couldn't for the life of me find any part for me to play. I was conditioned to thinking of myself as a comedienne; the dramatic parts I *knew* I could handle well seemed to be always denied me. I was completely floored when Billy Wilder, the director, said he wanted me for the part of the girlfriend to the hero."

Meanwhile in that same year Wyman was telling a *Motion Picture* interviewer, "I was my own worst enemy for years. I had the biggest chip on my shoulder that's ever been seen west of the Rockies. I had a little speech I made to myself every morning:

'Look out for yourself, and don't let anyone put anything over on you.'" She added that marriage and motherhood had mellowed her considerably, and that perhaps at twenty-nine she was fully ready for anything positive that might come her way.

While the picture that Brackett and Wilder wanted her for over at Paramount, *The Lost Weekend*, would change her life forever once she got around to it, the shooting was delayed until 1944. Before they went into production she had to fulfill her Warner contract obligations, which meant four mediocre films in a row, none of which did anything for her. Warners, as usual, continued to ignore the light under their assembly line bushel of assembly line fare. Back in "The Burbank Salt Mines," as one of her overworked colleagues had termed the lair of the Brothers Warner, she found herself cast in an item called *Make Your Own Bed*, a provocative title that the ensuing action did not spell out. In this Jack Carson makes like a private eye. With his girlfriend, Wyman, in tow as an accomplice of sorts, he poses as a servant to checkmate the machinations of some Nazi saboteurs.

The picture was chiefly notable for a vulgar ad run in major fan magazines that displayed Wyman,

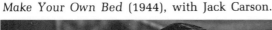

*Make Your Own Bed* (1944), with Jack Carson.

saucy-looking in a maid's uniform, and Irene Manning hitching up their skirts naughtily at the center of the layout. At the bottom a tasteless, cartoonlike Jack Carson was displayed, raffishly tearing the sheet off a bed that contained a coyly alarmed Jane and Irene while character performers Alan Hale and George Tobias, looking super-roguish, leer at the proceedings through an open door. Among the come-on lines were "Come on the Run for a Riot of Fun!" "You'll Whoop and Holler!" and "LAFF-FLASH! Theatres showing this picture reported laying mattresses in aisles—so customers can roll in comfort!"

Warners proved overly optimistic about the public and critical reaction. *Make Your Own Bed* was a witless 1944 also-ran, vulgar and repetitious. The forced situations and surprisingly humorless situations created a fadeout effect more hollow and enervated than bracing and alive—which of course was just the opposite of what the busy farceurs involved had intended. Wyman's performance is industrious and energetic, but despite her brightness it was evident her heart wasn't in it. Bosley Crowther of *The New York Times* wrote: "For all the contortions it goes through, [the picture] is a limp and labored endeavor to fetch laughs with a lot of old gags. And the humors it sometimes discovers are a feeble and unsustained lot."

In her next 1944 forgettable, Wyman joined Jerome Cowan, Eleanor Parker, and Faye Emerson in some nonsense about a vacationing private eye who walks into a murder trap. Wyman was Cowan's helpful vis-a-vis. *Crime By Night* was the title, and the real crime here was the imprisoning of audiences in a theatre for an interminable seventy-two minutes. Wyman looks listless and forced. She is obviously depressed about finding herself in the picture, and expert character actor Jerome Cowan promoted (or was it demoted) to a lead after supporting Bette Davis in such A pictures as *The Old Maid* (1939) and *Mr. Skeffington* (1944) seems to be working overtime to carry the picture as well as his three disspirited female leads, Wyman, Eleanor Parker, and Faye Emerson, to some kind of upbeat resolution. Downbeat, all the way, was more like it.

*The Doughgirls*, her third 1944 release, was a crock of frenetic nonsense about the housing shortage in wartime Washington. It was described in one of the ever busy Warners ads as "a romantic comedy

*Crime by Night* (1944), with Jerome Cowan and Stuart Crawford.

*The Doughgirls* (1944), with Ann Sheridan and Alexis Smith.

which revolves around three young ladies who get themselves into all sorts of complications when, for one reason or another, the marital status of each is proved illegal." Another ad read: "It's a honey of a funny—about love and money! 2 years on the stage— 2000 laughs on the screen! A screenful of screamful fun from Warners!" Jack Carson (again) and fey, pixieish comedian Charlie Ruggles were shown leering at Wyman, Ann Sheridan, Alexis Smith, and the then-ubiquitous Warner lovely Irene Manning—all of them prominently displaying their bosoms in spicy see-through lace get-ups.

Everyone worked hard in *The Doughgirls*, but the comic implications in the frazzled attempts to find housing *and* burgeoning relationships in wartime Washington had already been patented by *The More The Merrier*, the Jean Arthur-Joel McCrea-Charles Coburn smash of 1943, expertly directed by George Stevens. The retread of such tired situations, weakly helmed by an inexperienced James V. Kern, was more mishmash than smash this time around. Wy-

man and Carson by this time were running threadbare as a team, and in some scenes actually seemed to be irritated by one another—and not via a plot-induced gimmick. The only adrenalin provided came from a riotously miscast Eve Arden making hoarse-voiced accents as a Russian Army officer who for no reason that makes sense gets mixed up in the proceedings. Another problem was the dehydration of the snappy, often suggestive, Broadway script, which the bluenose Production Code, Hollywood's oppressive moral watchdog of the time, insisted be laundered, for dull results.

The Roman Catholic Church's bluenoses, as ever, lacking in a sense of the harmless hilarity implicit in many sexual situations, often cast a prudish pall over films of this period. The rules were strict: men had to keep one foot on the floor when embracing a woman in bed. Kisses were timed by the second lest they imply too much "lustfulness." Twin beds were thrown together, made with separate sheets and blankets, their occupants chastely attired in pajamas

The Doughgirls (1944), with Alexis Smith, Ann Sheridan, and Eve Arden.

and nightgown. On-screen sexuality in 1944 was a far cry from the erotic calisthenics taken for granted today. Wyman, in her pre-Catholic days, at times expressed to friends her impatience with this nonsense, but was not in any position to ameliorate it.

Wyman finally found a moneymaker for her last 1944 Warner effort, Hollywood Canteen, but here she was lost in a crowd of Burbank stars shown entertaining the boys in brown and blue before they took off for The Big Show in the Pacific. As part of the War effort in Hollywood at the time, the story of the canteen (which Bette Davis had originally sponsored) proceeded, through 104 minutes of frenetic flag waving and occasional human sentiment, on the frail thread of the story. Two servicemen (Robert Hutton and Dane Clark) spend a couple of nights at the Hollywood canteen before returning to duty in New Guinea. Prominently but briefly spotted, but not too long among all the other stars' turns, was a song and dance number featuring Wyman and Car-

son called "What Are You Doing The Rest of My Life?" Later, when a serviceman importunes Wyman for a date, she chirps "Not me. I've been Reaganized!" She got in a scene or two, strictly casual and in a crowd, with Davis—their only screen appearance together.

The war films of this period were simplistic items full of rah-rah patriotism, brave girls at home cheering on their intrepid heroes who smash the Japs and nab and nick the Nazis. Many were the saccharine scenes of soldier writing a letter while buddies snored, girlfriend at home wistfully checking the mailbox out by the lilac tree, all accompanied by Max Steiner's melodic inspirations at their mushiest and most banal. When Max the Musical Master was good (as in his Oscar winning Now, Voyager score) he could be very, very good indeed, but when forced, along with his musicians, to score a particularly silly war film, he could be consummately horrid. Wyman after the war told an interviewer that she was glad

*Hollywood Canteen*
(1944), with Jack Carson,
John Garfield, and Bette
Davis.

*Hollywood Canteen*
(1944), with Jimmy
Dorsey and Jack Carson.

The Lost Weekend (1945), with
Ray Milland.

*The Lost Weekend* (1945), with Ray Milland.

that in her roles she came into minimal contact with such treacle, though she had honest praise for the better war films.

With the last of *Hollywood Canteen* behind her, Wyman prepared to move over to Paramount for the finally ready *The Lost Weekend* with a sense of gathering excitement. Jack Warner had not hesitated to loan "little Janie" out for this; he knew little, and cared less, about the plans Wilder and Brackett had for what Warner called "that drunk film." Hollywood moguls of the time felt that any films that attempted to portray alcoholics in a serious light were poison at the box office. In their view drunks were always to be dragged in for comedy relief. That, they felt, would give audiences the reassuring, condescending, unthinking pleasure they came to the movie house for.

Billy Wilder over at Paramount was prepared to give them a rude shock. For his film of the Charles Jackson novel would show, with an unsparing,

nonsentimental brutality, the horrors of addiction to booze. For the lead they chose Ray Milland, an actor who up to that time had not been considered material for serious drama.

Things get going with a vengeance with the opening shot of Milland's bottle hanging out of a window via a cord. He is a New York City apartment dweller sharing a place with his conventional minded non-drinking brother (Phillip Terry), who supports him while he tries to make headway with his writing. He is thirty-three and pathetically dependent on his brother. While packing for a weekend in the country with Terry, he finds the craving for a drink too racking for denial. He persuades Terry, and his long-suffering girlfriend, Wyman, to attend an afternoon concert. Though he initially plans to see them later in the day, a tragic alcoholic odyssey ensues. The Milland character already has been confined to an institution for alcoholic bouts, and his brother is deeply concerned for him. As Doug McClelland wrote in *Cinema Notes*: "The script, and Milland, were especially skillful in capturing the unscrupulous, wily, diabolical desperation of the addicted."

Milland's Don Birnam steals the cleaning woman's money. Soon he is at his favorite bar, run by Howard Da Silva. Later, at the apartment, Wyman begs Terry not to desert Don. ("He's a sick person; it's as if there were something wrong with his heart or his lungs.") But the brother, fed up, leaves for the country. In a flashback Wyman and Milland "meet cute" at the opera when their clothing checks get mixed up. Even after she learns the truth, she stands by loyally, carrying devotion to practically masochistic extremes. One degradation follows another in his search for money with which to drink: he steals money from a woman in a restaurant; he pawns his typewriter; he begs money from a lady of the evening. Finally he ends up in the Bellevue alcoholic ward where sadistic attendant Frank Faylen acquaints him with the horrors he has observed among delirium tremens cases—a hallucination about a bat attacking a mouse, little turkeys parading in straw hats. He observes another patient frantically beating off imaginary beetles that swarm all over his body.

Out of the hospital at last, Milland hocks Wyman's leopard coat—but this time in order to purchase a gun; he plans to commit suicide. Wyman talks him out of it. In a less than convincing windup Milland contemplates the drink he is about to take, and instead drops a cigarette into the glass. Deciding he is, once and for all, off the booze, he begins to write a novel about his experiences. He will title it *The Bottle*.

In the Jackson novel the hero has homosexual inclinations. (Homosexuality was a favorite Jackson subject. Ahead of his time, he also write a frighteningly clinical novel called *The Fall of Valor* on the subject.) Homosexuality was considered too realistic and therefore *verboten* for 1945 film audiences. The prudish Production Code held it in ostrich-in-the-sand horror and banned even the slightest implication of it from the nation's screens. This side of the Milland character was dropped.

Described by one character as "an awful high-class young lady," in this role Wyman conducted herself with a resolute, ladylike integrity that jumped miles ahead of her chronic incarnations as chorus girl and "friend of the hero's best friend." True, things got rather thick, what with Wyman continually turning

the other cheek to the Milland character's neglect, abuse, and indifference—even to the point of sleeping on the steps outside his apartment awaiting his return from an all-night binge. However, Wyman gave an honest, sincere, tensely tragic performance in *The Lost Weekend*. Her compassion for her lost fiancee was portrayed tellingly, and her tormented inner churnings and indecisive moves as she planned her often futile strategies for his redemption are delineated with force and conviction. She was also well-dressed throughout, and in the snappiest 1945 styles, and made-up correspondingly, looking at all times her best. Since she had no drab outer aspect of costume or makeup with which to enhance her performance visually, she instead relied, with notable success, on her eyes, her gestures, her stances, and vocal intonations to communicate an inner misery under an enterprising and persistent exterior personality.

"It changed my whole life," Wyman later said of *The Lost Weekend*. Indeed, her fellow Warner player of the past, Olivia De Havilland, had first been considered for the role, and in fact Lillian Fontaine, De Havilland's mother, played the small role of Wyman's mother. Milland, too, had been a second choice for the lead. Wilder had wanted Jose Ferrer, but the studio heads felt that a more physically attractive lead would more fully ensure the sympathy of 1945 audiences. It almost didn't get made at all, this *Lost Weekend* "hot potato," as it was known during production. The several studios who had turned it down because they had mistakenly felt a serious study of a hitherto comedic subject would be boxoffice poison were confounded. After a disastrous preview with an audience in San Bernardino, who had obviously come seeking shallow escapist entertainment, the New York screening got a highly favorable reaction. The studio accordingly released it. *Photoplay*'s review stated: "They have created the mood, the tempo, and the horror of a man beset with a craving beyond and outside himself. . . . A new and dreadful kind of horror tale."

*The Lost Weekend* reflected credit on everyone connected with it. It won Ray Milland an Academy Award, and sent shock waves of awareness through Hollywood—an awareness that there was a responsive audience out there for films that were grainily realistic. It set the tone and style for the *noir verité* films that would follow in the later 1940s—productions like *Crossfire* and *Gentleman's Agreement*, movies *made* adultly *for* adults, that largely eschewed romantic escapism and pat solutions in favor of realistically tragic denouements and naturalistic acting. And Jane Wyman found that she had been on the ground floor for this new trend.

*The Lost Weekend* was to prove truly a watershed film for Wyman in that her acting was taken far more seriously by producers and directors. It was to lead to the film that would bring her to a new height of critical and popular esteem, *The Yearling*. And again, as has been so often the case in great acting careers out Hollywood way, the performer had to seek honor outside of her home territory. It was Metro-Goldwyn-Mayer, borrowing her from a still unaware of her potential Jack Warner, who provided the showcase for the greatest Wyman performance up to that time.

Metro-Goldwyn-Mayer had bought Marjorie Kin-

nan Rawlings' Pulitzer prize-winning novel, *The Yearling*, in 1938, but it did not make the screens of the movie houses until 1946. King Vidor was originally assigned to direct it, and he had high hopes for it, with Spencer Tracy and Anne Revere in the leads. But there were numerous delays. Tracy proved highly indecisive about the role of Pa Baxter, an impoverished Florida farmer living in 1870, who does perpetual battle with the harsh land, the recalcitrant crops, predatory beasts, and thieving neighbors. An unvarnished tale of hardship, the story also told about the Baxter son's passage into manhood. He is forced to kill a beloved yearling deer who has grown from adorable fawn to destroyer of the crops that literally keep the family alive. Vidor, as he told me, considered Anne Revere perfect for the role of the dour and stoical pioneering wife who has lost

With Ronald Reagan, 1945, at the California State Military Guard Ball.

At daughter Maureen's fourth birthday party, 1945.

With husband, Reagan, and children, Maureen and Michael, 1946.

With her husband, daughter, and son, 1946.

Husband Reagan gives her xylophone lessons, 1946.

*The Yearling* (1946), with Claude Jarman, Jr.

*The Yearling* (1946), with Gregory Peck and Claude Jarman, Jr.

Display ad for *The Yearling* (1946).

many children and is afraid to express her inner love for her one remaining child.

The projected screenplay, like the book, contained fascinating scenes: a hunt for a predatory bear, a near-fatal rattlesnake bite, a feud between two families resolved at the graveside of the boy's best friend, a frail cripple. The warmth and humanity of the project were, Vidor felt, irresistible if translated properly to the screen and if the actual locations were used.

Part of the holdup was Tracy's shilly-shallying about the part. He and Anne Revere and Vidor actually started on the film, but other obstacles intervened: changing weather conditions, fawns who grew too soon and lost their baby spots, the innumerable harassments of location shooting. In addition, high production costs and lack of studio unanimity about the project's worth also came up, and the film was abandoned.

Finally in 1945 director Clarence Brown and producer Sidney Franklin started up the project anew. Brown found an amazing child actor, Claude Jarman, Jr., in a Tennessee schoolroom and brought him to Hollywood for one of the three leading roles. Producer Sidney Franklin later reminisced about the selection of Gregory Peck and Jane Wyman for the roles of the pioneering parents:

"The important thing in depicting the parents," Franklin said, "was that we photograph their inner souls rather than their physical bodies. The thing that made you so moved, when you read the book and later screenplay, was not their physical appearance but their amazing courage and their undying love for each other, no matter how cruel life was in their remote wilderness clearing. In choosing Peck to play Penny and Jane Wyman to play Ma we felt we had picked the two players, man and woman, best able to present that amazing courage and that un-

Character study from *The Yearling* (1946).

dying love. Peck, tall, rawboned, looked the part of a wilderness pioneer. And quite frankly we picked Jane Wyman because of her work in *The Lost Weekend*."

Franklin added, "While there would seem to be a vast gulf between the modern, modishly attired girl who fought to save Birnam from drink, and the grim silent Ma of *The Yearling*, the two parts are emotionally very similar. Both women showed quiet strength in fights against implacable enemies. In one case, the enemy was liquor; in Ma's case, the wilderness."

Franklin and director Clarence Brown recalled discussing the story on separate occasions with Peck and Wyman, and actor and actress gave a resounding, eager *yes* within twenty-four hours. "Actors sometimes hesitate about roles that will tie them up for nearly a year in one picture, as was the case with

*The Yearling*," Clarence Brown recalled, "but both performers shared our faith in the story."

MGM publicists let it be known that the locations were a million and a half acres of Florida scrub country, in the Ocala National Forest. Brown and the stars described the inhabitants as "wonderful, warmhearted people. They have such a pride in their long lineage in the scrub country," Brown added, "that they were slow to get acquainted. But once you knew them they were real friends. We couldn't have made the picture without their enthusiastic interest and their trained technical assistance."

Wyman told me in 1948: "It was my biggest chance yet, and I was determined to make the most of it. I determined to act from the inside out, to disregard all surface effects, and delve into the character of a sturdy woman who endured hardship stoically and who concealed a deeply emotional nature under a frosty, pragmatic exterior. I meditated on the role at great length; I wanted to get to the bottom of this woman's psyche. And in doing so I dredged up all the early hardships and disappointments in my own life, looking constantly for some points of reference that would link our respective inner schemes."

The reviews were universally laudatory. Dorothy Kilgallen, the noted New York columnist, wrote: "Jane Wyman, demonstrating an amazing versatility, is the surprise of the picture. She plays the drab, nagging, miserable farm wife with such authority and definition as to make it almost impossible to believe that this weary creature and the glamorous little cookie of *Night and Day* came from the repertoire of the same actress."

The *Photoplay* reviewer wrote: "Chief acting honors indisputably belong to Jane Wyman as Ma Baxter. Devoid of glamorizing makeup, Jane doesn't *play*, she *is* a care-worn, embittered woman with one goal in life: food and shelter, and maybe a well outside her door so she needn't trek a mile for every drop of precious water." Rose Pelswick in *The New York Journal-American* said, "Miss Wyman's performance is surprisingly fine—surprising because for years she has been identified with pert ingenue roles and is here for the first time given a chance to show what she can do with a real characterization." And from *Parents Magazine*: "It is Jane Wyman as Ma Baxter who does the most creative acting for she suggests a whole lifetime of denial in the mother's fear of losing Jody if she loves him too openly. Her intense pride in rising above poverty and being beholden to no one is true of pioneer dignity. And she makes understandable the bitterness of backwoods women, the sameness of whose daily drudgery was rarely lightened by the hunting, the swapping, the relish of the seasons and their varied tasks that the men enjoyed. The talk is taken from the book and the actors have absorbed it so well that it comes out honest country speech instead of stage dialect. . . . The film is faithful to the spirit of a beloved book."

*The Yearling* was to win Wyman a nomination for the 1946 Academy Award—which she later lost to Olivia De Havilland for *To Each His Own*.

Clarence Brown as late as 1965 was telling columnist Ed Sullivan that Wyman was one of his three top-favorite actresses when it came to sheer talent and film authority, the other two being Greta Garbo and Katharine Hepburn. In 1977 Wyman would be among those honoring him at a Directors Guild of America tribute attended by many stars who had worked with him, along with top-drawer Hollywood notables. Brown said of her to me in 1972: "A great natural talent she had—and how much private unhappiness, defeat, and surmounting of personal disasters she must have dredged-up from her inner life of memories to have offered a rich portrayal that was so deeply felt and so wise in the ways of the human spirit."

Wyman later recalled to me and others that she had had a nervous and tense time of it in early 1945 while MGM was trying to persuade Jack Warner to lend her to them for *The Yearling*. Warner, at long last, had become fully aware of Wyman's potential and had already begun to look around for more solid fare for her.

Asked in later years why she felt the usually possessive (professionally) and stubborn Jack Warner had agreed to lend her to MGM for *The Yearling*, she said, "People who were rooting for me at Warners appealed to his self-interest by telling him I would come back to him an even more 'bankable' star after a solid part like that under my belt. I was *lucky* in *that* instance; he could be *very* tough with Olivia De Havilland and others on loanouts—or anything else, for that matter."

But before *The Yearling*'s formal debut in late 1946, Wyman had been forced by Jack Warner to finish several forgettable films due under her contract, *One More Tomorrow* and *Night and Day*, the Cole Porter biography, laughably bowdlerized to suit Production Code strictures which meant that all hint of Porter's well-known homosexual proclivities had been thoroughly laundered out of the screenplay. "The only asset for me in *that* film was that I got to play with Cary Grant," Wyman later said.

She added: "My role in *Night and Day* was that of yet another silly showgirl. (I was *32* by then!) And oh was I sick of playing dumb bunnies. Anyway, we were doing the big production numbers when the roof of the soundstage caved in. They had tried putting blocks of ice up there to stifle the heat and it didn't work. The sets had to be reconstructed, so when I finally reported for *The Yearling* I was both Ma Baxter and Gracie Harris for a few weeks. Rushing back and forth between the Warner and MGM sets unnerved me."

*Screenland* gave *Night and Day* precisely the frivolous, surfacy review it deserved: "Movie audiences who elect to see this Technicolor extravaganza will have a delicious feast of Cole Porter's songs, as well as a notable line-up of personalities: Cary Grant, who portrays the musical genius; Alexis Smith as his wife; Monty Woolley, Ginny Simms, Jane Wyman, Eve Arden, Mary Martin as the professionals who helped make his shows successful—and this film fine entertainment. Based on the composer's career, it's rich in incidents occurring in his exuberant days at Yale, his first production interrupted by war, the heartbreak of his broken marriage, his tragic accident and partial recovery, and finally his wife's return."

Of course the real Cole Porter, bitchy, tormented, wildly homosexual, compulsively promiscuous, never got on the screen—to his own secret amusement and the contempt of his in-the-know friends and associates, one of whom said, "If they weren't going to do it honestly, it would have been better if they had not done it at all."

"Oh, well," Porter was reported to have laughed. "They made me look like Cary Grant—and *that* was a bonus."

In 1957, when I interviewed Grant at the Harwyn Club in New York in connection with his film *An Affair to Remember* for which he was doing Twentieth-Fox publicity, I drew him out on *Night and Day*—and Wyman: "Up to then Warners wasn't beginning to tap her tremendous acting potential. Her role in *Night* was a nothing part, but she did the best she could with it. She was a most vital and arresting presence, really born for movies; I always thought her most vivid." I detected embarrassment in his eyes when the film itself came up. "We did the best we could with it." he said quietly. "Nobody expected it to win any Oscar nominations."

The critical consensus on Jane Wyman in *Night and Day*: "Her bubbly personality gave *Night and Day* spurts of life."

Her other 1946 film, *One More Tomorrow*, released before *Night and Day*, had her playing a distinct second-fiddle to star Ann Sheridan in a weak-tea remake of the 1932 film, *The Animal Kingdom*,

*Night and Day* (1946), with Cary Grant.

*Night and Day* (1946), with Cary Grant.

*One More Tomorrow* (1946), with Dennis Morgan.

which had starred (at RKO) Ann Harding, Leslie Howard, and Myrna Loy. Sheridan played the nice career girl (Harding's role), Dennis Morgan the rich brat who disillusions her (Howard was the original), and Alexis Smith was the insincere golddigger (Loy's role) whom he married—for a time—before returning to Sheridan and the realities of life outside the pale of the pampered rich. Wyman? She was in an unworthy, stupid, badly written role as the assistant-confidante of Sheridan. She did have a few bright lines, which she made the most of.

*One More Tomorrow* was to be cursed with yet another of those notorious Warner ad-copy brainstorms that were the perpetual embarrassment of the studio in that era. This one had to be seen (on a full-page mag layout—a fan mag, natch) to be believed. "WOW! WHAT A LESSON IN CARESSIN'! THE SCREEN'S FULL OF STARS WITH THEIR ARMS FULL OF LOVE!" went the garish legend, with Sheridan and Morgan smooching with "KISS KISS

KISS" superimposed over their adjacent lips and such observations as "Jack Carson—a weed in their garden of love," "Ann Sheridan and Dennis Morgan—Oh, what Annie Did to the *Xmas in Connecticut Kid!*" "Alexis Smith [complete with clinging black negligee]—Everybody's sweetheart—all at once!" And trailing the others (in a tight negligee-evening-gown-wrap-you-name-it), the hapless Wyman, with the legend, "Jane Wyman—She's been around so much she's dizzy!"

*Variety* said, "There are plenty of star names for the marquees but principal story play goes to Morgan and Miss Sheridan, with former garnering most footage. . . . Jack Carson, Morgan's unorthodox butler and friend, and Jane Wyman, friend to Miss Sheridan, also rate attention in more limited parts."

Ann Sheridan years later spoke warmly of Wyman to me, maintaining that Wyman's talents were far greater than her own, and she felt sorry that Warners had wasted them for so long—an opinion that Jerome

90

Cowan and other Warner players were also to volunteer. "She was a real pro," Sheridan told me. "I know she hated the parts they often handed her before her big breakthrough, but she was always game to make the most of them, and actually, given the dialogue and situations they inflicted on her in that earlier period, became quite a whiz at making *something* out of *nothing*."

Sheridan added: "When I worked with her, I wouldn't exactly call her a scene-stealer; she was much too considerate of other performers to do anything like that—in fact, always tended to build other actors up as best she could. But even when she tried to underplay to make the other performer look good, and I know she did that, she was really generous, her quietly implemented talent stood out for all to see."

Back at Warners, Wyman faced the dismal prospect of yet another inferior product, in which the still blithely condescending overlords expected her to star.

After the glories of The Yearling, Cheyenne (also known as The Wyoming Kid) was a distinct letdown for Wyman, although it gave her a chance to disport herself in some modified 1870s styles, courtesy of Warner's Costume Department. On hand again was her old standby Dennis Morgan, along with pert Janis Paige, stalwart Bruce Bennett, sardonic Arthur Kennedy, and old standbys Alan Hale, John Ridgely, and Barton MacLane. Director Raoul Walsh tried his best to apply his standard excitement, but the story by Paul Wellman didn't give him much to work with.

Bosley Crowther in The New York Times nailed the proceedings down, calling Cheyenne, "Just a Western in which romance and robbery are mixed in the usual fictitious proportions. . . . In an hour and

At a Screen Actors Guild meeting with Leon Ames, Joseph Cotten, Robert Taylor, and Boris Karloff, 1946.

forty minutes of rambling over the screen, *Cheyenne* unwinds a fable which is a little difficult to trail. But, as near as we could make out, it tells how an amateur sleuth unmasks the quixotic poet who is robbing the stagecoach strongboxes out Wyoming way. This sleuth is an unfrocked gambler, forced to sleuthing to save his neck, and in the course of his novel assignment, he meets the mysterious robber's wife. What could then be more convenient than that the sleuth and the lady should fall in love, that the badman should be eliminated, and that the lovers should claim each other and the reward?"

Crowther thought Morgan "jaunty" as the hero, Wyman "cool" as the wife of the robber, Bennett and Kennedy "dour" as the heavies—and Janis Paige "ridiculous" as a dance-hall girl.

Raoul Walsh told me years later: "I was off my stride with that one. No matter how professional one tries to be at all times, there are just times when it comes easily and naturally, and you know it's *right*— and times when you know it's all wrong, and can't do a thing about it. Also, the cast was unhappy with their assignments—I don't think one of them liked the picture—and that always shows, especially with an indifferently written screenplay."

Wyman had certainly not liked *Cheyenne* and felt it was just another example of Warner's indifference to how she was cast. "Don't ask me about that one," she once said to me, "I don't remember it—not a thing about it. . . ."

Critic Philip T. Hartung in *The Commonweal* tried to be nice about it, but was forced to note: "At times the script strains too hard with double-meaning wisecracks—a cheap device that was entirely unnecessary."

*Variety* said: "Morgan does a forthright job of his heroics, tempering melodramatics with an easy touch that helps. Miss Wyman's role is a bit more dour but well done and sweetens toward the end when she falls for Morgan."

In the years that followed I always found amusement in eliciting reactions from actors who had appeared in it. Counterpoising Wyman's "I don't remember it at all" dismissals was Barton MacLane, a veteran of numerous fare of this kind, who practically shouted in my face: "Remember anything about it! Hell, I remember too damned much about it—it was plain terrible! It was phony from start to finish, and the Wyoming locations were actually shot in Arizona!"

Years later on the set of *A Summer Place* Arthur Kennedy, when asked about *Cheyenne*, simply raised his eyes to the heavens with a dismissive shrug. Bruce Bennett simply glowered when I mentioned it. Janis Paige gave me a "forget it, honey" look, and John Ridgely made the comment that at that stage of her career it was a shame that Wyman had to waste her time with it.

Morgan reportedly commented that the only thing that might conceivably have saved *Cheyenne* would have been Eve Arden armed with super-snappy wisecracks—and even then it might have gone for a loss.

After the nothing results on *Cheyenne* Wyman went over to RKO Radio for the William A. Wellman produced-and-directed *Magic Town* with high hopes. Robert Riskin, who had done so well as writer for Frank Capra's pictures, was the co-producer, and later the great Capra himself admitted that he worked on the script without credit.

The premise of the story was intriguing, and James Stewart, Riskin, Wellman, Wyman, and the fine supporting cast fully expected to duplicate the success of the then recent Stewart hit *It's a Wonderful Life*. Certainly Wyman felt that here was the cinematic lift she needed in order to consolidate the gains of *The Yearling*. But something, somewhere, went wrong, and *Magic Town,* despite its good points—and intentions—never made it to the pantheon of top-drawer films.

The plot had Stewart as Rip Smith, an opinion pollster ambitious for the big time, who learns about "Grandview," a town with a special magic for poll folk because its opinions identically match those of nationwide opinion surveys. Stewart shows up in town to do some secret polling, but then encounters Wyman, a crusading lady editor, who wants to see the town progress out of its average rut. Of course the pair are shortly in conflict—and a burgeoning romance.

*Photoplay* said, "It's unusual enough to rate a cheer; it's unrealistic enough to rate a brush-off. Wyman is a good actress; her quiet handling of the role of small town 'Mary Peterman' is apt sometimes to put the mannered Stewart at a disadvantage."

And again from *Photoplay*: "The other small-towners are in the groove—Kent Smith, Wallace Ford, Regis Toomey, Ann Shoemaker. Touches of comedy come here and there from Ned Sparks and Donald Meek, and the boys' basketball team might

*Cheyenne* (1947), with Bruce Bennett and Janis Paige.

have been plucked from any town you'd point out on the map. But the goings-on are something else again, a bit too implausible to convince an adult audience, a bit too childish to be fantasy about Small Town, U.S.A. Mr. Stewart has something, so does the picture; but we wish both had used them a little differently to come up with a real winner."

The advertising didn't help much. One particularly vulgar ad appeared in a fan magazine with garish yellow lettering, neon-style, against a black background that implied, pictorially at least, that *Magic Town* was about Big, Bad New York, and along the sides were vignettes of Stewart and Wyman in various undignified and pseudo-romantic attitudes,

with captions such as: "Their meeting was saucy and flippant!" "Their Romance found birth in the magic of a sudden kiss!" and "Their love jeopardized the happiness of thousands!" To top all this, beneath the garish yellow lettering, Stewart was holding Wyman in an awkward but sexy embrace in which her up-turned legs dominated the surroundings.

In 1957 I asked Jimmy Stewart what he had thought of the film. "We really thought we were going to duplicate the success of *It's a Wonderful Life*," he told me. "Frank had even helped Riskin on the script, and I had a wonderful, responsive, crea-tive co-star in Janie, and the idea seemed fresh and unique. I just don't know what kept it from ringing the bell as loudly as I had hoped. The parts just didn't add up to a compelling whole. But we did give it an all-out try, and to this day I feel there were some sharp, clever things in it."

Kent Smith reminisced about the film, Stewart, and Wyman. "Jimmy and Jane really tried; they gave it all they had," he told me. "And I know Bill Wellman put maximum care into it. The cast was fine; they all looked like born-and-bred small-towners, but I remember Donald Meek saying quietly to me that something was missing, some spark, some extra something that, regrettably, spells the difference between a smash hit, something that endures, and an also-ran entertainment, the kind of thing the critics like to label 'pleasant, escapist fare.' I think the weakness may have lain in the basic story line. It was gimmicky and clever, yes, but weak as to motivation; it just didn't seem realistic. A film can be wacky and wild, but if there is that underpinning of realism it holds up. I never felt *Magic Town* did, really."

William Wellman felt that he had given the film his very best efforts, and when I talked to him about it some fifteen years later, he proved loath to admit that it had gone wrong. He kept citing cases of films that had been critically underrated at the time of their release and later won belated appreciation. But time has shown that *Magic Town*, for all its good intentions and the hard work that went into it, was not in that category.

When I discussed this film briefly with Wyman in 1948, on the occasion of our first meeting, she seemed to me to be damning it with faint praise, talking of how pleasant it was to work with Jimmy Stewart, the good actors and actresses who supported her, the vitality of Bill Wellman's direction, etc., but I failed to catch from her a spark of true enthusiasm about the film.

*Magic Town* is strained, reaching for dynamic effects that neither the direction nor the writing enabled it to attain. Jimmy Stewart tends to *overact*, and Wyman tends to *underact*, and of the two she comes out the more real and human. Stewart was obviously making a noble effort throughout to spark-up the picture via the highly expressive thespian dynamics he had applied to his earlier *It's a Wonder-*

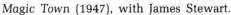

*Magic Town* (1947), with James Stewart.

*Magic Town* (1947), with James Stewart.

*ful Life* and other pictures that had made him legendary by 1947, but here he was making too much of a good thing. There seems to have been a self-conscious effort to create another thought-provoking, "Slice of Americana" confection, but the plot didn't allow for it, and Wellman, excellent as he could be in some related genres, didn't have the feel for this Capra-esque conceit.

Certainly *Magic Town* did Wyman no harm, but neither did it help her. But she certainly could afford a neutral effort, as in those four years from 1943 to 1947 she had risen dramatically, via *The Lost Weekend* and *The Yearling*, to a plateau of serious critical regard with a new audience alerted to her freshly dynamic, compelling mystique. Just ahead was an opportunity to take her to a position among stars of the first rank.

# 5

## The *Belinda* Bonanza
## 1948

The film that was to raise Wyman to the heights of stardom almost didn't happen. *Johnny Belinda* had originally been a 1940 Broadway play that starred Helen Craig (the talented wife of actor John Beal). Warners had purchased it in the mid-1940s, but didn't seem to know what to do with it. Many people have taken credit for getting it on the screen, but producer Jerry Wald, who had guided Joan Crawford to renewed fame in the 1945 *Mildred Pierce*, seems to have been the first to pick it from the Warner files and take note of its possibilities.

It is the story of a deaf mute in Nova Scotia who is taught to speak by a kind doctor. She is scorned and regarded as mentally deficient by the townspeople and even by her own family. Only the doctor offers her genuine friendship. Later she is raped by a townsman and becomes pregnant. When the baby is born, and the real father, whose name she has kept secret, sees that the baby is normal physically, he tries to take it away from her. She kills him. Eventually she is exonerated, and achieves a new understanding with her family and the town, and fortifies her friendship with the doctor.

Wald saw that the elements of commercially saleable melodrama were here. He also realized that if it were well done, properly photographed, sensitively directed, it might also be a major critical success. But even he did not comprehend what the eventual impact of the film might be. The film was put on the "go" list, and preproduction began in 1946. But by summer 1947 no lead had been chosen. Wald and the newly assigned director, Jean Negulesco, culled the possibilities. No major actor seemed chemically or pictorially right for the role. Then they thought of Jane Wyman.

The "new" Jane Wyman, so much more subtle, expressive, and quietly authoritative, had been unveiled in *The Lost Weekend, The Yearling,* and *Magic Town.* Wald noticed that she was wasted in the parts suggested for her at Warners, and he thought it ironic that her home studio couldn't give her something she could get her teeth into. It was on loanout that she was drawing parts that were so much richer.

So it was actually Wald who persuaded Jack Warner to put Wyman into *Johnny Belinda.* Everything in the record points to that. Not that Warner required too much persuasion; the Academy nomination Wyman had received for her powerful performance in *The Yearling* had not been lost on him. Lew Ayres, who had played Young Dr. Kildare in the series at MGM before the war, had made an impression as a psychiatrist in the 1946 *The Dark Mirror,* so he was assigned to the doctor role. Stephen McNally (originally Horace) had played the doctor in the Broadway play, but because his features looked cruel and he had the right chemistry, he was cast in the role of the rapist. Charles Bickford played Wyman's father (he was a leading character actor of the time) and rounding out the cast was Agnes Moorehead as her aunt.

Unlike most of the Warner films Wyman had acted in, *Johnny Belinda* was a first class production in which no expense was spared. It was filmed in an

*Johnny Belinda* (1948), with Agnes Moorehead, Lew Ayres, and Charles Bickford.

isolated, bleak section of Northern California because it closely resembled Nova Scotia's landscape. With Max Steiner assigned to do the scoring, and director Negulesco's attentive care to the details of atmosphere and photography, Wyman knew that for once her all-out effort was being matched and sustained by all hands in all departments.

The cost-conscious higher-ups began to get nervous, however. They thought Negulesco was fussing too much with camera angles and atmosphere. As Negulesco remembered it, "They actually took the camera away from me," at one point. An impatient Jack Warner started looking at the rushes. He complained that the picture seemed to be about seagulls and fogs. He wanted to see the melodrama and high-keyed histrionics emphasized. At one time he even threatened to fire Negulesco. "The way that guy fusses over this damned picture, you'd think he had another *Gone With the Wind* on his hands," Warner screamed at Wald. "For Christ's sake, it's only about a

deaf mute who gets raped, knocked up, and later kills the rapist!"

Wald made haste to cue Warner in on the fact that it was about much more than that—as Negulesco was directing it and Wyman was acting the star role, it was metamorphosing, before everyone's eyes, into art. "I've heard enough of that 'art' shit from Bette Davis," Warner screamed. "I don't mind it if the picture has some class, but I want it to *sell*, goddamn it!" However, as the rushes kept screening, even the irascible Warner began to mellow, and he admitted that it "seemed to have *some* class."

Meanwhile Wyman worked hard on her performance. She spent months studying the deaf, scrutinizing their mannerisms, their expressions, especially the look in their eyes, which she described to me in 1948 as "searching, wandering, vacant in a way but lit up, somehow." She added, "I tried to get that certain light into my eyes. When I saw myself on screen, I was humbly grateful to have, I think, succeeded in reproducing it." She made a special pal of one unfortunate young woman, who was both deaf and dumb. She observed her closely, in all aspects of her life, at mealtimes, in sleep, during moments of joy and stress, sorrow, and anger. Then she went for days on end with her ears plugged up with wax so that she could know firsthand the problems and tensions of someone so afflicted.

To prepare herself mentally, Wyman stayed by herself to get a sense of a deaf mute's isolation. "That was the terrifying time," she later remembered. "The silence was new, frightening." To fortify her resolve, she told herself that this was the way some people were fated to live all their lives, so if *they* could stand it for decades, *she* could stand it for a few weeks.

The deep thought and disciplined introspection Wyman put into her preparation for the role paid off. Cast, crew, and director were impressed. Negulesco remembered later that Wyman remained calm and self-sufficient during all the wrangles with the front office. "No matter what they do, the Oscar is mine this year," Negulesco remembers her saying. Nor did he or anyone else on the set disagree with her.

Jean Negulesco later recalled that when the crass but shrewd Jack Warner saw the film in final cut, his only immediate comment was "I have to take a leak." Later he expressed it as his opinion that narration over Wyman's closeups would tell the public what she was thinking. According to Negulesco, he talked Warner out of *that* brainstorm, but paid the price. Negulesco was never to do another picture for the studio. Incorrigible Jack Warner, however, was determined to have the last word on *something*. He assigned his gaudy ad copywriters to the film, and they delivered in their usual garishly tasteless style. The result was a full-page ad that ran in national magazines showing a gal-hungry male monster (a drawing, not a photograph), bearing down on a frightened-looking but nonetheless brazenly-belip-

*Johnny Belinda* (1948), with Stephen McNally.

sticked-and-berouged Wyman, juxtaposed with enormous white-on-black type that screamed: "SHAME CAME OUT OF THE SHADOWS AND CHANGED A YOUNG GIRL'S LIFE!" Nor was her gentle, refined scholarly co-star Lew Ayres spared, being listed in the ad as turning in "an endearing performance, as the doctor first to find her secret—first to share her shame!" This element in the plot seemed to perk up Warner at the screening. "Hey, that's *great*—they think the *doctor* knocked her up!" Jerry Wald remembered him cackling gleefully.

But Warner was still not all that convinced of the film's commercial appeal. With production completed in late 1947, he held up the picture through much of 1948. As Jane Wyman later remembered the tortured history of the *Johnny Belinda* project, "the story was at the bottom of the Warners bin. No one believed in it. It was thought too grim, too morbid, too offbeat. We proved them wrong on all counts, but it was a struggle to get it made, and then they first wanted to rush it out as a B movie—and then they wanted to stash it away for all time. Can you believe it?"

Months of 1948 went by, and Wyman, Negulesco, Wald, and company continued to sweat it out. Then Jack Warner's brother Harry happened to see it in a screening room at the Warner office in New York. He was impressed and pressured for its release.

After it came out and was a smash hit, critically and commercially, Wyman got a revenge of a sort. She made Jack take out a trade ad, in which he profusely congratulated the cast, crew, all connected with *Johnny Belinda*. To do Warner credit, he later commented, as he studied the fine returns at the box office, "Sometimes it's wonderful to be wrong!"

I will never forget, at twenty-five, my first viewing of the picture at a Boston press screening room, the very week I first met the star of *Johnny Belinda*. I was enthralled by the apposite score the gifted Max Steiner had summoned up out of his creative inspi-

*Johnny Belinda* (1948), with Lew Ayres and Charles Bickford.

*Johnny Belinda* (1948), with Lew Ayres.

rations. I found the supporting actors impeccable in their roles, with the rugged but sensitive Bickford particularly fine and Agnes Moorehead in great fettle as an embittered woman who conceals depths of understanding beneath a stern exterior. The photography was exceptional, catching all the ambience of a bleak but touching story in its evocations of sea, sky, and weather. Lew Ayres was ideal for his role—manly yet sensitive, dedicated and nurturing. And Wyman showed herself in this an artist of the first magnitude, mistress of many moods, with eyes that mirrored endless sorrows and an occasional smile that lit up the landscape. Her play of expressions were, throughout, perfectly modulated: abject animal fear when the rapist attacks, dawning tenderness when she looks at her new baby, a hopeful glow when she learns her first words. Her performance

was of the finest thespian tradition, natural and drained of false sentiment, and deeply moving. To this day I recall the hard-boiled Boston critics around me, usually so tart, restless, and frozen, responding visibly to the powerful emotions she projected.

When Louella Parsons, a fine reporter but a so-so writer, got around to reviewing *Johnny Belinda* in *Cosmopolitan*, she rose to what was, for her, a height of eloquence: "If stardom is what Jane Wyman wants most, [the film] will guarantee her this eminence. . . . Jane makes [her role] real and very touching. . . . She rises to every demand of tenderness and warmth."

While some prominent Hollywood figures claimed that they were astonished when at Academy Award time "little brown wren" Wyman won as Best Ac-

During a break in filming
of *Johnny Belinda*, 1948.

tress of 1948 for *Johnny Belinda*, her triumph was
not as much of a surprise as legend would have it.
Despite strong competition, her performance had
given just a little more—some said a *lot* more—in
humanized, universal terms than those of the formidable talents with whom she competed that year:
Irene Dunne (*I Remember Mama*); Olivia De Havilland (*The Snake Pit*); Barbara Stanwyck (*Sorry,
Wrong Number*); and Ingrid Bergman (*Joan of Arc*).

Standing on the stage before her peers, with
camera bulbs flashing, her eyes brimming with tears,
the triumphant but fundamentally unassuming
Wyman was dressed unobtrusively in a gown of
white crepe with a high, round neck. Her hair was
simply coiffed. Her big brown eyes had a new light in
them that night. Nervously she clutched the Oscar in
both hands and said, "I accept this award very grate-

fully—for keeping my mouth shut once. I think I'll
do it again."

Lew Ayres, who had escorted her that night (she
and Reagan were estranged at this point), was
waiting for her when she came into the wings, after
one of the briefest acceptance speeches on record. He
kissed her on the cheek and gave her a gentle but
tender hug. Jerry Wald, Walter Huston, many others
she knew and loved, tendered their heartfelt congratulations. Clinging to her award as if she would
never part with it again, she proceeded to field a
barrage of reporters' questions, declaring at one
point, "I've never been so frightened in my life.
When Ronald Colman [the 1947 winner for *A Double
Life*] called my name and I walked up to that stage, I
was scared to death."

After congratulating Claire Trevor, who had won a

Above: At the premiere of *Johnny Belinda*, 1948. Below left: Jane Wyman wins Best Actress Oscar for her fifty-fifth film, *Johnny Belinda*. Below right: Ronald Colman, 1947 Oscar winner, and Jane Wyman, 1948 Oscar winner.

Oscar time, with Douglas Fairbanks, Jr., Claire Trevor, Jerry Wald, and Walter Huston.

supporting award for *Key Largo*, Wyman went on to a party at the Champagne Room of the Mocambo, with Lew Ayres on one arm, Jack Warner on the other. Warner at the party announced to one and all that for his 1949 lineup he was considering for her such projects as *Ethan Frome*, a projected film version of the famed Edith Wharton novel, which Bette Davis had coveted and which was never made, and *A Streetcar Named Desire* (which finally went to Vivien Leigh and was produced by Warners in 1951).

Now that he fully realized that he had a major talent on his hands, Jack Warner left nothing to chance. Jane Wyman was promptly signed to a new ten-year contract with Warner Bros. Her friends warned her that she was being extremely unwise in doing this, that Bette Davis and others were availing themselves of the services of the toughest, shrewdest agents in town so as to get the best deals possible. To all the protestations Wyman had a stock answer: "Seven years was the legal limit, that's true. But heck, I was damned grateful to Warners for all the years they stuck by me. I was never one to walk out,

raise hell—I was suspended only a few times, while some of my colleagues seemed to be on walkouts half the time. I respected their reasons, which I am sure were valid enough for them, but that kind of stance was not for me." She was given Bette Davis's trailer, at Davis's express request, when the latter left Warner Brothers in mid-1949. And she told reporters she thought of Warners as *home* after thirteen years. Many of the terms of the new contract appealed to her, including clauses that stated that she could do one picture a year on the outside. Later, in the 1950s, the contract was to undergo revisions.

Thus early 1949 found Jane Wyman, thirty-five, at the peak. All the years of patient waiting, of loyal service to the studio, of unassuming hard work, of increasing dedication to her art had paid off. But into every life some rain must fall, as the adage goes. Sadly enough, the evolution of her personal fortunes—or rather *misfortunes*—in this period contrasted tragically with the brilliant professional fulfillment she had attained.

# Personal Ups and Downs

Wyman's newfound joys at the studio contrasted with the atmosphere at home, which over several years had steadily deteriorated. Wyman's and Reagan's personal and professional interests diverged ever more sharply, what with his increasing interest in the Screen Actors Guild and its attendant labor problems, and her ever growing absorption with her career. Even lovely little Maureen, always present to remind them of the freshness and beauty of what they had once shared, and the small boy, Michael, whom they had adopted in 1945, seemed unable to provide the continuing adhesive that is the lifeblood of a mature, evolving marital alliance.

Friends tended to date the beginnings of the ever widening fission to early 1947, when *The Yearling* had won her an Academy Award nomination. The strain was becoming apparent, for they were quarreling in public—something they had rarely, if ever, done before. By March 1947, when the Oscar ceremonies were held (Wyman had lost to Olivia De Havilland for *To Each His Own*), much public attention was given to Wyman's sudden and startling metamorphosis into a full-fledged dramatic actress, and it was obvious that Reagan had found himself suddenly jolted out of his hitherto half-patronizing half-pleasantly indifferent attitude toward his wife's career.

The fan magazine writer and longtime Warner publicist Jerry Asher, who knew the Reagans intimately for a time, once told me: "Ronnie was a kind, gentle, and understanding husband, but he was busy with his SAG activities and other off-screen causes that had become increasingly important to him, and let's face it, he neglected Jane." Obviously they were still trying to save what they had, for early in 1947, with the acclaim continuing to ring in her ears for *The Yearling*, Wyman discovered that she was again pregnant. For a short while the Reagans deluded themselves that yet another round of parenthood would solidify their marriage.

Then a peculiarly grim fate took a hand. While shooting *That Hagen Girl*, yet another of the mediocre films through which Reagan walked casually while his wife was working at her acting as never before, he contracted pneumonia, which worsened, and shortly he found himself at thirty-six, in a hospital literally fighting for his life. At home the pregnant Wyman, worried as she was about pending career choices, was suddenly confronted with a seriously ill husband.

She was thirty-three in 1947, and the pregnancy, then five months along, was neither easy nor comfortable physically. Her worry over her husband's condition, and her knowledge that his recovery was being slowed by his concern over not being by her side, kept her nerves at fever pitch. Suddenly she felt the beginnings of something ominous. She called to be taken to the hospital, where, on June 26, 1947, her baby girl, a frail wraith whose advent had come much too prematurely, came into the world—and died within hours. The tears came then, profusely and often. All the tensions that in an attempt at inner discipline she had dammed up, broke through their stoic barriers. Her floods of tears were followed by

Maureen and Jane,
Mother's Day 1946.

ominous melancholic silences, and friends found her inconsolable.

At a different hospital with his own health still in jeopardy a helpless, bedridden Reagan knew a profound despondency that was uncharacteristic of his usual sunny, positive self. Here was his wife, enduring her sorrow and attendant physical weakness alone across town without the husbandly consolation that might have somehow lightened her agonies. After several bleak, gray weeks both Reagans had shakily completed their separate recovery routes. They went home to a house governed by long silences.

Reagan eventually staggered back to the still-uncompleted *That Hagen Girl*, which had been running up costs due to his absence, leaving at home Wyman, who moped about her bedroom locked in the grip of a profound depression that for weeks she couldn't shake.

"Those terrible weeks were the beginning of the end for Jane and Ronnie," Ruth Waterbury later told me. "Both began to realize that there was nothing there anymore. Ronnie felt she was remote and

indifferent to him and his interests. Jane felt that he didn't appreciate her and still neglected her.

"And let's face it," Waterbury added. "He was only human and couldn't help resenting the fact that his wife's acting career was taken far more seriously than his." This was compounded when he overheard friends saying in effect: "Ronnie's *bright*, but Jane's *creative*." *Creative* was never a word that had ever been applied to Reagan's acting efforts, either by critics or admirers.

When friends warned him that something had to be done to knock Wyman out of her growing seclusion, Reagan began making her go out dancing with him. He tried to rekindle memories of the first days of their courtship by taking her to intimate supper clubs. But nothing worked. Their evenings ended early, with both retiring to their separate quarters— and their thoughts.

"Work is the only answer for her," Jerry Wald told friends. "It will take her mind off things." By late summer she was throwing herself into the role of the deaf mute in *Johnny Belinda*. She lived the role twenty-four hours a day. Reagan, while relieved by

110

his wife's resumption of her career, noted that she seemed even more withdrawn. During August through November of 1947, they both kept so busy with their separate pursuits that they hardly saw each other. "Life at the Reagan ménage became icily polite," Hedda Hopper commented later. "It was hi, how are things going, coming in, going out, passing in the hall. All the mortal symptoms were there. So I, for one, wasn't all that surprised at what happened soon enough."

Meanwhile, on the set of *Johnny Belinda*, Wyman had found a new friend—Lew Ayres, her co-star. At first they hadn't particularly liked each other. Wyman said she'd rather have had someone like Joe Cotten as the understanding doctor who takes her out of her dark night of isolation. Ayres said that he had never thought of Wyman as anything but the hey-hey blonde ingenue that he remembered re-

motely from the 1930s. (Obviously he had not yet seen either *The Lost Weekend* or *The Yearling*.) But as they worked together, he observed firsthand Wyman's artistic dedication to her characterization, and his interest deepened. And so, reportedly, did hers.

"After all, Ronnie was gadding off on his SAG business," Jim Reid, the writer-publicist who knew both, told me. "And Lew was right there, a fellow actor, working and struggling along with her to help make *Belinda* the greatest performance of her career. It began with a common interest, with Lew's steady supportiveness—and then it blossomed."

There has never, in fairness to Wyman, been any indication that she ever violated her marriage vows during the period her friendship with Ayres was deepening. His understanding warmed and distracted her, though, and because he sensed the first-

Lew Ayres and Jane Wyman, 1948.

class intellect and creative potential in Wyman, he introduced her to books, music, and painting, on a scale she had never indulged before.

Ayres, who had reached stardom at twenty in 1930 with his touching portrayal of a bewildered young German soldier in Remarque's *All Quiet on the Western Front,* had had a checkered Hollywood career through the years. His star had faded in the mid-1930s because his innocuous "nice boy" image had temporarily gone out of vogue. He had two abortive marriages, one to Ginger Rogers, the other to Lola Lane. Those two Hollywoodites ran in a faster lane than he. Ayres had a renascence of sorts as Dr. Kildare in the MGM series of that name, thanks to Louis B. Mayer, who liked sentimental serialized concoctions (*Andy Hardy,* et al.) and decided Ayres would make a perfect foil for Lionel Barrymore's Dr. Gillespie.

In World War II Ayres had shocked Hollywood and the country by registering as a Conscientious Objector. A pariah at first, he suddenly emerged as a heroic medico in the thick of the Pacific fighting, much loved by the men, and commended for his valor under fire. He came back to Hollywood in 1946 a hero, and soon found rewarding roles in major pictures awaiting him. He dated numerous Hollywood lovelies, but his only ongoing close relationship was with actor William Bakewell, who became his friend when they played young German recruits in *All Quiet*—and who was to remain his friend through a lifetime.

It was this scholarly, deep-spirited man who now claimed the major share of Jane Wyman's attention aside from her work. "It was platonic, yes—but it was intense," Jim Reid, the studio publicist, said.

Meanwhile at home, during the fleeting times when she was there, Wyman lived her role in *Johnny Belinda* day and night. Reagan was seldom there to notice. When the picture ended in November 1947—and with it, for a time, the close daily association with Ayres, Wyman grew even more restless, and when she and Reagan, in efforts to make some time together, went night clubbing, they were caught quarreling publicly more than once. Even two-year-

Halloween art from Warners, 1948.

old Michael and six-year-old Maureen seemed unable to offer Wyman any true comfort. "The role of Belinda had taken so much out of her she seemed to take months to unwind," Ruth Waterbury remembered.

Suddenly, on impulse, Wyman took off for New York—alone. While there she gave a statement to the press, a reckless statement that the Warners publicity people, watchful and protective as always via their New York office, could not head off. She told a reporter, who had expected to hear conventional tales of moviemaking and domesticity, that she was unhappy, that things had been piling up on her emotionally, one after the other, and that she would talk over her problems with her husband in the hope of avoiding a separation.

When the wire services carried this shocker back to Los Angeles, it hit Reagan "like a ton of bricks," as a friend recalled. Surprised and shocked, he didn't at first know how to react. Louella Parsons was the first to get to him. "What's really wrong with you and Janie, Ronnie?" she asked. To the woman he and Wyman regarded as a substitute mother since the days they had courted prior to their marriage, the woman they had toured with at movie theatres and who had happily announced their engagement, Reagan gave the scoop:

"Right now, Jane needs very much to have a fling, and I intend to let her have it. She is sick and nervous and not herself." He added that Wyman had told him that while she loved him, she was no longer in love with him, a distinction that the never overly subtle mind of Reagan found bewildering, at least at first.

Reagan proceeded to inform one and all that Wyman told him she was bored by their life together, his SAG activities and his endless political bull-sessions with his brother, Moon, and others. Wyman let it be known that he was patronizing and indifferent to her career efforts, with "that's fine, Janie, fine" his typical comment on her acting laurels.

Back in Hollywood in December, Wyman announced a separation. "She's just depressed," the increasingly confused and hurt Reagan told friends. "Why, we'll be married for fifty years! We love our kids—we love each other! We really do!"

But Reagan saw the 1948 New Year in with friends at a party, and at one point broke down in tears. "Now it was his turn to be depressed and defeated, and that was just how he felt," Ruth Waterbury commented. "Ronnie was a builder-upper, not a

tearer-downer; he hated to see anything he had engaged in come apart."

By February 1948, yielding briefly to his entreaties to try to patch things up for the kids' sake as well as their own, they were back together again. By May 1948, finding their life together—or rather, for all practical purposes, apart—intolerable, Wyman and Reagan separated for the last time. This time with divorce in the offing.

Reagan, despite the neglect, condescension, and incomprehension he had evidently exhibited, seemed to get all the sympathy with "she was a fool to leave him she'll never get a good solid man like that" pretty much the gist of what Hollywood was saying about them. But obviously, for Wyman in 1948, "goodness" and "solidity" were admirable as far as they went; the trouble was that they didn't go far enough. She was bored and sated, and she wanted out, for keeps.

Again Reagan sat down for an interview with Louella Parsons. His comments on Wyman were generous and restrained: "Please remember that Jane went through a very bad time." He added, to another reporter, that the loss of their baby girl the previous June had thrown them way off emotionally.

Michael was only three, and later remembered not comprehending the enormity of what had happened, but Maureen recalled the terrible emotional jolt she had received when both her father and her mother made the standard "we won't be married anymore but you're still our little girl and you'll see us both always" speech. She remembered crying often, and wandering through the house feeling rootless and lost.

By summer 1948 Wyman had acquired her interlocutory degree; a property settlement, child support, and complete access to the children for Reagan had all been respectively worked out. "My impression of Janie at that time," fan writer Gladys Hall later said, "was that she couldn't wait to have it all over and done with, couldn't wait for off with the old and on with the new, whatever, and whoever, that might turn out to be." For Reagan it was a period of grief and disorientation.

A corner of the veil over their incompatibilities and assorted problems was lifted during the court hearing, when, according to one Los Angeles newspaper, Wyman informed the judge that while he knew she had no interest in his political activities, Reagan insisted that she join him at meetings. And when she tried to offer ideas, she added, her husband

Christmas card painted
by Jane Wyman, 1950s.

tended to treat her thoughts as of no importance. She finished with the observation that in the end, they found they had nothing in common.

Wyman obtained her final decree in the summer of 1949. The world being a large place, but Hollywood being a small one, they often met socially at friends' homes, by accident of course, and Reagan made full use of his visiting privileges to see the children. Wyman contrived to be absent from these reunions more often than not, and soon she was seeing Lew Ayres again regularly and spending quiet evenings at the Ayres ménage "listening to music, painting, studying, and being consoled," as the 1949 fan magazine terminology would have it.

Some of her friends during 1949 felt she wanted to marry Ayres. But if this were so, she soon found herself disillusioned. For the essentially shy, schol-

arly Ayres, who despised the more garish ways of Hollywood, had no intention, at least at that time, of taking a third wife. "He functioned well as friend and consoler and escort, sure," Jerry Asher told me, "but Lew had had enough of marriage—Ginger and Lola had taken a lot out of him. His palship with Bakewell was more congenial to him than any heavygoing relationship with a woman, at least then, and he was happy to be Janie's friend, and always there for her. Anything heavier was more than he could cope with."

The on-again off-again Wyman-Ayres relationship (such as it was) continued through 1949 and 1950, then was suddenly over. Soon Wyman was telling interviewers about Ayres, "Oh Lew, swell guy, we see each other from time to time."

Meanwhile Reagan, after a year of what one of his

pals styled "racking loneliness and hopelessness," perked up when he met a young actress named Nancy Davis. Completely unlike Wyman in temperament, and certainly far her inferior in acting talent if not in brains, Davis did not take her career seriously, and was primarily geared, emotionally, for a home and a man. She put her man first, as she told more than one writer, and had no ambitions for herself but as a man's helpmate. Juxtaposed suddenly with a woman who shared all his interests and lived only for him, Reagan delightedly began courting Nancy Davis "and in the good old-fashioned style," as one of his friends put it. "No sneaking around for *this* guy, no shack-ups, nothing like that. He treated Nancy like a *lady* and wooed her like a *gentleman*."

Meanwhile, on the rebound from Ayres, Wyman was restlessly "dating around." "She was in love one day and out of it the next," one friend said of the Jane Wyman of 1950 and 1951. First there was a handsome young golfer, at least ten years her junior, named Clark Hardwicke. Hardwicke shared with her a cute button nose, a winning smile, and a capacity for fun. By July 1950, such magazines as *Movie Life* were chirping: "Latest in Jane Wyman's string of admirers, golfer Clark Hardwicke, tossed off some witty chatter while giving her a whirl on Romanoff's dance floor. Two were among group merry making at a dinner party."

In August 1950 *Movie Life* rhapsodized, "The all-star preview of *The Glass Menagerie* was a personal triumph for Jane Wyman, escorted by golfer Clark Hardwicke, still a top contender for her affections. Before the film was shown, Janie was saying she wanted light comedy for her next; but spontaneous applause of rival stars convinced her drama's her best bet."

No one in Hollywood who knew her well took Wyman's fling with young Clark Hardwicke seriously. "She used him to distract herself; I never heard her say anything really deeply felt about him," Ruth Waterbury remembered. "Let's face it, he was a cute, sexy kid with a good athlete's body; Janie was feeling light and giddy and Clark filled the bill for *that* mood. She was enjoying being a major star and all the acclaim, and except for her kids—and she *was* a good, attentive mother—and her friends, I think she had had enough of serious emotions—for a time." Soon Clark Hardwicke disappeared from the Jane Wyman record—never to be heard of again.

Wyman maintained her "single" status straight

With golfer Clark Hardwicke, 1950.

through 1951, with one man after another rumored to be *The One*. Sheilah Graham gushed in *Hollywood Romances* under the heading "JANE'S TRAGEDY: SHE CAN'T SEEM TO PICK UP THE PIECES: The name is in lights, but the girl is in the dark. If she'd never really been in love, things would probably be different. As it is, even though she and Ronnie don't want each other anymore, she still knows what it feels like to be solidly crazy about somebody; the emotion may be gone, but the memory lingers on, and she can't be taken in by counterfeit. Maybe that's why she goes from date to date, looking for something she doesn't know how to find."

Wyman seems to have thought she had found it in handsome, sexy Hollywood attorney Greg Bautzer, whose boudoir tactics were said to be as nimble and graceful as his courtroom performances. Bautzer, at the time the movie colony's most elusive bachelor, had served as "romantic interest" to such as Joan Crawford (their fights and reconciliations had become part of Hollywood legend) and Ginger Rogers, with whom he had had yet another tempestuous affair. Lana Turner, reportedly, had also found Mr. Bautzer to be All-Man in any and all situations.

"I don't quite know what attracted Wyman to Bautzer," Jim Reid recalled. "Everyone was dumbfounded when she proceeded to fall deeply in love with the guy. He was certainly not marriage material in those days; Mr. Love-em-and-leave-em, they called him. Jane must have known what she was in for, that it wouldn't work out. If she had treated him as a fun-toy, as she had young Hardwicke, she'd have had all of the joy and none of the grief."

Soon she was reportedly coming on so strong to Bautzer, having him over for evenings with the kids, hinting about marriage, that he began to withdraw. "She led with her heart, and got socked again," Ruth Waterbury said. "But why didn't she *see* that Greg was wrong for her?"

Soon Hollywood was titillated—and a little saddened—to note that Bautzer and Wyman—at the premiere festivities for her *The Blue Veil*, were sitting, double-date style, at the same table with Ronald Reagan and Nancy Davis, a far more staid and quiet twosome, who were already talking marriage. "I think it embarrassed Ronnie," a friend recalled. "He really wasn't the sophisticated 'let's all be friends and introduce our new date to each other' type." Reagan had come to *The Blue Veil* premiere as

With Greg Bautzer, 1950.

a gesture of friendship to Wyman, but had not expected to figure in a sophisticated-foursome photographic session. Nancy Davis, too, seemed embarrassed. Wyman's attitude was that she and Reagan had to see each other all over Hollywood whether they liked it or not, so what was a friendly foursome now and then.

Soon, she began to realize that Bautzer couldn't be had, at least not in a marital way, and next she was seen on the town with director Curtis Bernhardt, who had guided her so expertly through *The Blue Veil*. At the same time rumors had her stealing handsome, muscular actor John Payne away from his steady gal, Rhonda Fleming.

Confronted with news pictures of Wyman with both Bernhardt and Payne within the space of one week, her friends began to shake their heads and whisper "*What* has happened to Janie?"

Then, later in the year, there was more gossip. Wyman, it seemed, had not extinguished her torch for the womanizing, footloose Bautzer, and when she attended a party at which she had to watch him dancing in intimate style with Ginger Rogers, with whom he had resumed, she reportedly ran into the ladies' room and wept violently.

But the worst was yet to come. Reagan and Nancy Davis announced their engagement and were married on March 4, 1952. Jolted by the fact her ex had found what appeared to be solid happiness and humiliated by Bautzer's withdrawal from her, which he had finalized, Wyman began dating Travis Kleefeld seriously. She had met Trav, as she called him, at a Christmas party. A week or so after the Reagan-Davis marriage, she announced her engagement to him. More than one columnist commented on the coincidence of Wyman's telling the world she would marry young Kleefeld only a week after the Reagan marriage.

The news of the engagement alarmed her friends. Kleefeld was twenty-six to her thirty-eight. He was a nice-enough young man, with an urchinish, sexy face, and he harbored singing ambitions. (Five years later, as Tony Travis he would launch a singing career, with little long-range success.) Kleefeld came from a prominent contracting family, worked in the family business, and was rumored heir to a considerable fortune.

The fan magazines of early 1952 proceeded to gush Niagaras of purple prose about Wyman and her new young man. Much of the copy she saw in the press hurt and humiliated her. Her friends tried to break up the relationship, warning her that Travis was too young for her, that she was making a laughing-stock of herself. Then the Kleefeld family made known their disapproval of their young son as potential husband to a famous thirty-eight-year-old movie star of sophisticated prior experience, who had already been married three times, and who had failed all three times at bat.

Ruth Waterbury later recalled: "The situation was identical to what she was to act out in her picture *All That Heaven Allows* three years later, the older woman and younger man in love, with the whole town out to break them up. Was Jane in love with Kleefeld? I think she was, after a fashion. But she couldn't take the pressure. Within a month she had broken off with him—for a while, anyway. *Then*, a few months *later*, agreeing they weren't right for marriage—with each other, anyway, they began going around together—as friends, they claimed."

But before they "settled down to a quiet friendship," as Louella Parsons put it, *Modern Screen* was running such gushy items as: "Travis Kleefeld put a down payment on a mink coat for Jane Wyman just before the engagement was called off. Incidentally, relations between Jane and Kleefeld's mother were what you might call strained when we were going to press on this issue."

With young Kleefeld "put in his place," Wyman went back to work at Columbia, for a musical, which was prophetically to be entitled *Let's Do It Again*.

With tennis player Tony Trabert, 1951.

Since for her singing and dancing she would need the cooperation of Columbia's music department, she found herself in the constant company of Freddie Karger, the pianist, composer, and music supervisor at the studio.

Soon the shop talk was taking a more personal turn. A romance developed. Karger, the son of Maxwell Karger—a deceased pioneer producer in the old Metro Company, later to be Metro-Goldwyn-Mayer, and the child of a vaudeville family on his mother's side—was a year or two younger than Wyman and had been divorced from an entertainer who later became a lawyer. He had one daughter Maureen's age.

"They had music in common, and had a lot of laughs together. Since he was practically her age, she didn't have to go through any more older woman and younger man publicity. He was as lonely as she was, and unlike Bautzer, wanted to remarry. He lived at home with his family, felt rootless and disoriented, and wanted to get back into domestic harness again. At the time everyone thought he was perfect for Jane. Even Ronald Reagan approved of him." This from Hedda Hopper.

Since Karger's daughter and Maureen and Michael became friends in short order, and seemed anxious that they all become one family, Wyman and Karger sneaked off to Santa Barbara on November 1, 1952, and were married.

Trouble began almost at once. Wyman's salary and social status were above Karger's and this made him feel inferior. They couldn't decide where they wanted to live. Their career schedules conflicted. Restless in the role of wife-and-mother, Wyman, as in the past, threw herself into her by then high-powered career with even more ruthless intensity. The kids were put in boarding school, and Wyman saw them on weekends. Separations and reconciliations followed all through 1953 and 1954 in bewildering tandem, and finally Wyman threw in the towel for keeps. At her divorce suit in 1954, Wyman claimed that Karger had a fierce temper and frightened her by throwing furniture around. The divorce was granted. Both seemed relieved and went their separate ways.

Confronted with her fourth marital failure, a depressed and enervated Wyman, influenced by the devout Catholicism of her close friend Loretta Young, began taking instruction in the Roman Catholic faith and within the year had converted to it.

With Travis Kleefeld, 1951.

With her fourth husband,
Freddie Karger, 1953.

Loretta Young said a year or two after that: "I think the rituals, practices, and philosophy of the Catholic faith gave Jane a balance, a consolation, an inner peace that she had been looking for in the wrong places. I think she is much more emotionally settled and fulfilled now." By then forty, Wyman wrapped her life around her kids and even had them instructed in the faith. They, too, converted.

But the Freddie Karger chapter was not quite over. They began seeing each other socially, and Wyman was reminded that Karger had been brought up a Catholic, had once been a regular practitioner, but had lost his faith. In their dinner conversations, they talked Catholicism at a blue streak, and Wyman had the satisfaction of bringing Karger back to the faith. Like herself, he had not remarried, and he felt equally at loose ends.

Their friendship deepened, and to Hollywood's surprise, seven years later, in 1961, they remarried. This time around, the marriage lasted four years, but seems to have broken up because of the same career and emotional incompatibilities that had dogged them the first time.

Wyman was never to remarry. "I guess I just don't have a talent for it," she told friends after the second Karger divorce. "Some women just aren't the marry-

With Ethel Merman and hubby Freddie Karger, 1954.

ing kind—or anyway, not the *permanently* marrying kind, and I'm one of them."

Meanwhile ex-husband Reagan and Nancy Davis were busily proving that they *were* the permanently marrying kind, welcoming a little girl, Patricia (later Patti) in late 1952, and a boy, Ron, Jr., in 1958.

Wyman's attitude toward them as the years went on was philosophical and fair. "She gave him what I couldn't—good luck to them," seems to have summed up her reported attitude during the 1950s and 1960s.

Wyman and Karger remained friends—of a sort. He remarried, happily, and died of leukemia in 1979.

# 7

## The Quality Varies
## 1948–1955

The year 1949 brought Wyman three movies—all courtesy of Warner Bros.—that did nothing whatsoever for her. Jack Warner assured her he was looking around for more serious fare for her and promised that if she were a good girl, for the time being, she would find it worth her while eventually.

*A Kiss in the Dark*, her first release of that year, was a trivial and foolish comedy conceit about a concert pianist (David Niven) who finds himself the owner of an apartment house. The ex-owner (Victor Moore) keeps hovering about the premises, making a fussy nuisance of himself. Niven sparks up when he sees Wyman, a photographer's model, is one of the tenants. Love influences him, and he switches from classical music to swing, for a time anyway, while trying to reeducate Wyman's lowbrow tastes. To make a dull story short, he finally wins the lady away from her meathead boyfriend, Wayne Morris, and, as the *Modern Screen* reviewer summed it up, "He knocks down his manager, who is trying to prevent the romance, and then knocks down Morris. Maybe while he's on tour, he'll discover he prefers socking people to playing the piano, and then we'll have a sequel in which he plays a boxer (man, not dog)."

Wyman was wasted in this frothy concoction. Clad in some twenty-five changes of wardrobe and required to sashay about in evening wear, sports apparel, and severely tailored business garb in her role as a model, Wyman appears bored and distracted much of the time, and her efforts to inject some vitality and spontaneity into the proceedings are at times painful to watch. Additionally, Niven's arch playing is not of much help.

*A Kiss in the Dark* was to be the final picture of the famed character actress Maria Ouspenskaya, who played a famous musician-teacher who advises Niven not to let the piano dominate his life as it did hers. Both Wyman and Niven had fond memories of Ouspenskaya. In 1951, when I interviewed Niven in New York during the run of his stage comedy, *Nina*, with Gloria Swanson, he paid tribute to Ouspenskaya's unique force of personality and fascinating mannerisms born of Moscow Art Theatre training and years on the stage in America. "Jane and I were deeply moved by her," he said. "She was very tiny, very wizened, looked like she'd shrivel up before your eyes, but oh the force in that little lady. She just glowed."

Of Wyman he said, "She had a natural comic timing; certainly it was sharper than either mine or Ouspenskaya's, who had won fame, of course, as a dramatic actress. Jane could handle anything the script threw at her. Of course Delmer Daves was not a McCarey or a Gregory LaCava, and his comedic inspirations were—to be charitable about it—rather limited, but Jane was a self-starter, always. I thought that by that time I had the rudiments of comedic style and timing fairly down pat, but that woman surprised me. I found myself reacting to her sudden bits of inventiveness. I know it helped my own performance."

Not everyone held the Wyman and Niven comedic efforts in high esteem. *Time* magazine's April 25,

*A Kiss in the Dark* (1949), with Maria Ouspenskaya and David Niven.

1949, review was brief—and acidulous: "[The film] is a daffy romantic comedy apparently intended to prove that 1948 Oscar-winning Jane Wyman is not really a deaf mute. . . . The only real laughs are provided by quaint Victor Moore, who as erstwhile owner of the house, clucks about among his tenants like an anxious Leghorn. The artistry of his quavering frustrations and waddling dignity make the rest of the shenanigans look plain silly." *Photoplay* tried to be dismissively nice about it: "It's all as light and carefree as a spring day."

Years later Wyman told me that the best thing about *A Kiss in the Dark* was its contrast with the dramatic *Johnny Belinda*. While the picture was no world-beater, it did demonstrate her versatility in a light-comedy departure.

The next 1949 item on Wyman's agenda, *It's a* *Great Feeling*, was one of those all-star affairs that Warners seemed to enjoy throwing together (an apt term) from time to time. In one of its occasional excursions into self-reference, the studio instructed its writers to set up a fairly amusing dialogue exchange between Jack Carson and Dennis Morgan, who wander through the picture. Carson is out to convince Morgan that his new girl sidekick-protégé, Doris Day, has ability. "I'll see to it that she's as good in this as Jane Wyman was in *Johnny Belinda*," Carson declares. Morgan scornfully rejoins: "She didn't even talk in that one." To which Carson replies: "Well—you can't have everything."

The nonlinear proceedings were written by Jack Rose and Mel Shavelson on a day to day basis as they were being filmed. Shavelson has recalled that one day he and Rose heard director David Butler guiding a previous scene just outside their window and hollered out: "Slow up, David—we haven't written the next scene yet, so take your time, *please.*"

The wafer-thin connecting plot had Doris Day taken under the wing of the Morgan-Carson team, playing themselves as movie stars grooming *her* for stardom. Warner Brothers stars appear in vignettes throughout. Wyman's fans got a special kick out of her daughter Maureen's appearance in one scene. Maureen, then nine, comes to her mother's aid with a glass of water when she faints after being told by Bill Goodwin, playing a producer, that she is to do a film starring and directed by Carson. Ex-husband Ronald Reagan appears with Carson in a barber shop scene.

Filmed in technicolor, *It's a Great Feeling* is rather lightweight and silly. It moves along pleasantly enough, but one wonders why Warners made it. One theory is that it kept some of their personalities contractually busy while better fare was found for them.

*A Kiss in the Dark,* weak though it was, could be excused as Warners' attempt to display Wyman's virtuosity in light comedy after the gothic heaviness of *Johnny Belinda.* But Wyman's fans wondered what possible excuse could have been forthcoming for *The Lady Takes a Sailor,* an insubstantial romp in which she co-starred with Dennis Morgan. One significant note in the ads: she was, for the first time, billed over Morgan. Eve Arden, mercifully, was the saving grace of the thing this time around, with

*A Kiss in the Dark* (1949), with David Niven.

Eight-year-old Maureen Reagan acted with her mother and Jacqueline DeWitt in *It's a Great Feeling*, 1949.

screenwriter Everett Freeman giving the irrepressible Eve some bright lines which she delivered—with aplomb.

The ads in the fan magazines tended to be vulgar, while still depicting the Oscar statuette, with the caption "She's the Lady who took the Oscar for *Johnny Belinda*" thus begging the question, as one Hollywood wag put it, of just why Wyman had spent all of 1949 in forgettable "comic" turkeys while the Warners powers-that-be fiddled. Among the tasteless lines in the ads were: "Man the LaughBoats!" "What maneuvers! Jane's got the navy all at sea over the man she wants to land," "Dear Admiral, please send the whole fleet!" and "It's the laughin'est lovin' ever from Warner Bros." Nor was director Mike Curtiz in top form for this one. "I felt his mind was elsewhere all through it," actor Allyn Joslyn told me some time later. "Mike was a dynamo usually, but he seemed to slink through this one with a hangdog air, as if Jack Warner were punishing him for something or other. And the results showed it."

Another supporting actor in *Sailor*, Tom Tully,

told me: "A four-letter word comes to mind for *that* one—*limp!*"

*The Lady Takes a Sailor* dealt with a director of a buyers' research institute (Wyman) who goes sailing on Long Island Sound. Her boat is overturned by what appears to be a one-man submarine. She is rescued by the submarine owner, and he puts her ashore after drugging her. Having photographed the submariner (Morgan) and his craft, she complains to the Coast Guard about him, but can't substantiate her allegations because she can't show the photographs, which were mislaid.

It appears in time that Morgan is actually engaged in secret naval work and found it his duty to remove Wyman's film from her camera. There are assorted misunderstandings but in the end Wyman finds love is more important than literal truth telling.

As the rundown of the plot demonstrates, there is considerable confusion in the writing, and weak performances are given by Wyman and Morgan. The conflict of his secret government work and her insistence that truth must be told results in a none-

*The Lady Takes a Sailor* (1949), with Dennis Morgan and Eve Arden.

Welcoming Marlene Die-
trich to the set of *Stage
Fright*, London, 1949.

too-comic effect. Neither of the stars seemed to have their heart in the thing, and it came and went, with dispatch.

Eve Arden did what she could as Wyman's friend, though she was not afforded the snappy repartee when needed to back up her always amusing looks, gestures, and stances. Tom Tully has a few lively moments as a private detective who can't make head or tail from the proceedings.

During production, the film had been called *The Octopus and Miss Smith*, a title far more original than the one employed, especially since the picture needed every possible hype from cover to gag lines

to Arden's freshest comic inspirations to keep it alive and afloat. When I first saw the film in 1949, I could not help but speculate that those Warner-Dolts-on-High had spent all of 1949 proving to their now hopefully sated satisfaction that Wyman could weather even inferior comic fare as well as she could dramatize. But 1950 would bring some improvement in the assignments that came her way, and it was none too soon.

Seeking to expand her creative horizons, especially after the weak fare accorded her recently, Wyman went to England in mid-1949 to star in Alfred Hitchcock's *Stage Fright*, some of which was filmed at London's Royal Academy of Dramatic Arts. When *The London Express* tendered Wyman a thousand-pound prize for her performance in *Johnny Belinda*, she donated it to the Royal Academy. "There are some prime talents budding there," she told one reporter, "and I want to do my bit toward assuring breaks for them." Asked by the same newsman how she felt about her Oscar—a question she had been asked a thousand times by then—she replied: "Still pleased, of course, but mostly busier than ever before," and implied that she found it psychologically constructive to keep trying to top her prior efforts.

*Stage Fright* was challenging, but mostly because of off-screen tensions. Wyman and Alfred Hitchcock seem to have gotten on with a "pleasant uneasiness." Associates of both felt that their chemistries were not really suited to each other, though Hitchcock realized that Wyman was trying to expand her range, and did his best to help. Then there was Marlene Dietrich, Wyman's co-star, who reportedly resented Wyman's being billed over her. Marlene's highly

theatrical personality and garish if chicly effective makeup and wardrobe made Wyman look like The Little Brown Wren by comparison. Since the plot called for Wyman to pose as stage star Dietrich's maid in order to expose Dietrich as a murderess, it was necessary for Wyman to assume a cockney accent and play down her clothes. There were reports that Wyman resented this and wanted to improve her appearance, thus going against the character, and that Hitchcock was annoyed with her about it.

Hitchcock is reported to have said: "Jane's a very attractive woman in her own right; she's one type; Dietrich is another. Also, she's twelve years Dietrich's junior and the camera will catch that—so why is she worrying?"

Another complication was that Wyman, though English by birth in the plot, is given an ostensibly American education to explain away her American accent. Then, on top of this, she was to essay a cockney manner of speech. "Mattam" (for Madam) was, according to one British critic, about the only

*Stage Fright* (1950), with Marlene Dietrich.

Cockney enunciation she managed to get out correctly.

Michael Wilding was another source of irritation to Wyman, as he tended to mutter all his dialogue. This, combined with his British accent, made most of his lines unintelligible, and later considerable redubbing was necessary.

Speaking with Michael Wilding some years later, I found his memories of Wyman and the film affirmative in a gentlemanly style typical of him. "I never felt that *Stage Fright* was a good picture for Hitch or any of us," he told me. "*Under Capricorn*, which I did for him earlier that year, was, I felt, a better picture—though I know it was badly received. Jane Wyman was under a handicap in being almost the only American in a British cast, and I thought she carried herself off with dignity and poise, and held her own beautifully."

Wyman later defended her desire to look reason-

ably attractive as the Cockney maid with the assertion that using too much unattractive makeup and clothing would only have called undue attention to itself. She felt that putting over the character and personality of the maid was more important than fussy makeup. Possibly, at age thirty-five, she was going through a phase where she wanted to look good, especially with Dietrich up against her as contrast.

Dietrich, colorful and feisty as always, nearly stole the show with her often recalled music hall number, "The Laziest Gal in Town." It was especially written by Cole Porter for her in that film, and featured such lyrics as: "It isn't that I wouldn't, and it isn't that I shouldn't, but I'm the Laziest Gal in Town." Dietrich accompanied this song by constant seductive shiftings from one chaise longue to another across a wide stage of a theater in the story.

The plot has Wyman, a drama student, trying to

*Stage Fright* (1950), with Marlene Dietrich.

*Stage Fright* (1950), with Marlene Dietrich.

save her boyfriend, Richard Todd, from a murder rap. He's under suspicion of killing Dietrich's husband, but *he* claims Dietrich did it, which is why Wyman is stalking her. In the course of rather convoluted action, Wyman falls in love with Michael Wilding, the detective on the case, and learns, almost too late, that Todd is the actual murderer.

Wyman's work in the film was sincere, proficient, well thought out, but she lacked the subtly wry, backhanded style of the more successful Hitchcock heroines, and the Wyman-Hitchcock—to say nothing of the Wyman-Dietrich—styles collided rather than colluded. Since Dietrich had all the glamour and the clothes and the makeup pertinent to her music-hall star role, she sems to have been reasonably content (for her) during the filming, but when asked later if she enjoyed working with Wyman, she must have

remembered the billing, because her answer was an indifferent shrug.

Wyman was surrounded by good actors in this, including such British character stalwarts as Alastair Sim, Kay Walsh, Dame Sybil Thorndike, and Joyce Grenfell. Alastair Sim, who had acted with the best, later commented that Wyman was a naturally gifted performer.

In a *Cinema Notes* review Doug McClelland pointed out: "Hitchcock must have been impressed by his star's darkly expressive eyes, so widely praised in *Johnny Belinda*; he makes good use of them via innumerable closeups. [Wyman] in *Stage Fright* is much better photographed than most actresses in the less than lush British-made films of the day. Her eyes are best utilized near the end when Wyman as well-meaning meddler and Todd are

131

The cover of *Photoplay*, 1950, announcing Wyman and James Stewart as the year's Gold Medal winners.

hiding in a theater prop room. A voice suddenly booms out to proclaim that Todd, the murderer after all, might now kill *her*. She plays almost this whole tense scene with her one-time beau in close-up, shadows enveloping all but her great eyes, now an almost poetic mixture of sorrow, pity, and terror."

*Photoplay* offered an amusing anecdote relating to Wyman's offscreen life during the shooting. She woke up one Sunday morning at her hotel with a very sore throat. At her request the manager hailed a leading throat specialist. The specialist insisted on bringing along his small son on the way to a cricket match. He sold the visit to the boy with the argument that he would get to meet his favorite screen star, and that he would leave the door slightly ajar so he could peek in on her.

During the examination the child suddenly rushed into the room and announced, "We missed the matches for nothing. That's not Jane Wyman!" In the middle of explaining her symptoms to the doctor, Wyman asked him why he thought she wasn't Jane Wyman. "Because I saw her in *Johnny Belinda* and she can't talk at all!" the boy rejoined.

Asked when the *Queen Elizabeth* docked in New York in October 1949 if she had enjoyed working with Hitchcock, she replied cryptically: "We all did the best we could."

Within a week of her return from England in the fall of 1949, Wyman went to work on *The Glass Menagerie*. Certainly she had won the plum role of the year as the fragile, crippled Laura, who lives in an imaginary world of small glass animals and who must cope with the overly anxious and aggressive efforts of her mother, Gertrude Lawrence, to make of her what she herself once was, a "belle of the ball" in Mississippi. Arthur Kennedy was assigned the role

Receiving the *Photoplay* Gold Medal with James Stewart, 1950.

*The Glass Menagerie* (1950), with Kirk Douglas.

of Laura's poetic, frustrated brother Tom, who longs to escape from his factory job to the great wide world of the merchant marine, and Kirk Douglas was his factory friend, the "gentleman caller" who had been Laura's crush in high school and who raises brief hopes in her that are to be disillusioned.

There was much criticism that the delicate, subtly characterized theater piece that had brought renewed fame to Laurette Taylor in 1945 had been Hollywood-ized, with the stark poignancies muted and a false happy ending—or anyway, the implication of one, tacked on. Tennessee Williams himself co-authored the screenplay and did what he could to preserve the piece's original essence—not always successfully. The final results, despite director Irving Rapper's and the cast's best try, did not make the playwright happy, and he did not count it among his favorite transcriptions to film. (*The Roman Spring of Mrs. Stone* (1961) with Vivien Leigh was his favorite movie version of one of his original works.)

In describing her characterization of Laura, Wyman said: "It takes more than a limp to play a lame girl. . . . It takes a definite frame of mind, in which you project yourself into the part so fully that you even think like a handicapped person and act like one. In *Menagerie* I wear a specially designed shoe that makes my left foot turn in and that actually forces me to limp."

She added, "As a result of playing such roles I have gained a new respect for handicapped persons. Those of us who are fortunate enough to be in perfect health often take that health for granted. But generally you will find people who are not so lucky have much better dispositions. They bear a greater load with more cheerfulness."

The specially made orthopedic shoe that forced her to limp made it unnecessary to think about her walk or general stance, leaving her free to concentrate on dialogue and characterization. But often she found the pain and pressure on her foot so intense that she resorted to a rubber padding around her ankle to avoid cutting from the shoe. At the end of every shooting day, as a precaution, she got a foot massage from an orthopedic specialist and later recalled, "At the end of the day, I limped even without the shoe."

After cutting her hair somewhat short, Wyman tried a long blonde wig that went below her shoulders. Some critics were to find it artificial, and pointed out that in some scenes it appeared obviously synthetic. While trying for the general appearance of the original Laura, Julie Haydon, Wyman determined to bring her own interpretation to the role. An interesting sidelight to her role in *Menagerie* was the fact that in private life Wyman herself had enjoyed collecting glass animals, and she even lent some to the studio for the film.

During the shooting, Michael, then four, became sick with virus flu and had to be hospitalized. Wyman left her work when scenes involving her were not called for, spent much time with him, and nursed him every evening after her stint was completed. When warned by the head office that she stood in danger of catching flu from Michael and endangering the shooting schedule, she calmly rejoined that she took whatever precautions were necessary but that her role as mother to Michael was, in terms of importance, on a par with her acting duties. Luckily, she escaped infection.

Director Irving Rapper, who had guided Bette Davis through her ugly-duckling scenes in *Now, Voyager* eight years before, was conscientious to the point of frustration. Wyman and Kirk Douglas were later to recall as "the longest six days of our lives"

With the glass animals in *The Glass Menagerie*, 1950.

Holding the broken glass animal in *The Glass Menagerie*, 1950.

their sitting-on-the-floor scene. Rapper insisted it be rehearsed to perfection.

Perc Westmore, the makeup genius at Warners, had his problems reassuring Wyman that her head didn't look too big. Every morning when he fit her wig, she complained that it turned her almost into a caricature. It was Westmore who, to reassure her, designed her short hair into a fluffy bob, which she liked so much that she wore it for some time thereafter.

There were the usual outraged-reader reactions to the ad for *Glass Menagerie*, with the vulgar-minded copywriters not able to resist such large-type verbiage as "SHE WAS TOO SHY FOR TOO LONG. . . . AND THEN CAME 'FRESH GUY.'" After an outcry from the public, the Warner ad department pulled in its horns and went to the other extreme with a coy observation to the effect that "SHE THOUGHT IT WAS REAL LOVE" followed by the conservatively (for them) worded: "YOU'LL VOTE IT PICTURE OF THE MONTH, OF THE YEAR, OF THE DECADE!"

Prior to her demand to be let out of her Warners contract in the midst of completing *Beyond the Forest* in the summer of 1949, Bette Davis had been prominently mentioned for the role of Amanda (Laura's mother), and many felt she would have done more justice to it than Gertrude Lawrence (especially with her *Now, Voyager* director, Irving Rapper, on hand to guide her). There was to be much criticism of Lawrence's exaggerated, airy portrayal, with complaints that she had even let a touch of Cockney (she was English) slip into her Mississippi-St. Louis accent. Some reviewers felt, too, that Lawrence had played it too much for comedy, stinting on the poignant dramatics and fey subtleties that Laurette Taylor had brought to the role on Broadway.

Arthur Kennedy and Kirk Douglas received due praise for their highly professional renditions. Wyman, while some reviewers disagreed as to the merits of her performance compared with the stage original of Julie Haydon's, seems to have come out of it very well, especially with retrospective critics over the past thirty-five years who have had to suffer through many an inferior Laura.

In *The Glass Menagerie* Wyman again displayed to telling effect her profound understanding of the wells of the human heart. She suggested here that there were no limits to her artistic range. As Laura she probed every subtle nuance of the character of an unhappy, introverted, and emotionally warped girl

who still contains in her inmost nature a keen awareness of the true, the good, and the beautiful.

She did much of her acting with her eyes, especially in the candlelit scene with Douglas. Each flicker of her eyelashes, each glance seemed a mosaic of contrapuntal mood changes, from hope to despair to hope again. One gets the feeling that she directed herself in that crucial scene. Douglas, who in films like *Lust for Life* indicated reserves of sensitivity not always associated with his more pedestrian roles, complemented her beautifully and generously allowed the scene to build around her moods.

*Time* said of this: "Miss Wyman is constitutionally incapable of looking so ethereal as Julie Haydon did [in the Broadway version]. But with the help of shoulder-length hair and a childlike smile she gives the part of a girl half her age an almost equally poignant sincerity."

When I discussed *The Glass Menagerie* with Wyman a full decade later, she said: "I worked harder on the character of Laura than anyone will ever know. I wanted to get her right. I didn't want to model my interpretation on anyone else's. I felt there was a deep-down truth to this girl that I would discover through my instincts—and I feel they served me well. I also had the benefit of a good director and creative co-actors."

As per her Warners contract, Wyman could do outside pictures, but one wonders who chose them for her as some were ill judged. In one of her rare excursions to Metro-Goldwyn-Mayer, Wyman took over an airline stewardess role originally intended for Lana Turner. Lana bowed out, and June Allyson was next slated for it, but an impending Blessed Event knocked Allyson out of the running. After being sent the script, Wyman decided to accept; her chief motivation was that she needed a change of pace after the poignant dramatics of *The Glass Menagerie*.

The picture was called *Three Guys Named Mike*—the three Mikes being Van Johnson, a research scientist she encounters on a flight; Howard Keel, a pilot; and Barry Sullivan, an advertising executive.

There were complaints that the picture seemed to be one big advertisement for American Airlines, what with small-town girl Jane training to be a stewardess, then getting into comedy incidents during flight service (forgetting to load the food for passengers and crew, "sterilizing" the pilot's microphone with gardenia perfume, etc.). All three Mikes are allowed to make their respective romantic over-

*Three Guys Named Mike* (1951), with Van Johnson, Howard Keel, and Barry Sullivan.

tures, and part of the fun is figuring out which Mike will end up with Jane.

One critic, jumping on the "concealed advertising" theme, wrote: "[It] will have girls all over the country racing to the airlines' employment offices. All is thrilling and wonderful; it's fun to watch. But killjoys [the pot called the kettle black here] will be asking why they should pay to see a film that features a real life airline from start to finish—American—and which reaps millions in publicity for the private company thereby. What the rival airlines will have to say is something else again. This device," the carping critic continued, "adds fuel to an argument that has been aroused by concealed advertising in previous films; this one, however, is more obvious than any in the past."

Metro-Goldwyn-Mayer's flacks promptly let it be known that airline promotion had nothing to do with the Sidney Sheldon-scripted film, the gist of their argument being that if a film is to portray aspects of American life realistically it follows inescapably that some inadvertent and totally unintended coverage occurs. After all, they averred, life is not lived in a bandbox and film is a searching medium that pries into various areas and that is part of its intrinsic merit.

All three of her co-stars enjoyed working with Wyman, and all spoke well of her. Johnson, still married at the time, was all wrapped up in his and Evie Wynn Johnson's small daughter, Schuyler. Wyman later recalled that offscreen Johnson spent most of his time (he was a dedicated artist) creating small, exquisite paintings and drawings for Schuyler when she reached eighteen. Barry Sullivan in 1965 expressed to me his admiration for Wyman's expert and easy shifting from drama to comedy. "She played comedy as to the manner born," he said. Keel also admired her greatly, and said she was most helpful and understanding with his efforts in one of his rare nonsinging parts which, he reminisced, "I carried off with flying colors thanks to Jane."

In order to feel at home in her role in *Three Guys Named Mike*, Wyman, in a stewardess outfit, made a real-life flight from Los Angeles to Phoenix and met Ethel (Pug) Wells, a real-life American Airlines stewardess. She formed a good and lasting friendship with Wells.

*Time* said of the film: "As the Mikes in her life turn up, the script offers three versions of boy meets girl, gives each suitor a chance to show his wares and make his pitch. The thin idea is spread pretty thin. But actress Wyman, well-supported by her leading men and occasionally sprightly dialogue, buoys *Three Guys* into good-humored entertainment."

Charles Walters, who was more notable for his 'MGM' musicals, kept the film admirably paced with his shrewd directorial ideas. When things got tense on the set, Walters and Keel enjoyed teasing the other cast members by threatening to break into a song and dance act, not that this lively picture needed it.

From Metro-Goldwyn-Mayer Wyman went over to Paramount on yet another outside deal. She said at the time, with rather wry humor, that whatever energy she expended traveling from studio to studio,

it was refreshing to "see new sights and meet new people."

In *Here Comes the Groom* Wyman co-starred for the first time with Bing Crosby. In this she demonstrated her singing and dancing abilities, reminding everyone yet again of her wide range as an entertainer. She and Crosby made a sparkling pair onscreen, and so obvious was their good-humored chemistry that rumors of a possible romance between them immediately began.

The Bing Crosby the world knew—calm, serene, almost lackadaisical, and solidly domesticated—was not the Crosby of private life. A privately unhappy, restless, and discontented man wed to a former actress, Dixie Lee, who had given him four sons, he was ridden with dour Catholic guilts—which he tended to take out on those around him. He was given to compulsive adulteries. For the famous Der Bingle, as he was affectionately known to his fans, there were more than a few women in the wings only too happy to jump into bed with him. He and Dixie were not happy; they had grown apart, and she reacted to his coldness and withdrawal by developing psychosomatic illnesses that were to result in her death a year later—plunging him into new depths of guilt.

Crosby found Wyman, who by 1951 had already

*Here Comes the Groom* (1951), with Bing Crosby.

weathered three marital debacles of her own, a tonic for low spirits. Not only did she do everything to make him smile, sensing as she did his melancholic private temperament and domestic unhappiness, but she even initiated (or so friends averred) a platonic flirtation to make him understand that emotions as well as sex were important to man-woman interplay, and that friendship and camaraderie and mutual moral support were the most important things of all. Der Bingle responded readily to this approach, what with most women around him either trying to use him or offer him sex (or a combination of both). He found the synthesis of Wyman's worldly wisdom and breezy humor both novel and bracing. Later he told friends, "And when I realized that this girl had unsuspected singing and dancing skills that she had seldom used in recent years, I was really sold on her."

Because prudish "guardians of Hollywood morals" and their allies, the watch-dog lawyers (who forever reminded studio heads that the morals clause in studio contracts could always be blithely invoked to get rid of players who were unwanted for other reasons), were very much around in 1951 Hollywood, Crosby and Wyman found it necessary to quell the inevitable gossip (some of it happily egged on by studio flacks who smelled free publicity in it). Bing had long since accustomed himself, despite his religious scruples, to "sneaking around," but it wasn't Wyman's style at all. Everything was up front with her, and there were the two children to consider. It bothered her somewhat. *She* might know that their relationship was a fundamentally refreshing and wholesome one, but would the gossips and bluenoses see it that way? She became even more uneasy when some indiscreet scribes began talking

*Here Comes the Groom* (1951), with Bing Crosby.

about their "budding romance" with allusions to the possibility of Bing leaving the ailing Dixie and taking up with her full force.

Certainly director Frank Capra must have sensed some growing emotional involvement between them, for in his later autobiography he said, "When a love story rings true on the screen, it catches up both audiences and players in its wonderment. An emotional chemistry happens between two people that transcends the film itself. And now it happened again—in a wild comedy—between Bing and Jane. They fought, argued and scratched. But when they were alone, the world didn't exist. They loathed each other, yet were one another's favorite entertainers and audiences. They were in love. And love, as we've all found it, bewitches and ennobles everything—even hokum comedy." Capra went on to speak of "the charming chemistry" that developed between them. Wyman he described as "short nose, big heart, and all talent. She had a rarely used flair for singing and dancing. The news about her song 'Cool, Cool, Cool of the Evening' was Jane—the way she traded her crying towel for a glamour-girl's raiment and becomes a dish to behold!"

Whatever the flacks, the public, and Hollywood—and Capra—may have thought of the romance, Wyman and Crosby obviously entered into some form of mutual agreement to terminate it—whatever it was—upon completion of the picture. They were both sensible people; there were her kids, and his wife and kids, to consider. Even had matters progressed into ever-deeper waters emotionally, Crosby would never have affronted his Catholic faith by divorcing and marrying her, and hers was not the temperament for back-street involvements. But they remained great friends, and in subsequent years always referred to each other with bantering affection. They were even to do another picture together.

The plot of Here Comes the Groom was forgettable enough. Crosby is a newspaperman in Paris. After a three-year stint he comes back to the U.S. with two war orphans he has adopted to resume, he thinks, with his waiting lady, Wyman, but she now has other plans, having become engaged to her boss, Franchot Tone. Crosby pulls every trick in the book to win her back. That is the sum total of the plot, but the star performances make the audience forget there even is a story. Alton Cook in The New York World-Telegram and Sun said: "Now that Jane Wyman has her Oscar safely tucked away, she is back at being our most pixieish comedienne and making her share

of things very mirthful as a fisherman's daughter out to crash Boston's most blueblooded circles. . . . When director Frank Capra is in exactly his best mood, he and his writers have the maddest and funniest flights of fancy ever produced on this continent."

Wyman told me years later that she welcomed Here Comes the Groom as a change of pace from heavy dramatics. She describes it as "a breezy, amusing romp, and Frank Capra was someone I had always wanted to work with. Bing was a delight, so humorous and upbeat; I heard tales of how moody he could be, but I rarely found him so on this picture. Of course, Capra kept everybody bubbling with his infectious high spirits, so it was impossible to keep a long face around that set—or even to develop the makings of one."

Franchot Tone, when I talked with him in the late 1950s, remembered how kinetic a team Crosby and Wyman made. "They had a chemistry there, those two—they made only one other picture together later, and they should have made more. Everybody got caught up in the fun they were obviously having together."

In October 1951 Wyman appeared with Crosby on radio in his Bing Crosby Show. Hoagy Carmichael, Ken Carpenter, and the John Scott Trotter orchestra complemented them ably. "With Miss Wyman, Crosby did an unusual amount of kidding," Variety noted. "It's a delightful show, easy on the ears, in a program that provides a maximum of relaxation."

It is true that the chemistry between Wyman and Crosby is very much in evidence in Here Comes the Groom. Their obvious enjoyment of each other comes through. And they play together as if they had been doing it for years, though it was their first picture together. Neither upstages the other; they give each other equal time and even show more than usual consideration for each other's moments of sole camera attention.

In her next picture Wyman was to shift from lighthearted comedy and musical capers to serious dramatics for what was to be one of the finest pictures of her career, one that would win her yet another Oscar nomination.

Wyman journeyed from Paramount over to the RKO studios for a picture she had initially been hesitant about. It was The Blue Veil. Producer Jerry Wald, who had guided Johnny Belinda, had for some time been searching for another "blockbuster Wyman drama" and had brought it to her attention.

By then an RKO producer Wald asked her to look at the French film version, *Le Voile Bleu*. (An item of apparel common to French nurses, the blue veil is the emblem of their vocation.) Wyman at that point was winding up the lively *Here Comes the Groom* and as writer Ida Zeitlin was later to recall, "Working with Crosby, Capra, et al. was like drinking vintage champagne—all zing, sparkle, and a heady sense of well-being. Drama [Wyman felt] twisted your nerves and left you limp as a dish clout. Who needed it?"

Even before she left the *Here Comes the Groom* set she discussed the role—a nursemaid who devotes her whole life to children, foregoing marriage, money, friendship, everything for it—with Bing, who encouraged her to do it. But for some time she remained indecisive, remembering *Belinda* and *Menagerie* and the toll they had taken of her emotions. A short time later Crosby had to go into the hospital for a minor operation, and when she checked on his health she told him she had decided to do *The Blue Veil* after all. She remembered later that a lot of truth is spoken in jest when he had sallied, "I knew it! Wyman smells a great role and unfurls her feathers to the breeze!"

It seems that Jerry Wald had won her over with the words: "If it flops, we'll all pick our whistlestop. If not, we'll all take our bow. But it's a challenge, so you can't turn it down." Jerry Asher in *Screen Life* wrote after she began in the role, "Beneath the animation, the humor, the friendliness, lie depths of reserve. You can go so far and don't cross the line. She belongs to herself. It's a self that admits few intimates but loves humanity with a steadfast sense of responsibility. This feeling demands release and finds it in the kind of pictures she makes."

Wyman herself explained the inner idealism that propelled her toward *Belinda, Menagerie,* and *Veil.* In 1951, while making the film, she said, "We're put into this world; nobody knows why. Sometimes I don't like it. Sometimes I'd rather be in heaven or elsewhere. Meanwhile I'm here for a certain span of years. Nothing adds up for me except how much good you can be to how many people during that span. Without a goal you don't live, you drift. I've set myself quite a few. This is the only one that's ever made sense."

Warm, tender, and unaffected, *The Blue Veil,* as guided by the sensitive director Curtis Bernhardt,

*The Blue Veil* (1951), with Charles Laughton and Vivian Vance.

*The Blue Veil* (1951), with Richard Carlson.

was somewhat apart from the usual run of 1951 movies. It had no sex, did not dwell on any major love story, thoroughly de-glamorized its heroine, yet succeeded in wending its way into the hearts of millions across the country. Certainly it contained one of Wyman's most sensitive performances. In it she played a character obviously engaged in a continuing romance with the great wide world—especially a succession of children who over the years come under her care as a nursemaid. For that is all she is, from beginning to end—a humble, simple, drab, totally unaffected nurse who loves children. In fact in her later years she is even reduced to being a janitor, but that is all right with her, too, for it's in a school where she can be near kids.

The film was also deeply moving as shown, with Curtis Bernhardt mounting it for maximum assaults on audience emotions; and with Wyman, a past mistress by then of this sort of thing, manipulating

the sensibilities again and again during the 113-minute running time. The picture also boasted a literate Norman Corwin screenplay, fine photography by Frank Planer, and one of the most touching scores eminent screen composer Franz Waxman had ever come up with.

In *The Blue Veil*, Wyman had to age from twenty to seventy. The aging worried her—she was anxious to get across the stance, the mannerisms, the inner psychology of an aged person. Perc Westmore was there to make her old on the surface, but how could she feel old from within and act that feeling to the surface?

She was lucky to have as one of her co-stars the distinguished actor Charles Laughton, then past fifty and with his own share of inner torments. She asked him one day about it. "I have to know why old people walk the way they do. What happens to their minds and nerves and muscles? Why do their hands

*The Blue Veil* (1951), with Natalie Wood.

move more slowly? What makes them unsure of their steps?"

Laughton advised her that the answers were only partially to be found in medical books. Then he tapped her forehead. "It's to be found *there*," he said quietly. She recalls Laughton talking with her for days about the role, and about the gradual aging process. He brought her books, which he carefully marked. Though Laughton was only in the film for a couple of weeks, Wyman, who had never met him prior to that time, remembered him with lasting gratitude. Later she said, "From this man whom I'd never met before, I learned more in ten days than I could have learned in ten years knocking my own blundering head against the walls. He made me *feel* old." At the time Wyman was thirty-seven.

Wyman always said that Laughton was a deep one, a man with a great private sorrow that had made him

crotchety and snappish, yes, but that had also invested him, by empathetic osmosis, with a profound understanding of the depths of the human heart. When the later posthumous revelations of Laughton's tortured and humiliating homosexuality came out to shock readers via various biographies, Wyman reportedly was one of the few in Hollywood to react with compassion and understanding—as she was to do later with a star even more famous. In *The Blue Veil* Laughton was moving indeed in his role, conveying most sensitively the middle-aged loneliness of a suddenly widowered man hunting for a fresh lease on life and love.

Wyman broke one of her longstanding domestic rules for the premiere of *The Blue Veil*. She took her ten-year-old daughter Maureen to see it. She had never allowed Maureen to view *Johnny Belinda*, later telling friends, "My comedies, yes—but not my dramas. Maureen and I had had all we could take when she saw *The Yearling*. Of course she was only seven, but she wouldn't speak to me for two weeks because I'd killed the deer! And of course I felt that the subject matter of *Belinda* was too mature for her at the time."

Dressed like her mother in fetching black velvet, Maureen watched the first sequences of *The Blue Veil* with ladylike dignity, but soon sobs were racking her. "Mother, it's so sad," she wailed, to which Wyman rejoined, "The saddest is yet to come. Especially if you don't hang on to yourself." Maureen promptly choked off her sobs and the audience turned its attention again to the film. But at the end she was a wilted mass of emotion.

In great amusement Wyman told a friend some days later that she had heard Maureen telling a pal about how moving the film was, but deploring the fact that her mother, sitting right next to her, never shed a tear—and didn't *understand* drama. . . .

In 1957 I discussed *The Blue Veil* with the actor Everett Sloane, now deceased. He figured in a scene as a district attorney who has to reprimand the aging nursemaid for her attempts to hang on to a beloved child neglectfully abandoned to her care for years and whose mother now wanted him back. "I'll never forget the impact of that scene," Sloane told me, "in which Jane made a touchingly direct and true statement that she had been with that child through all manner of sicknesses and childhood sorrows, and that was what a *real* mother did, and what would the other woman know of all that?" He continued, "Jane was a wonderful dramatic actress; she never pressed her points, never overstated, just simply let out the emotions in restrained but telling ways that were pure Wyman. Like all artists, she is very much an *individual* in what she imparts."

Other actors in that film were Richard Carlson, Joan Blondell, Cyril Cusack. Carlson played a young tutor in a household where Wyman is a nursemaid.

*The Blue Veil* (1951).

He almost elopes with her, but then backs off. Blondell is a self-centered actress who almost loses her daughter, Natalie Wood, whom she neglects, to Wyman, until the latter, with supreme unselfishness, warns the real mother that she will lose Wood forever if she doesn't pay her the needed attention.

Cusack, who had acted with the greatest companies in the world, said of Wyman to me: "There is no limit to what she could have done—the stage, anything. She was an artist of infinite resource."

An unnamed viewer in *Modern Screen's* 1951 *Hollywood Yearbook* nailed down the essence of Wyman's *Blue Veil* contribution (for which she earned another Oscar nomination, losing to Vivien Leigh's Blanche Dubois): "[Three cheers for] Jane Wyman in *The Blue Veil* because, though she was playing one of those sad, soap opera creatures who is left in poverty and loneliness in her old age, Jane refused to descend to tear-jerking histrionics in her performing. The temptation to make a field day of *The Blue Veil*, to chew the scenery, to pull for the loud sobs from the customers, was scornfully rejected by this intelligent actress. Instead she gave us Lulu, the governess, going through thirty-five years from fresh young womanhood to forlorn old age with complete, sincere respect for the dignity and worth of the woman. She affected us more than if she'd tried phony tugging at heartstrings."

*Time* magazine, never easily pleased by movie fare, said: "[All the roles] are reliably performed. Miss Wyman, carrying the main burden, ages convincingly and plays a necessarily subdued role with deep feeling. And considering the flagrantly sentimental nature of his material, director Curtis Bernhardt deserves credit for using restraint in the face of obvious temptation."

Years later, discussing her varied roles with her and getting assorted shrugs and nods in the process, I noted that her eyes lit up with honest retrospective feeling when *The Blue Veil* came up. "*That* I was proud of," she said.

With 1951 came yet another of those Warner all-star films in which Wyman did brief stints. Actress Ruth Roman originated the idea to bring all-star entertainment to the boys at Travis Air Force Base near San Francisco. This was in the second year of the Korean War, and some of the boys were getting ready to ship overseas; others lay wounded in the base hospital. Louella Parsons pushed the idea in her column, and Warners then proceeded to make a movie, called *Starlift*, at the base with such Warners

personalities on hand as James Cagney, Gary Cooper, Randolph Scott, Frank Lovejoy, Virginia Mayo, and Gordon MacRae. Wyman, too, climbed aboard, for a delightful singing sequence in the base hospital (accompanied by a serviceman accordionist) with Doris Day. Wyman demonstrated that she could hold her own in the warbling department with Day, the most formidable singing talent at Warners—or any other studio. Neither overshadowed the other.

One reviewer commented: "Despite its good intentions and a host of the studio's top stars in guest appearances, [this] was a pretty feeble effort."

And from another: "A couple of writers padded it out to a full ninety-one minutes and trumped up a young-love story. Janice Rule is the star torn between loving and loathing an Air Force corporal, played by Ran Hagerthy. . . . But it's dependable Doris Day and Jane Wyman, just singing some oldies, and a nightclub comedy act, Noonan and Marshall, who steal this show of patriotism."

John Klorer and Karl Kamb were the writers, and director Roy Del Ruth tried to keep it moving, and lively, but the results were so-so. Gary Cooper, one of the stars in attendance, said later that the star-serviceman combo did not seem, somehow, as effective during the Korean conflict as in World War II, perhaps because in the earlier year, with the Hollywood Canteen and all, the idea had seemed more fresh and novel.

Wyman said she felt good about her stint, as it brought back pleasant memories of similar work during World War II. And she and Doris Day got to share such popular standards as "Liza" and "S'Wonderful" by George and Ira Gershwin; "It's Magic" by Sammy Cahn and Jule Styne, and "What Is This Thing Called Love?" by Cole Porter.

Wyman remained at Warners for her next film, in which she would do her co-star an unusual favor.

In her one Warner Brothers release for 1952—a hiatus from constant loanouts—Wyman took what was essentially a secondary role and made it stand out. Many wondered why Wyman had agreed to only technically co-starring in *The Will Rogers Story*, opposite Will Rogers, Jr., an amiable enough man, who looked and talked much like his famed father. Rogers had been a Congressman and had just enough of his father's aura to have proven to be the one logical person to play him, but his acting limitations were very evident, and he later credited Wyman, rather than the sometimes impatient and peremptory director Mike Curtiz, with saving the day for him.

Wyman was tired at the time, what with a tough radio schedule and the to this day unexplained cancellation of a picture called *Broadway Revisited*, for which she had high hopes. *The New York Times* had announced it as forthcoming on her Warner schedule. According to the *Times*, *Broadway Revisited* would deal in "a romantic vein" with the professional and personal life experiences of a movie star who returns to the New York stage.

Rumor had it that Jack Warner had asked Wyman, as a favor, to lend her box office clout to the Rogers film. In the tradition of Bette Davis, who had done the same favor for Warner, playing second-fiddle to Paul Lukas in *Watch on the Rhine* (1943) and Monty Woolley in *The Man Who Came To Dinner* (1941), thus assuring top grosses, Wyman went along with the idea.

A friend at the time said: "I also think she felt the film would be a hit, and she reasoned that it was better to be second-banana in a hit than top-banana in a fair picture or a failure."

*The Will Rogers Story*, though it was a pleasant-enough entertainment that captured the original's distinctive quality, was no world-beater, either with the critics or at the box office. Wyman seems to have had a change of heart about the film later, too, for one column item of the time said that she had positively refused to help publicize the film in any shape, manner, or form. There were rumors that she didn't like the way her role was constructed by the writers and felt the film didn't give her enough opportunities and kept her characterization overly "passive" and "on-looker-simpering."

Other rumors had it that she had found the inexperienced Rogers, Jr., a trial in more ways than one. But Rogers himself had nothing but praise for

*The Story of Will Rogers* (1952), with Will Rogers, Jr.

her, both during and after the picture. "Jane is wonderful," he told one writer on the set. "She shows me how to read the dialogue and has taught me plenty about camera angles." In that same interview he confessed that none of his Congressional campaigns, tough and physically demanding as they were, compared to the ruggedness of the acting business and cited an unusual scene in the movie where he was playing his father present at his own birth.

The film, centered almost entirely around Rogers, covered his rise from a lariat-twirling cowboy in the Ziegfeld Follies to the Hollywood heights and his ever growing status as America's prime humorist. During most of this Wyman stood by, ever loving and ever supportive, looking rather drab and housewifely in unbecoming period costumes. Her friends—more than a few—said later in 1952 that Wyman heaved a huge sigh of relief when the film was over and said it had so depleted her that—unless

an exceptional role [such as Mildred Cram's supernatural romance, Forever] came her way—she'd like to go to bed and stay there for months.

The critics, for the most part, were kind—condescendingly so—to young Rogers's charming inadequacies and gave Wyman points for her heroic efforts to shore him up at various sections of a saggy film. Bosley Crowther in The New York Times wrote: "Considering the warmth and affection with which Will Rogers was held in American hearts, not to mention the simple sweetness and sentiment of the man, it is not surprising that Warner Bros. has choked up and blubbered just a bit in filming [this]. . . . It cannot be said that this rundown on Mr. Rogers's life is dramatically absorbing or exciting, in the ordinary sense of those words. It sticks to a narrative pattern, it rambles around quite a lot, and, like its beloved hero, it is full of leisurely talk." Crowther spoke of Wyman's "pleasant and gentle attitude" in the film. Otis L. Guernsey Jr. in the New

*Just For You* (1952), with Ethel Barrymore and Bing Crosby.

*Just For You* (1952), with Bing Crosby.

*York Herald Tribune* wrote: "Jane Wyman makes a likable figure." Such damning with faint praise doubtless soured Wyman on the film.

Feeling at that point the need to vary the dramatics with some lighter fare, in order to get herself some needed spiritual renewal and refreshment, Wyman went over to Paramount. She has always credited Bing Crosby with getting her back into the singing and dancing groove of 1951 and 1952. In her new picture with him, *Just For You*, she played a musical comedy star, and for Decca Records recorded some songs. *Variety* in its June 11, 1942, issue, carried a review of songs by such as Georgia Gibbs, June Valli, Don Cornell, Toni Arden, Tony Martin, Rosemary Clooney—and Jane Wyman.

Reviewer Herm Schoenfeld of *Variety* wrote of Wyman: "'Checkin' My Heart,' 'He's Just Crazy for Me' (Decca) are two cute tunes from the Paramount pic *Just for You* and make good material for actress

Jane Wyman. 'Heart,' a rhythm number with a clever lyric, is bounced by Miss Wyman in okay, if not standout, style. In a slower tempo, 'Crazy for Me' gets a more colorful slice by Miss Wyman but the dragging beat requires several spins before it catches on. Dave Barbour's backing is first rate."

Co-workers remember that the overall atmosphere on *Just for You* over at Paramount was a little quieter than at Columbia for *Here Comes the Groom* the year before, for Crosby's wife Dixie was dying and he was feeling an uneasy mixture of guilt and concern for her, which he only partially disguised with somewhat forced comedy playing. In *Just for You* Crosby was a successful composer-producer on Broadway too busy being famous to pay proper attention to his teenage kids. His adolescent son, Robert Arthur, falls in love with stage-musical star Wyman, thus presenting his father with a triangle. It seems the kid resented Dad's tepid attitude toward his songwriting

Showing off her gams in *Just For You*, 1952.

attempts. Soon he is encouraging his son's creativity and getting his daughter (Natalie Wood) admitted to an exclusive girls' school run by fey headmistress Ethel Barrymore. Eventually all complications are resolved, and the right people end up together which, considering the plot's general predictability, was no surprise.

Critic Jack Karr of *Showplace* wrote: "This artificial hocus-pocus is made palatable by the continued nonchalance of the Groaner in the producer role and, to a lesser measure, by Ethel Barrymore who, when she isn't forced to be outrageously cute, is as comfortable as an old shoe in the part of the swanky school's headmistress. As for Miss Wyman, she bobs about ingratiatingly, mainly in abbreviated togs, displaying an elegant figure. She also pipes prettily

some of the film's songs, sometimes alone, sometimes in duet with Bing. 'Zing a Little Zong' and the title number are probably among the best."

Mae Tinee of the *Chicago Tribune* wrote, "While the plot of this film isn't too sharp, the cast presents it so smoothly that the rough spots disappear in an aura of warmth and good fun. Miss Wyman sparkles like Lake Michigan on a sunny morning and the studio provides her with some of the most becoming costumes a woman could have."

*The Christian Science Monitor* reported, "As the fetching Carolina, Miss Wyman is abundantly qualified to strike a young man's fancy—or, as the story dictates, a young man's father's fancy. She plays with genuine affection the scenes in which Carolina tries to promote better family relationships among the

Blakes, and with tender understanding the difficult passages in which she discovers that she has inadvertently encouraged [the young son] to fall in love with her."

On the set of *Just for You* (original title: *Famous*, from a Stephen Vincent Benet story), Wyman told Bob Thomas that her long apprenticeship at Warners had paid off for her in versatility terms and that people tended to forget that she had started off originally as a singer and hoofer. "Why, do you realize," she reminded Thomas, "that since Bette Davis left the lot I am the oldest gal left there? And only Errol Flynn among the actors has been there longer. I started in 1936 and he preceded me by only a year."

She was lavish in her praise of Crosby, and told Thomas that her new career as a recording artist had really happened by accident. "It was Bing's doing," she explained. "After we did [*Here Comes the Groom*] together he asked me if I wanted to come over to Decca and cut a disc of 'In The Cool, Cool, Cool of the Evening.' I said, 'Are you kidding?' but he wasn't and so we did the thing together."

A number of records followed and soon they were dubbing her "A Dinah Shore of Tomorrow." To this Thomas quoted her as rejoindering: "Well, let's say the Dinah Shore of the day before yesterday."

Asked why she was going in for light singing-dancing-comedy fare circa 1952, Wyman declared: "Audiences don't want to see [heavy dramas] just now. They have enough troubles of their own, without going to see more problems on the screen. That's why [for the present] I want to sing and laugh in the movies I make." Her role in *Just for You* had originally been designed for Judy Garland, who, what with weight and drug problems, to say nothing of numerous emotional crises, had been having an up and down time since her 1950 film, *Summer Stock*. Crosby and others had hoped that *Just for You* would be just the tonic Garland needed, but she simply wasn't in shape to film, so Wyman was drafted in her stead. One year later, Garland was on her way to a big comeback over at Warners in *A Star Is Born*.

Wyman was away from the Warner home base for yet another picture. This time it was for a comedy she felt might afford her added range. A number of Wyman's friends and associates, however, ques-

*Let's Do It Again* (1953), with Ray Milland.

*Let's Do It Again* (1953), with Ray Milland.

tioned her judgment in essaying the remake of the Irene Dunne-Cary Grant 1937 hit, *The Awful Truth*, a four-star comedy if ever there were one. For it, director Leo McCarey had won an Academy Award, and it had proven a perfect blend of that highly talented director's humorous and sentimental qualities. The new picture, sixteen years later in 1953, was given the saucy title, *Let's Do It Again* (meaning: let's get married again, *not* let's-do-that-again).

Wyman had the Dunne role, Ray Milland the Cary Grant stint, Aldo Ray substituted for Ralph Bellamy as the oafish "other man," and Alexander Hall superseded McCarey. Hall was pure McCarey, and while the remake was creditable enough, it didn't match the earlier picture in any way. Wyman was delightful, however, not only as a comedienne but also as a leggy, voluptuous singer-dancer and farceur. She was in Technicolor here—and in the wildest, sexiest gowns designer Jean Louis could dream up.

A retired musical star, Wyman acts as "perfect wife" to composer Milland, who has a wandering eye. She seeks to teach him a lesson by romancing suave producer Tom Helmore and crudely attractive Klondike nugget millionaire Aldo Ray. Divorce is in the offing, but "the awful truth" (as the original was aptly titled) emerges: that they are only happy and fulfilled in a monogamous relationship with each other.

Valerie Bettis is on hand for some sexy singing-dancing pyrotechnics as an entertainer whom Milland finds attractive (up to a point), and when she does a hot number called "Call of the Wild," which involves some inventive gyrations designed "to separate the men from the boys," Wyman, a captive audience, takes secret notes for future reference. Toward the end, at a stuffy party thrown for Milland and his snooty socialite "second intended" Karen Booth, Wyman shows up unexpectedly, stops the

152

party cold, and sends the guests fleeing with a wild reprise of Bettis' shenanigans.

As Doug McClelland said in his review, "This basic episode had afforded Irene Dunne her finest moments in *The Awful Truth*. Indeed Dunne's over-all comedy performance has never been surpassed in pictures. The scene was updated (from 1937 to 1953) for Wyman, who played it sexier, a trifle coarser, less screwball, keeping her voice in seductive lower-register throughout . . . her farcical skill earned favorable comparison with Dunne, than which there is no higher praise."

*Let's Do It Again* was a film in which Wyman cut loose musically, as she has seldom done before or since. She got to do the 1953 dance rage, the mambo, and was in great form with such Lester Lee-Ned Washington numbers as "It Was Great While It Lasted," "I'm Takin' a Slow Burn Over a Fast Man," and "Anyone But You." Milland made like a singer, too, on occasion, though his voice was dubbed by Paul Frees.

Milland did his level best, being no slouch in comedy, but he was not quite up to Cary Grant's original conception, and when called to wear some female attire, he could not quite summon the light, unselfconscious, fey quality of which Grant was a past master. Milland has warm memories of the film—and Wyman. "It was yet another of those things she did in the early fifties that reminded everyone yet again what a versatile artist she was," he said in 1970. "She could sing and dance with the best of them, and her comedy timing was top-notch. She was a wonderfully cooperative person on the set, inspired everyone around her to give their best, and she was very down-to-earth and democratic in her expressed appreciation for the 'pro' contributions of even the humblest associates on the picture."

Aldo Ray has recalled her kindness and understanding toward him. He was relatively new in films at that point, and Ralph Bellamy's hilariously hayseed conception of 1937 was a tough act to follow. He remembered director Alexander Hall and Jane counseling him to play himself, gravel-voiced, masculinely charismatic, and rough-edged, and stamp his own conception on the role. This he did with marked success.

When I talked to director Alexander Hall about the film in the late 1950s, he said, "I felt it was a solid effort, but the times were against us somewhat. In

So *Big* (1953), with Sterling Hayden.

1937, screwball comedy was fresh and new, and there was what I can only describe as an innocence and directness and spontaneity to the genre, and of course McCarey was a past master of that. But by 1953—well, there had been a horrible world war and postwar readjustment and then another, smaller, war, and people weren't quite as ready to abandon themselves to the escapisms that had so distinguished the 1937 film. Given the times and the material we had, I think we did as well as we could have, but even I have to admit I wondered at times if a remake of that classic original was warranted, or worth it."

Wyman he praised. "That gal can do anything she sets her mind to; she is one of the most creatively versatile performers the screen has ever boasted.

Why, that same year, she was drably noble in a picture of quite a different stripe, *So Big*, and superb all the way. You wouldn't have thought it was the same actress. And she was such a good sport—some of the singing and dancing and clowning stuff required a lot of effort, and she was always game for retakes when required." Wyman's memory of the film is tersely to the point: "I did the best I could."

After two pictures away from the home lot, Wyman went back to Warners for *So Big*, the third film version of Edna Ferber's Pulitzer prize-winning novel. Colleen Moore and Wallace Beery had co-starred in the silent (1925) version; Barbara Stanwyck had graced the 1932 rendition, and Wyman's was the third turn at bat. The film showcases Wyman at her most poignant and affecting; it is yet another in

*So Big* (1953), with Sterling Hayden.

*So Big* (1953).

her distinguished gallery of brave women who triumph against all odds.

The story is a simple and touching, if occasionally convoluted, one about true vocational values versus commercialistic expediencies. Selina (Wyman) has been brought up to believe that there are two kinds of people—the emeralds, or creative folk, and the wheats, those who do productive work. Orphaned by an improvident father after a finishing-school education, she finds herself married to a rough but decent farmer (Sterling Hayden) who is obviously a wheat. When their son, who is nicknamed "So Big," is born, she senses he is destined to be an emerald, and encourages him in that direction.

After the death of her husband, who dies admiring but never completely understanding his far more intelligent and creative wife, Wyman brings the truck farm slowly and painfully to success with the help of family friends, and sends her son (grown up to be Steve Forrest) to architectural school. He, however, disappoints her by choosing the quick, easy way in sales promotion, but the love of an artist, played by Nancy Olsen, brings him back to his true, emerald destiny. His long-suffering mother has the satisfaction of seeing her dreams fulfilled.

*So Big* has a number of interesting subplots. Wyman encourages a sensitive musician, an emerald lost among the wheats, who grows up to become a famous concert pianist. Also she befriends an overworked, miserable wife of a neighboring farmer who tries to run away several times from her crude and brutal husband and who, as the Wyman character ruefully notes, finally succeeds in escaping all the way—into death.

The picture, coming so soon after Wyman's sparkling comedy performance in *Let's Do It Again*, demonstrates her versatility most strikingly. There was, however, much criticism in the trade and among the public of Warner's crudely salacious ad for the film. Warners, especially in the 1940s and 1950s, seemed to distrust the capacity of some of its more tasteful and literate pictures to sell themselves on their merits alone. A notorious instance had been the 1945 ad for *The Corn Is Green*, a dignified Bette Davis drama about a staid Welsh schoolteacher of advanced years (played by Ethel Barrymore in the stage version) who inspires a crude young miner to make the most of his exceptional literary gifts. The Warner advertisement (those boys were at it again) pictured a young, beautiful Bette Davis (devoid of her middle-aged makeup and dowdy costuming) and a handsome boy gazing at her with adoration. The legend read: "DEEP IN HER HEART, SHE KNEW SHE COULD NEVER HOLD HIM!"

Eight years later for *So Big* the vulgarians in the Warners promotion department had obviously been racking their brains (or anyway the lower lobes of them). The ad, which ran in magazines and newspapers nationwide, showed Wyman being grasped roughly and lustfully by Hayden, with her looking mighty scared and with him looking mightily lecherous. The legend read: "HE STOOD THERE SO BIG. LOVE HAD COME, INTENSE, UNASHAMED—SHE WAS READY TO FORGET SHE'D EVER BEEN A LADY."

Since So Big was the nickname she had given her son and certainly did not refer to the physical properties of Mr. Hayden, and since her descent from being a lady had to do with the harsh work of a farm rather than the vicissitudes of the primrose path, the ad, disgraceful to begin with, proved downright misleading. Fans wrote in protesting vehemently. (This was to hold the world record for tasteless movie ads until 1966, when the Jennifer Jones-Michael Parks older woman and younger stud movie, *The Idol*, was to surpass it with the super-teasy legend: "TO BE IDOLIZED, A MAN MUST OFFER THE UNUSUAL . . .")

Be that as it may, the critics forgave Warners all malfeasances when the Robert Wise-directed film went on display in screening rooms across the country. Helen Bower, in *The Detroit Free Press*, spoke for most of her colleagues, writing, "[*So Big*] is a picture of solid worth, solidly performed by all concerned. Miss Wyman retains for Selina the undying spark of dreams that sustain her through the years of rugged farm toil."

Lydia Lane, of the *Miami Daily News*, visited Wyman in Hollywood during the making of *So Big* in 1953 and asked her "what had helped her most to make her dreams come true." "Honesty," Wyman replied, adding: "You can't cheat whether you're offering talent or something you've manufactured. You have to come through with your best." Asked how much emphasis she placed on appearance, she replied, "It's very important. It helps to establish YOU. When I am doing a picture, I work especially closely with the designer. The first impression you create depends largely on your key outfit. You establish character with it."

Speaking to another reporter on the *So Big* set, Wyman demonstrated a surprising (and to her interviewer, unwarranted) humility about her character range. "While I've been lucky in managing a pretty wide range of screen roles," she said, "there are plenty of things I can't do. Suspense drama, for one thing. The kind of performances which Barbara Stanwyck gives so beautifully. You know, the ones that wind up audiences like a spring. I can't do them, so I stay away from them."

When I interviewed Richard Beymer, who played one of the children in *So Big*, in 1962, he spoke glowingly of Wyman, telling of her natural ease and supportiveness with children. "She had true maternal instincts," he said. "Not the artificial, assumed, plastic maternalism so many actresses, even bad ones, can summon, but the real article. She was a wonderful actress—a natural talent. And she knew how to calm down nervous kids, and she had her share of them in that picture. Kids are supposed to be cool naturals in front of the camera, but it isn't *always* so. We were lucky *she* was in the picture; she was our mainstay."

Director Robert Wise rated Jane Wyman high on his list of favorite performers. He told me: "As a director who believes that a pleasant and 'up' atmosphere on a set is terribly conducive to better results, it's always a plus to have leading actors who do have a sense of humor and can help in keeping the atmosphere from getting too heavy. This was one of the strongest attributes that Jane brought to the making of the picture, apart, of course, from her fine talents as an actress."

He added, "She has a definite approach to the role from her own standpoint, but was always most receptive to suggestions and help from me as the director. She never resented direction nor became temperamental at any point. She is a very talented, highly intelligent, 'fun' kind of person to work with." Over the years, Wise drew more than his share of prima donnas and temperament-freaks, and his favorable opinion was not given frivolously. He seemed honestly grateful to have worked with Wyman.

The Wyman performance in *So Big* demonstrated a quality in her playing that has often been overlooked: her sheer *strength* of personality, her presence. Audiences who were to compare her strong matriarch of the 1980s *Falcon Crest* television series with what they regarded mistakenly as her more "soft and muted" past self on screen had an imperfect memory of her. While she always tended to underplay—no bravura grandstanding for her—she radiated authority and granitic personality resolve in *So Big* and *The Yearling* among other films, and more often than credited.

Wyman's next picture, again on loan to another studio, this time Universal-International, was to put her at the very top of the Box-office Christmas Tree. The remake of the Lloyd C. Douglas novel, *Magnificent Obsession*, first done in 1935 by Universal-International with Irene Dunne and Robert Taylor, catapulted Wyman into her strongest box office

position to date. What seemed poignant and meaningful in 1935 came across as studied, garish, and artificial in 1954, though Jane Wyman's performance won much praise for its simple sincerity and emotional honesty amidst a plethora of technicolored camera goo, artificial-looking sets, and sentimentally forced situations.

However producer Ross Hunter, who had a pronounced leaning toward fluffy, overproduced remakes of 1930s hits, seemed to instinctively understand, whatever his deficiencies in taste, that no one ever went broke underestimating the taste of the American public—an old saying that has proven true in era after era. And those ads! Universal-International positively outdid Warners in tastelessness with these, and Wyman's top-grossing audience appeal in *Magnificent Obsession* was, many suspected, due not so much to her sterling performance, but rather to the impact generated among the great and vulgar and unwashed out there by such advertising copy as: "THIS WAS THE MOMENT UNASHAMED. . . . WHEN THIS MAN AND THIS WOMAN FELT THE FIRST ECSTASY OF THEIR

With doctors in *Magnificent Obsession*, 1954.

*Magnificent Obsession* (1954), with Rock Hudson.

MAGNIFICENT OBSESSION!" These scarlet words, accompanied by an illustration of an ecstatic Wyman, eyes closed, being busily nuzzled by co-star Rock Hudson, whose eyes were also closed but whose expression could have been construed by the prurient as "gathering-steam lecherous." Oh, the ecstasy of it all!

And what did the title *Magnificent Obsession*, in both book and the two films, actually refer to? Well, it seems there is this heroic doctor who follows a certain mystic credo: do people good, but tell no one about it. The rather implausible but salably lachrymose plot had Rock Hudson as a playboy whose life is saved during a lake accident by medical attentions required for the altruistic medico who is left unattended during a fatal heart attack. The worthless man survives; the do-good doctor dies, leaving widow Jane Wyman behind.

Though aware of this, Hudson continues his careless ways, then inadvertently is responsible for Wyman being blinded when she attempts to evade him and steps into the path of a speeding car. Enter a sort of Christ-Mr. Jordan figure, Otto Kruger, who tells Hudson of the doctor's good works and his secret formula (*do* it but don't *tell*). Like Saul on the road to Damascus, Hudson, magically reformed and filled with newfound purpose, resumes his medical studies. Before too much more running time has elapsed, his hair slightly grayed at the temples, his features composed into granitic resolve, he becomes a famous surgeon. When he meets Wyman again, she doesn't know who he is. He gives the blinded

Wyman a romantic interlude in Europe, where she has gone to get the best medical advice. She leaves him when she discovers his identity. He tracks her down where she is dying of brain pressure from the original accident, operates on her (with Kruger playing Svengali from the operating-room window), and behold—her sight is restored, and true love conquers all.

Hudson told me many times of the gratitude he felt toward Wyman for all the help she had given him, recounting stories of her patience and subtle hints to him on methods of enhancing and deepening his portrayal. Doug McClelland, in his review of the film, was unimpressed, however. "Hudson, in perhaps the most demanding role, was a comic-strip handsome hero but thrashed about with no special distinction, his scenes lined up with all the depth and subtlety of great colored blocks." Of Wyman, McClelland wrote: "[Her] intelligently subdued theatrics gave [the film] the veneer of quality."

Jim O'Connor in *The New York Journal-American* wrote: "An actress of rare skill, Jane Wyman fairly glows, playing with dignity and simple sincerity.

Especially is she effective in the scenes where she is blind."

In *Current Screen* the author wrote: "Producer Ross Hunter wants to give the screen back its original glamor, at least the glamoratics of the emotionally operatic 1930s, but he seems to imagine that garish technicolored effects, prettily upholstered settings, gooey music, and overblown writing will duplicate the economy, taste, and authentic feelings of his thirties models. Not so, Ross. The marvel is that Miss Jane Wyman's unaffected sincerity, tasteful underplaying amidst the bravura effects of her experienced supporting players and the sadly amateurish flounderings of Mr. Rock Hudson, and clever knack of making the meaningless story and situations seem somehow significant and humanly credible, lift the fluffy, pretentious goings-on far above its intrinsic merits."

Just forty when she made *Magnificent Obsession*, Wyman won her fourth and final Oscar nomination for it, losing out to glamour girl Grace Kelly for her drab, long-suffering wife role in *The Country Girl*. Many Wyman partisans felt that she deserved the

*Magnificent Obsession* (1954), with Agnes Moorehead.

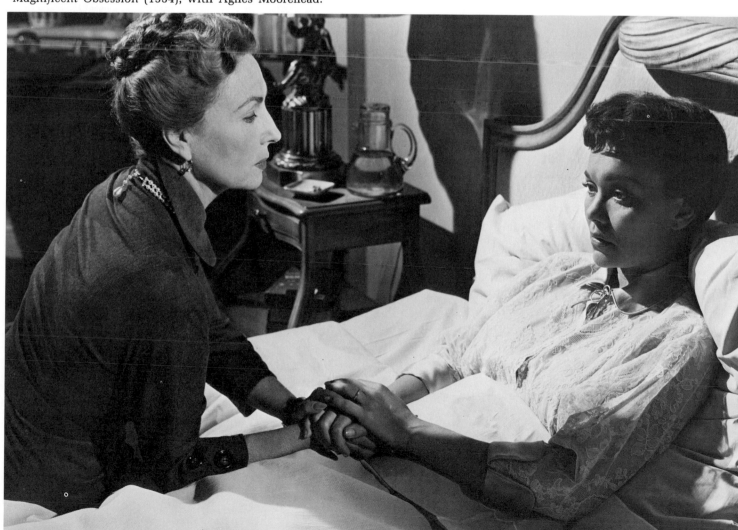

Oscar far more than Kelly, who coasted through a good picture with glasses, drab makeup, and a severe hairdo doing much of the acting for her, while Wyman had lifted an artificial, soapy, pseudo-mystical mess like *Magnificent Obsession* to a point where it looked, often, like the intelligent, meaningful film it thought it was.

Even so, there were some protests in print over the fussy efforts to glamorize Wyman in *Magnificent Obsession*. Gordon Gow wrote with some exasperation that after being blinded, Wyman continued to appear "with makeup applied so impeccably that she might have been presumed to seek supernatural relief every hour or so to fix up her face at the mirror."

I talked to two of the prominent character performers in *Magnificent Obsession II*—Otto Kruger and Agnes Moorehead. Kruger, surprisingly, felt that Rock Hudson was a far better potential actor than he was given credit for being, and that by the time of his second picture with Wyman, *All That Heaven Allows,* he had improved immensely. Moorehead concurred, adding that the second Wyman-Hudson picture had been more intelligently written, made more sense, and gave both stars and character players more to work with than *Magnificent Obsession*.

"There was something starry-eyed, something out of balance, about *Magnificent Obsession*," Moorehead told me thoughtfully. "And I don't think director Sirk really believed in it while he was doing it. The coincidences were stretched, the situations unbelievable, and I, for one, felt it was very hard to play. I didn't feel I was at *my* best in it, but Janie was wonderful, as always, making silk purses out of sow's ears at every turn. And I don't think Rock Hudson had the material to work with here that he did in his next with Janie. He was under another disadvantage, too. Let's face it, no one will ever give a very handsome man credit for acting ability; there's a subconscious envy there, a feeling that the gods would be unfairly generous were they to give him *talent* along with *beauty*."

Kruger said he felt ill-at-ease in his mystical role, the piercing-eyed purveyor of Dr. Philips's give-in-secret philosophy. He felt that gentle, sensitive Ralph Morgan of the 1935 version had been much more suited to the part. "Also, some of the lines didn't really hit the mark," he added, "but as a character player who did as he was told, I was in no position to suggest rewrites. But I recall that naming Jesus Christ as having died on the cross for secret do-

gooding was wrong, as Christ made no secret of any of his good works or miracles during his three-year ministry. I felt this was just one of the examples of bad research on this film."

What with an Academy Nomination for it and a Top Ten Box-office Stars listing, Wyman could not complain of its effect of her career, but from what she said to me and others, I always felt she had some reservations about *Magnificent Obsession*.

"That was my period for remaking other stars' stuff," she told one reporter in 1962. "I redid two of Irene Dunne's [*The Awful Truth* and *Magnificent Obsession*], one of Barbara Stanwyck's [*So Big*], and I never felt a recycled picture could ever capture the freshness of an original inspiration. I, for one, wish they had remade some pictures that had flaws and were not so well-received in their time; it seemed to me it would have been far more creative to improve on a bad original than on a good one. But actors propose and you-know-whos dispose in Hollywood."

At any rate exhibitors and the hanky-wielding

With Charlton Heston between shots on *Lucy Gallant* (1955).

*Lucy Gallant* (1955), with Charlton Heston.

public were not complaining. Weepy situations, handsomely winsome Rock, Technicolor, and fudgy music, all of it, in fact, strengthened by Wyman's sterling performance, rendered *Magnificent Obsession* one of the biggest money makers of 1954.

Next the Wandering Wyman trekked over to Paramount for a film that was to do her little good—and would, in fact, generate the kind of publicity she *didn't* need. Latter-day feminists find Wyman's 1955 film *Lucy Gallant* an anathema, for it dealt with a career lady in the Texas of the 1940s who starts a successful dress shop, but must be constantly bailed out financially by an intrepid, resourceful male, Charlton Heston. He finally persuades her to forget business and settle for domesticity. How could the women's movement approve of that dénouement?

Bosley Crowther in *The New York Times* commented: "Some of it catches sudden flashes and briefly revealing glints of the crudities and vulgarities of the Texas nouveaux riches. The ostentation of such things as lavish spending and going to backyard barbecues in evening gowns is subtly satirized . . . but essentially, this fable takes a warm view of female extravagance and ultra-chic, lavish interior decoration and the absolute elegance of plush."

Crowther wrote of its stars: "Jane Wyman does as well as anybody could do with the material at hand, and Charlton Heston is not unbelievable as a hardheaded Texan who wants a wife. But the boy-meets-girl, boy-loses-girl routines through which they have to go are too much for the talents or the patience of the longest-suffering actors in the world."

Some time later, after *Lucy Gallant* had proven a limp item at the 1955 box offices, it found itself inexplicably retitled *Oil Town*, with Charlton Heston getting played-up in the billing and Wyman getting played-down—accompanied by an ad legend—courtesy of some oversexed, possibly overbeliquored copy writer that rhapsodized about "A STORY WITH THE FORCE AND POWER OF AN EXPLOSIVE GUSHER."

Wyman's clerical pal, Father Robert Perella, tells a story in his book about Wyman warning Heston

With director Douglas Sirk on the set of *All That Heaven Allows* (1955).

during the shooting to "lose that fat rear you're carrying around." Heston had a good enough body for most purposes, but studio executives, and some of the fans, had noted that the rear quarters of the soon-to-be Moses and Ben-Hur tended to be on the pudgy side, as against his imposing stature and well-developed musculature in other physical departments. Heston seems to have accepted her advice without complaint or even any display of chagrin. ("I do try to be detached and objective about all aspects of my career and my personal life," he told me in 1956), and four years later, as *Ben-Hur* attests, Heston had developed a slim, tight rear to conjure with, one that held its own with any actor's around. Wyman, as another friend told me, never hesitated to be short-term cruel in her observations to others, if the result promised to result in a long-term kindess, as in the Heston case.

Heston spoke warmly of Wyman when I interviewed him in New York a year or so later, shortly after his smash hit in DeMille's *The Ten Commandments*. "She gives not one hundred percent but one hundred and twenty percent to whatever she is doing. She is a conscientious artist, determined to do her best at all times," he said. "She was also a lot of fun, very down-to-earth, and unaffected."

When I asked him what he thought of *Lucy Gallant* in retrospect, he immediately replied: "It was rather thin." Then, remembering that we were in the company of watchful Paramount publicist Charlie Earle (later to be one of the best-liked of independent press agents), he continued cautiously, "There *were* a lot of fine talents connected with it." Then, his intrinsic honesty overcoming his scruples about panning a picture that had come from Paramount along with the two he was plugging, *The Ten*

*Commandments* and the about to be released *Three Violent People,* he finished off with: "I just don't think *Lucy* made it—not really."

I also found Wyman lukewarm on the effort, for when I brought it up to her years later, the look and shrug she gave me when it was mentioned spoke volumes of negative response.

Many of the critics cross-country agreed with Crowther that fashion-maven Wyman and oil-man Heston as a romantic team represented the proverbial mixing of oil and water. Director Robert Parrish later told me, "I tried on that one, I really tried," but I always felt Parrish hadn't tried hard *enough. Lucy Gallant* was false in its situations and phony in its characterizations, as written, all the way through. Heston had in high gear that stoical, monumental, posturing style that would carry him right up to Mount Sinai as Moses a year later (he was still doing it as late as 1986 on TV's *Dynasty II: The Colbys*), and Wyman was giving her sincere best to material essentially unworthy of her talents, trying to be affirmative, feminine, and ambitious at one and the same time. I, for one, was relieved when over the years they didn't get together again professionally. In *Lucy Gallant* their diametrically clashing styles almost cancelled each other out.

One piece of Paramount ad brainstorming ran: "HE'S COLD—SHE'S HOT—SHE WARMS HIM UP!" But audiences' temperatures cross-country never got above lukewarm.

William H. Pine and William C. Thomas, the Paramount producers Crowther dubbed The Dollar Bills, had made money on their he-man sagas, which while not pretending to art at least had a rough-hewn production integrity about them, but in *Lucy Gallant* they deserted their true and natural métier to dawdle with women's high fashion in an oil boom town setting, and they even (possibly out of sheer desperation) included a flashy fashion parade, introduced by Texas' governor Allan Shivers, and narrated by costume designer Edith Head.

While neither the good-ole-boy governor nor the dour Miss Head set themselves up for any 1955 supporting Oscars in this, one Texas exhibitor, possibly with an eye to The Big Chief in Austin, gushed in his trade report: "An excellent sentimentalized drama that all women, and many men, will love for its romance, its very human sentiments, and for the fashion show that is extravagantly staged at the climax. While the story is sentimentalized, the sentiment is mostly very true to human nature and the picture is so capitally acted by the principals that everyone enjoying realistic and very human action will accept the story unquestioningly."

Or as Joe E. Brown would have put it: "That guy said a mouthful!"

In early 1955, succumbing happily to the public's insistence on another Wyman-Hudson film after their smash box office results with *Magnificent Obsession,* Universal-International cast the pair in a romantic masterpiece that is one of my all-time favorite Wyman movies. Castigated at the time of its late 1955 release as soapy and "women's-picture-ish," it has picked up a cult following over the past three decades and is now regarded as one of the highly creative, long underrated Douglas Sirk's better efforts. Sirk had directed the film in the spirit of two of his favorite writers, Henry David Thoreau and Ralph Waldo Emerson, who in the nineteenth century had counseled individualism. Wyman personally had long been fond of Thoreau's *Walden,* which contained an aphorism that appealed to her in the conduct of her own life, about obeying that different drummer. This certainly expresses the spirit of the fine and sensitive *All That Heaven Allows.*

Living in a small New England town, Wyman plays a widow who is lonely and disoriented in her inner life. Middle-aged, with children in college, she inhabits a handsome house on the best street in town but eschews shallow socializing to dream reclusively, unsure what she is waiting for. Hudson, a young gardener, prunes her trees periodically. She is drawn to him. He is an idealist, a noncomformist who wants only to grow trees in his isolated nursery and live his life according to his own precepts. He has no interest in sleeping around, cocktail parties, gossip, snobbery, or the coarser varieties of roistering with the mediocrities of the town. He is obviously all-man, however. At first Wyman fends off his shy, tentative advances, feeling that she is too old for him (she is supposed to be about forty [she was forty-one when she shot the movie], and he about twenty-eight).

Gradually they come together. On a visit to his free-wheeling friends, Charles Drake and Virginia Grey, Wyman finds herself in a refreshing rustic atmosphere among people who have adopted as a code of life the separation of the essential from the inessential, a firm adherence to Rousseau's concepts of individualism and personal integrity and a scorn for the commercial rat race. But as the romance of the middle-aged widow and the young gardener deepens, so does her dilemma, and when she encounters the shocked reactions of her children, and the ridicule of her conformist friends, she retreats, leaving the young man she loves and who loves her for the death-in-life loneliness she had known before. But the two grown children who had demanded that she keep up a front go on to lives of their own, her sense of isolation deepens and she wonders if it had been worth the sacrifice. When she consults the family doctor on her obviously psychosomatic headaches, he gives it to her straight, counseling that she stop running away, cease living by the opinions, smiles, and frowns of others—adding that she was ready for a love affair, but not for love.

Seeing the light, she goes to find Hudson, who has been languishing in the old mill he had handsomely refurbished for what he had hoped would be their married life together. He falls down an embankment into a deep snow while trying to attract her attention. Things look grim for a while when it appears he may not survive. But he pulls through, and as she kneels by his couch in the living room of the mill, she promises never to leave him again. A deer, outside the picture window, frolics in the snow.

Wyman gave one of her top performances in this film (my other four Wyman favorites being *Johnny Belinda*, *The Yearling*, *The Blue Veil*, and *The Glass Menagerie*). Her portrayal of the despondent and lonely widow was deeply felt, thoroughly convincing; she made the character a genuine human being, investing her with a reality that was as subjectively intense as anything she was ever to generate on the screen.

Obviously she had drawn on the painful, heart-rending memories of bitchy Hollywood's snide and unkind reactions to her earlier efforts to find real-life happiness with the much younger Travis Kleefeld and other attractive men who were, as the Biddies and Boobs of Beverly Hills never let her forget, "undignifiedly" too far behind her in years. In the 1950s older woman and younger man arrangements were frowned on in a way liberal 1980s attitudes would find fantastic—and outrageous. Wyman was

*All That Heaven Allows* (1955), with Rock Hudson.

*All That Heaven Allows* (1955), with Rock Hudson.

ahead of her time in this, and in actual life she had paid the price. In the superior screenplay of *All That Heaven Allows,* she had found a creatively fulfilling means with which to have the last word—and she did. The screenplay by Peg Fenwick, an overlooked talent, was literate, poignant, and penetrating. The sets and artwork were tasteful, the Technicolor hues handsome and subdued. Care was taken in all departments. The musical direction was clever and sensitively aware, adapting as it did, some of the more romantic melodic inspirations of Franz Liszt and other classical composers to point up the movie's ambience. Replete with emotional power and a romantic exaltation unusual in its intensity, even for that era, *All That Heaven Allows* has been seen frequently in television reruns, where it has the strange faculty of looking fresh and novel thirty years after it was made.

There was much in the screenplay and ambience that suited Rock Hudson's mystique. When I interviewed Rock ten years later, he spoke in eager, glowing terms of this particular film. "I felt comfortable, happy, and relaxed while making it," he told me, "and working with Jane was always an inspiration. Just playing to her brought out more of my capacities than I suspected were there. The picture was handsomely put together, with a host of fine actors in support, and it is one of my favorite films."

I had interviewed Rock on a number of occasions, and knew him quite well for years. In private life he was far more serious and introvertedly thoughtful than his public persona usually allowed. He was simpatico with *Heaven* because the character he played was much closer than usual to the inner spiritual realities of his own life.

Rock's homosexuality was known, of course, to all

*All That Heaven Allows* (1955), with Virginia Grey.

Hollywood insiders. His studio, Universal-International, went out of its way, via its enterprising and inventive publicity department, to cover up this part of his life. The mores of 1955 forced him to hide behind a macho front. His brief marriage to his agent's secretary, Phyllis Gates, had been arranged that same year in order to eliminate any public suspicions. But the real man was very like the gardener of *Heaven*. Like him, he was a nonconformist of a particularly extreme persuasion, but in this case it was a form of nonconformity that would be ruinous to his career if exposed. Like the gardener, Rock was romantic; he wanted life to be like the movies, and of course it wasn't. He was forever forming liaisons with handsome young men who hurt, betrayed, and bitterly disillusioned him, yet he was always ready for another go-round. There are several scenes in *All That Heaven Allows* in which the transparently hurt expression in his eyes when he runs up against sexual hypocrisy, displays, quite flaringly, his own tortured inner feelings. Wyman

knew about his real-life mystique as did everyone else, and she went out of her way to help and protect him. He brought out, in his vulnerability and fundamental gentleness, a maternalism in her. Liberal about other peoples' lives, with a fine tolerance and live and let live philosophy, she felt a genuine concern for Rock, a fear that through some unfortunate accident, he would fall through the thin-ice public persona forced upon him. One story I heard in Hollywood years ago had a rather stuffy friend of Wyman's pontificating about Rock's "unfortunate sexual bent." "I wish he would *triumph* over it, somehow," the friend said. "*I* wish he would find *happiness*," Wyman is reported to have replied.

After Rock's death in October 1985, amidst a welter of garish publicity about his AIDs affliction and the revelations of his homosexual life-style, Wyman, who had had her own jousts with falso conformity, publicly spoke warm words of praise for Rock's fundamental integrity—as actor and as man.

After *All That Heaven Allows*, Rock Hudson and

Wyman never acted together again. He went on to make memorable romantic comedy films. Wyman was to do one more feature film before she embarked on her television career.

Wyman went to New York for location shooting on *Miracle In The Rain*, written by Ben Hecht and based on his original story. It dealt with a poor little office girl in the New York of 1942; she is plain and drab, with a whining, querulous old mother at home, a zilch job, and zero social life. She meets a young soldier on leave, Van Johnson; they fall in love; he goes overseas and gets killed. Though not particularly religious, Wyman begins going to St. Patrick's Cathedral to pray for him. One day, despite the rain and the pneumonia she has contracted, she goes to the Cathedral, as usual, and the alleged "miracle" takes place.

In the original version Wyman was to die in the cathedral; in a later revision (this was the version released) she survived. As written by Ben Hecht, a tough ex-newspaperman who could oddly wax sentimental in some of his work, the "miracle" con-

sisted of the dead hero Johnson appearing as a ghost in the cathedral, where he proceeds to give her a good-luck coin she had given him before his departure to war—and the beyond.

Such brazenly saccharine material was already out-of-date in 1956—it would have had trouble squeaking by in *1946* for that matter—and only Wyman's touchingly sincere playing gave it any semblance of human validity. Johnson, too, was affecting as a wholesome innocent sent off to the slaughterfields of France, and director Rudolph Maté tried to give it a lot of New York human interest and local color. Although it was a "Nice little picture" that sent the less sophisticated denizens of New York rattling home in the subway feeling pleasantly teary, it was no world-beater in critical terms.

While Wyman was on location in New York, enterprising twenty-year-old reporter Doug McClelland of the *Newark Sunday News* licked the ban on all interviews set by the Warner publicity department by becoming friends with Wyman's wardrobe woman. McClelland found Wyman at Saint Patrick's

*All That Heaven Allows* (1955), with Rock Hudson.

Cathedral, worn out from the endless location shooting around New York that spring of 1955, and the
sudden rain-storms that plagued the shooting had
not helped her disposition. They were shooting the
original ending (later discarded) and Wyman had to
stagger into the cathedral again and again to die in
the arms of the young priest (Paul Picerni). Re-
peatedly they reshot the scene under director Maté's
fussy tutelage, sometimes with real, sometimes with
fabricated rain. Then a dry spell came, and stayed,
and while the rain-making machines were being set
up for the umpteenth time, Wyman told McClelland
with a wrily tired look, "This is the way we do things
in Hollywood."

Caparisoned in blankets, two sets of underwear,

and two raincoats (it was May, but still she had the
shivers), she gratefully accepted a cup of tea. "At
least I know I'm dead now, once and for all," she
laughed, since that appeared to be the last shot. Her
expression indicated that at least she hoped she was!
Oddly enough, after all the fuss over the scene, the
final release print would have her lying on the cold
pavement inside the cathedral, clutching Johnson's
coin, with the question of whether she lived or died
left up to audience imaginations.

On this occasion Wyman detailed some of the
production hitches. The company couldn't get en-
trance to St. Patrick's before ten in the evening, and
they had to be out by five in the morning. And with
the delays in setting up cameras and lights, they

Discussing a scene in
front of St. Patrick's Ca-
thedral with director
Rudolph Maté and Paul
Picerni for *Miracle in the
Rain* (1956).

*Miracle in the Rain* (1956), with Van Johnson in St. Patrick's Cathedral.

didn't get started until one A.M. The prop department had to make grass and trees grow at a spot in Central Park when none had been planted. With the help of local nursery men they had to resod five thousand square feet of park for just one scene. According to Warners publicity, the shooting inside St. Patrick's was the first ever permitted a studio by the Roman Catholic Church. More than half of the picture remained to be shot on the West Coast, with Wyman anxious to get back to fourteen-year-old Maureen and ten-year-old Michael, who would be out of school for the summer. She planned to get the kids ready for holiday time, with Mike being sent away to camp and Maureen slated to "stay home and help with house chores."

Wyman watchers felt that her recent conversion to Roman Catholicism had influenced her choice of this role. But by that year Catholic miracles, either of the supernatural or theatrically romantic kind, were so distinctly out of style that the picture did not do well, and Wyman later blamed Warners, claiming that they had stinted on promotion and advertising so as to be able to afford the mammoth hype they proceeded to accord the Elizabeth Taylor-Rock Hudson *Giant*, released about the same time.

The incorrigible Warners flacks, as usual, were on the lookout for come-on ads that emphasized sexual innuendo at the cost of delineating a film's actual leitmotiv. This got the Hollywood wags gleefully playing around with ad-copy ideas, one of which—the most popular among the gagsters—ran: "You'll be *stupefied* by the *unusual* thing that *Van Johnson* did to *Jane Wyman* in the *darkness* of St. Patrick's cathedral!" "Do you like it?" one Warners adman reportedly asked another with the reply going: "It's swell! But it needs two or three more exclamation

Relaxing on location in New York's Central Park during shooting of *Miracle in the Rain* (1956).

points at the end. [So read that!!!]" In actuality, of course, Johnson had appeared as a wraith from the beyond who handed Wyman the aforementioned coin.

*The New York Herald Tribune* was rough on Wyman in this: "Miss Wyman's secretary is a glum portrait unrelieved by any sense of depth of character or humor. She is sad even when she realizes she is in love. There is hardly a change of expression when she learns of the death of Johnson. . . . [The picture] is straight-faced and uncompromisingly dull."

It was unfortunate that Wyman's final theatrical release for some years had thudded. She went out of films into television with a whimper rather than a bang. But there would be bright moments coming up in the new medium, and she looked forward to the change.

# 8

## Tackling Television
### 1955–1980

On August 30, 1955, Wyman turned full-force to a medium that was to occupy her, with time out for occasional films, for the next thirty-one years. She seems to have felt, after completing *Miracle In The Rain*, that television was the next logical step for her because it offered a more permanent security than films, which sent her critical and popular fortunes fluctuating from picture to picture. Also she felt that the kind of picture she wanted to do was passing out of vogue. She may have realized this only as a matter of hindsight, but it has been written that she sensed it in mid-1955.

She was not, of course, unfamiliar with the worlds of television and radio, having tried her hand fleetingly in both over the years. In 1952 she worked on the WMAZ radio program *Hollywood Star Play-house*. Before that, in 1947, she appeared with her then husband Ronald Reagan on *Lux Radio Theatre*, and in 1948 showed up with George Murphy and Eddie Bracken on the *Let's Talk Hollywood* show (NBC). At that time she indicated that radio and/or TV were far from being her favorite media. For some years after that a number of prominent Hollywood stars, faced with the post-1948 increased competition in television, avoided the medium either because movie contracts stipulated no two media appearances or because they were obeying an unwritten law not to compete with their screen selves.

In 1955 all that was in the past, and Jane Wyman took over as president of the company that produced TV's *Fireside Theatre*, an anthology series that had already been a going concern for seven years. As chief policy implementer, she announced that the series would offer a variety of comedy and drama. Shortly after she took over as chief executive, the name was changed to *Jane Wyman Presents the Fireside Theatre*. As chief executive in charge of planning and creative projects, she had the final say on everything, and enjoyed her new status as top woman. The season was announced as thirty-four half-hour episodes. Wyman was set to star in fourteen of these. A CBS-TV presentation, sponsored by Procter and Gamble, the premiere offered her in a piece called *Technical Charge of Homicide*, advertised as "The tense and tender story of a woman torn between conflicting sympathies." The critics were for the most part admiring and respectful of her debut in the new medium, calling her performance "wise and controlled," "a fine exhibition of her proven acting skills," and also citing her "well-projected sympathy" and "honest feeling."

Asked by reporters at the time why she had taken such a risky plunge, especially since she had just refused a co-starring spot with Gary Cooper in a prestigious production *Friendly Persuasion* (the role in this theatrical film went instead to Dorothy McGuire), she explained that while she would have loved to have had the opportunity to work with William Wyler, who was to direct the film, she felt that a move into television full-time was right for her then. She added: "There is more latitude, I feel, in the choice of stories for TV. For example, a charming vignette that isn't suitable for a feature-length movie might be ideal for our *Fireside Theatre*. Or a short

With Bill Goodwin on a General Electric TV show, 1955.

story with tremendous impact can be worked into a half-hour film, whereas, lengthened to eighty or ninety minutes, it loses in the transition."

If mistakes were made she, as overall head of production, insisted on assuming the responsibility for them, and she praised her production crew, adding, "I'm having the time of my life, even while working harder than ever before." That fall Wyman was being hailed around the country as the first major screen star to attempt to combine a regular TV series with a movie career. Actually, the films had gone into limbo indefinitely.

In late 1955 it was estimated that Wyman stood to gross some four-and-a-half million dollars from the series over the next three years, but much of the money went into the show. She didn't penny-pinch. "She's a sort of pretty Sam Goldwyn [a film producer

noted for his emphasis on quality]," a friend said. "She always asks 'What's the best way to do it?' Never the cheapest."

By fall 1956 it was decided to change the name of the series to *The Jane Wyman Theatre*. "They say the first year of marriage is the toughest," she said then. "Well, so are the first twelve months of TV, and I'm very glad to have them behind me." The series continued for four years, ending in 1959. Wyman starred in nine episodes in the 1958–59 seasons. She cast many friends from the movie business, including Joseph Cotten, Linda Darnell, and Paul Henreid.

Eventually the show was cancelled because of fallen ratings. Also it had proven difficult to find good stories. Wyman, to her credit, had kept the quality quite high, and many of the stories were well chosen. The acting was also exemplary, as was the

174

direction, and Wyman can take pride for having given her show, on many occasions, a "quality movie" look.

For those four years she had spent most of her time reading outlines, scripts, and short stories. Once, after going through a typical pile of *Fireside* story possibilities, including pieces from national magazines and original scripts submitted by top writers on both coasts, she found one script she particularly liked, and learned that it was written by none other than her secretary, Stephanie Nordli. "Imagine!" she chortled. "Steph was an established movie writer before she was employed by me! Isn't it a small world in more ways than one?"

Wyman, interviewed in the mid-fifties, spoke of her crew. "When we first started working together, we were all uncertain—strange to one another. Now we've done so many shows, we almost automatically anticipate one another's requirements. I don't think it's any exaggeration to say we're like one big, happy family." Wyman delightedly reported that even during the summer vacation, when crewmen can't wait to get away and forget all about the boss, she received a number of postcards from various places where they were relaxing with their families, some of them looking forward to the next season with the "Boss-Lady."

Gene Barry, who worked with her in 1957 on a show, commented, "I don't know where that lady got her energy! She could attend to a hundred different things connected with a program—and they were always pitching her something—and still manage to get in front of the cameras fresh as a daisy and letter-perfect, and looking like a million!"

After the show ran its course, Wyman, back in movies again for a while, still found the time to appear in such quality CBS-TV specials as *America Pauses for Springtime* in which, as one of a star-studded cast, she recited with great poignancy and poetic authority some of the loveliest verses of Emily Dickinson. One critic described the program, telecast on April 1, 1959, "All of Monday night's performances were transformed into choice adjectives describing this wondrous season, which Emily Dickinson called 'an outward sign of inward grace.' This excellent hour production not only hailed the time of year when nature is reborn, but it also brought back to life the magic that was once such an integral part of the TV medium." Kay Gardella in *The New York Daily News* wrote of Wyman's performance, "The very best part of the telecast came at the finale

when Jane Wyman read the beautiful poetry of Emily Dickinson while nature's miracles unfolded before our eyes. 'It almost speaks to me,' intoned the actress, reading the immortal lines of the writer."

Offscreen Wyman was centering her personal life on old friends like Loretta Young and Barbara Stanwyck, as well as members of the Catholic clergy. She had become friendly with a number of them since her conversion in the mid-1950s. While she admired and respected the priests and nuns and Catholic charities workers she came to meet in increasing numbers in the mid and late 1950s, she never stood on ceremony with them, treating them as equals.

One of these friends, Father Robert Perella, has recalled that Wyman began to get more prudish and rigid after her conversion, sometimes vehemently so. There had been the case of a handsome young actor who had appeared with her on her television show in 1958. Wyman was then forty-four. The actor had been "coming on strong" with her for some time off the set. She had tolerated his shenanigans with what grace she could summon, not wishing to hurt him with a direct rebuff, but when the actor, who in their scene together was supposed to kiss her lightly and

With Jeff Morrow on a *Jane Wyman's Fireside Theatre* TV show, 1957.

tenderly, gave her a big, wet "soul-kiss" replete with much tongue-and-teeth action (and in complete disregard of the director's instructions) she fired him immediately.

Sometimes she would regale her friends with harmlessly humorous tales of the Reagan marriage, and how "exasperating" it had been at the time to get up early with a hard day at the studio facing her "and have someone at the breakfast table, newspaper in hand, expounding on the far right, the far left, the conservative right, the conservative left, the middle-of-the-roader," ad infinitum.

Once, in about 1960, Wyman and some friends were passing an imposing mansion set back from the street, and she told everyone to tip their hats. "We just passed Mother Superior's house," she laughed. Mother Superior was Loretta Young, a friend she dearly loved, who had in recent years become more Catholic than the Pope. This occasioned considerable amusement among her friends because Loretta's racy younger period in the 1930s had featured assorted varieties of Hollywood hell-raising, includ-

ing "romances" with such as married Spencer Tracy, with whom she had starred in a 1933 film called *A Man's Castle*, and married Clark Gable, with whom she had had a torrid involvement while making a 1935 film aptly titled *Call Of The Wild*.

After this three-year hiatus, Wyman returned to the movies. She played a mother, in *Holiday for Lovers*, following Myrna Loy and other by then fortyish stars who played the loyal, loving and long-suffering wife to prissy, irascible Clifton Webb. In *Holiday for Lovers* he does more of his fussy, carping *paterfamilias* stuff, as a New England psychologist who takes a trip to South America with wife Wyman in order to superintend the love lives of his budding daughters, Jill St. John and Carol Lynley. Travelogue style shots of such South American cities as Rio de Janeiro, São Paulo, and Lima take up roughly half the footage, but these were mere background and process shots. The picture, par for the course of 1959 customs, was shot in Hollywood.

The thin plot has Webb fussing, more *maternally* than *paternally*, over his daughters' love choices. St.

*Holiday for Lovers* (1959), with Clifton Webb.

*Holiday for Lovers* (1959), with Clifton Webb.

On the set of *Pollyanna* (1960).

John's beau is a young artist, son of handsome, smooth Paul Henreid, whom her father at first suspects of cradle-robbing. Lynley falls in love with an air force sergeant, Gary Crosby.

Much of the proceedings are dishwater dull, winding up with Webb getting drunk and finding himself on an airliner—whereupon he decides that maybe the girls know more about handling their lives than he does. Result: the two sets of lovers get to pair off.

Wyman's principal function in all this is to console, advise, succor, and steady this confused family, and this she does in a quiet, controlled, underplayed style that recalls her best previous work without duplicating its solidity and characterizational depth—solely because the script gives her no opportunities. Sydney Johnson in *The Montreal Star* wrote: "Jane Wyman has a stooge role that is almost as incomprehensible as Mr. Webb's but she plays it

beautifully like the lady she is and makes one wish she was given something more intelligent to do."

Many reviewers dismissed Wyman as "pleasant" in her role; some referred to "her imperturbable smile," but Mae Tinee in *The Chicago Tribune* did somewhat better than that, writing: "Jane Wyman's part as mama relegates her pretty much to the role of an innocent and patient bystander during all the goings-on, but she's perky and pretty as ever," adding "the girls are attractive but seem overly and suddenly susceptible to the charms of their respective beaus, and the whole business doesn't add up to much more than just another movie."

Even in 1959 there were some sly digs at Webb's fussiness, as it was well-known (but then kept quiet) that he was a homosexual who developed "crushes" (as the euphemistic 1959 term had it) on every third man he met. He was also a classic mama's boy who lived with, and went everywhere with, his mother, Maybelle, until she died in her nineties. He made such an issue about mourning Maybelle that Noel Coward, in tart, common-sense terms, saw fit to remind him that deploring one's orphan state while one was in one's sixties was—well, overdoing it.

Wyman, who had found another tortured homosexual, Charles Laughton, a treasure house of creatively helpful advice eight years before in *The Blue Veil*, had the same relaxed, tolerant view of Webb, whom she found testy and temperamental but a brilliant actor. She liked to recall, humorously, that she, as a former hoofer, probably appreciated more than most his terpsichorean turn at a complicated South American dance in one sequence. Webb, of course, had won his first Broadway fame in youth as a dancer, appearing opposite such as the incandescent Libby Holman, one of the stage's most eminent and/or notorious femmes fatales.

Paul Henreid recalls that he watched Webb and Wyman, doing the samba, and felt they should do another movie as a middle-aged Astaire-Rogers team, so lithe and limber were their steps. When told this Wyman reportedly commented, "Now that's the best casting idea I've heard in some time!" But it never happened.

Asked years later why she had returned to the screen in such a secondary, thankless role after four television years, Wyman replied that it was the best thing offered her at the time and served to limber her up for another serious go at theatrical films. At forty-five she looked handsome, and ten years younger, with her face clear and unlined, and her figure as trim as ever.

There was some reason to believe in 1959 that Twentieth Century-Fox, in view of Wyman's young appearance and polished acting skills, was contemplating an offer of a term contract. But despite gossip in the press, it never happened.

By 1960, age forty-six, Wyman was choosing her roles with great care—she was after a "wholesome" image, as befitted a good practicing Catholic and the single-but-devoted mother of teenagers Maureen and Michael. Walt Disney Productions came forward with an offer for her to star in *Pollyanna*, a film version of the 1913 "novel for nice young ladies"

*Pollyanna* (1960), with Hayley Mills.

that had helped make a genteel nice-nice reputation for a rather prim New England lady named Eleanor H. Porter.

At the time the film was released, in the spring of 1960, *Time* in its review was calling the original book "an irresistible tearjerker that drenched the pillows of grandma's generation and added to the language a new word for the sort of softheaded optimist who can see no evil, especially in the mirror, and who hysterically insists on confusing goo with good. The story distilled Victorian sentiment to its treacly essence, and readers of all ages lapped it up."

With what one commentator was to call "his infallible instinct for what will fill the public's sweet tooth," Walt Disney poured some 3,200,000 dollars into *Pollyanna*. According to *Time*, he "photographed the little horror in throbbing colors, bloated it with big names . . . and generally calculated its gasps and sniffles, homilies and heehaws with such shrewdness that *Pollyanna* emerges on the wide screen as the best live-actor movie Disney has ever made: A Niagara of drivel and a masterpiece of smarm."

The picture, which follows the original book with ninety-eight percent accuracy, has to do with Pollyanna, an eleven-year-old orphan daughter of a goody-goody clergyman "who had gone to heaven to be with mother." She comes from the West Indies to live with her Aunt Polly (Wyman), who inhabits a mansion smack in the middle of an Eastern town and from which all power flows. Wyman doesn't really want Pollyanna, but takes her in as part of her duty.

Pollyanna (Hayley Mills's second film), despite her rags and poor-relation aura, shows herself a relentlessly cheerful, positive-spirited do-gooder. Despite being put in an attic room and icily patronized by all comers, Mills proceeds to initiate anyone who will listen into her "glad game" which consists of finding "the silver lining in every cloud, the gold tooth in every shark."

While a number of critics of *Pollyanna* called it "bathetic" and "hypersentimental to a sickly degree," I found myself disagreeing. There is a foolish tendency with films of this sort, ever more prevalent since the cynically decadent 1960s, to downgrade anything that is warm, emotional, and affirmative. Some of the 1960 critics, and many since, were so afraid of honest emotion that they felt they had to put down *Pollyanna* for fear of being regarded as soggy sentimentalists, but the film, in my view,

understood, and stayed artfully within that fine line between sentimentality and honest feeling, and did so with consummate professionalism from all hands. Wyman as Aunt Polly was at the top of her acting form.

In a letter actress Anne Seymour offered some interesting reminiscences of Wyman as of the *Pollyanna* period: "What a wonderfully warm woman she is," Seymour wrote, "such a pro with such humor, concentration, and strength. The first time I ever worked with Janie, or knew her, was in *Pollyanna*. As she was a superstar, I was a little in awe of her. The first time I watched her work was when Janie [as Aunt Polly] found Hayley Mills [as Pollyanna] injured on the ground after her fall from a tree.

"I was impressed with the way she did it. And then amazed, after I told her so, that she was humble and grateful. I think that's when we became friends. When we were on location in Santa Rosa, California, we went out in groups for dinner. One evening I said I'd like trout, but I didn't know how to bone it. Janie immediately announced, 'Annie is having trout and I am boning it for her!' Which she did expertly and then asked me if I were able to *eat it* alone!

"I think that was the night we were driving back to the motel and Janie started singing. She had a lovely, true voice. We kept begging for more; she thought we were putting her on.

"When we worked at the studio, we ate in Mr. Disney's private dining room reserved for stars and VIPs. By then we were one big happy, mad family. Poor darling Aggie Moorehead and Ed Platt, Reta Shaw, Leora Dana, Adolphe Menjou, Karl Malden, and beloved Donald Crisp. My, what a cast! And Hayley, naturally, with John and Mary Mills, her parents. Because we were happy actors, we were noisy actors. We constantly tasted each other's food. Finally, Mr. Disney sent word that he loved having us there, but would we please be a little more quiet. We distracted his clients. Naturally, Janie was the ringleader.

"After the picture I went back to New York, where I lived then, and, almost immediately, had to come back to California to do something else. So I called Janie and asked if I could have her small apartment in Beverly Hills that she used only when she was working—she really lived in Newport. She said 'of course,' bless her. She was in and out a lot. I distinctly remember her saying once, 'Never throw an empty can away without rinsing it!' I put detergent in the percolator one morning and she bawled me out—'The coffee will taste like soap!' She was very neat, which was a lively challenge, thoughtful, wanted to know how my day had been. She was angrier than I when I didn't get a part in a picture I wanted.

"She was a very good Catholic, too. I was impressed by her sincerity and deep belief."

Seymour and Wyman worked together nine years after *Pollyanna* in *How To Commit Marriage*. Seymour remembered Wyman had just bought a Rolls Royce. "Someone had asked her how she was doing, and she said, 'A Rolls doesn't run on water!' She always had a quick, funny answer to everything.

"She was as demanding of others as she was of herself. She hated anyone who held up shooting. That's one of the reasons she's a star. She is a perfectionist about her work, and she expects others to come up to her level. She'd help in every way

possible—but if they were impossible, they just weren't *there*, for her."

Among the other performers in *Pollyanna* who reminisced about Jane to me were the veteran Oscar-winning actor Donald Crisp and Hayley Mills, both of whom I talked to in the mid-1960s.

Hayley spoke of Jane with deep respect. "I was new at film acting then, and she was wonderful to me, so patient and kind. I feel that my good reception in that film was in great part due to her. She was wonderful to play off and to, and I found my own standards rising to meet hers. She was a no-nonsense lady. Oh, she could be lots of fun when time came to relax, but on the set, with the urgent business at hand of making a scene pay off, she led one a merry chase. I am grateful to have known her."

Donald Crisp, who has acted with the best, from Lillian Gish to Bette Davis, thought Jane a profes-

*Pollyanna* (1960), with Richard Egan.

"When Hell Froze"
(1966), on *Bob Hope
Chrysler Theatre* (TV).

sional of the first order. "You don't see such expertise, usually, in people without stage background,
and she had none, but what she got on the screen
was remarkable. I knew her slightly at Warners for
years and think it a shame they didn't build her into
a major star long before they did."

On a tour to plug *Pollyanna* in May 1960, Wyman
told *Washington Post* critic Richard Coe over lunch
at the Mayflower Hotel: "You can imagine the fun we
had making [the film]. Somehow we'd all acted
together before [a Wyman inaccuracy; she had *not*
acted with *all* of them before]; all knew each other
well and we used to try to guess what each one
would do with a particular scene. We'd try to have
surprises in how we'd do things because the roles are
all so clearly defined. The result was a very lively,
alert set.

"Hayley . . . was a joy to us all. What a person to
act to. She acts right back. She'd been beautifully
brought up, too. Polite. Almost curtsies when she
meets you, if you know what I mean. What a grand
theater family those Millses are!"

Wyman went on to tell Coe that "making a real
movie again was fun, too. I've just spent four whole
years producing and acting in my own TV show.
That was hard work, hardest I've ever done and I
don't think I'd try it again. I'd like to be able to enjoy
the beach home we have on Lido Island."

In New York she spoke to entertainment reporter
Henderson Cleaves: "I don't know why they should
come out crying. It is really a very funny movie in
many places. Of course the ending is rather affecting.
When Pollyanna wins over her Aunt Polly, the
old bag I play." Someone remonstrated, and she

snapped, "Well, that's what she is," adding, "I think people need this movie. I think they're tired of sickness and violence. I know I am."

Whatever private hopes Wyman might have had for more worthy theatrical films, she was not to do another for two years. Instead she returned to television.

As Wyman moved into the 1960s, directly after appearing in *Pollyanna*, her television appearances tended to be spotty and infrequent. *Lux Playhouse* presented her in "A Deadly Guest" in 1959, for which she had received reviews of the usual calibre, and in 1960 *Checkmate* presented her in a drama called "Lady on the Brink"; her performance was called "creditable." In 1961 she did "Labor of Love" for the *GE Theatre*, "Death Leaves a Tip" for *Investigators* and "Twenty-five Santa Clauses" for *Rawhide*. In 1962, on *Wagon Train*, she did "The Wagon Train Mutiny," and in 1963, age forty-nine, she was in "The S.A. American Dream" for *Naked City*.

Critics of the time commented that as fifty approached her performances, which mostly amounted to guest spots, were on the whole taking on a mechanical and perfunctory quality, as if she didn't believe in the material or was tired of the endless production grind. While she continued to photograph startlingly well for a woman at the half-century mark, it was obvious that she belonged henceforth in middle-aged or character parts—not that she seemed to care particularly. In 1963 she told an interviewer: "I don't care a hoot about so-called glamour—I just want a good, meaty part I can get my teeth into—and they're getting harder to find. The writers don't seem as disciplined now, and they are getting careless about writing to suit the performer's personality."

The reruns of *The Jane Wyman Theatre*, seen during the early 1960s, seemed to go down well enough with TV audiences and advertisers, but a dramatic series starring Wyman in the role of a backwoods doctor called, tentatively, *Dr. Kate*, and which had been projected for a regular weekly show after a pilot, came to nothing. Based on the life of Dr. Kate Newcomb, an intrepid female medico who worked in a lumber camp, the idea was based largely on Dr. Newcomb's book about herself, *Angel on Snowshoes*. The project had at first seemed promising to Wyman and her associates. Script troubles were said to have contributed to its undoing.

Of Wyman's *Wagon Train* segment, *Variety* wrote: "[It] shaped up as a wholly arresting hour . . . the yarn unfolded swiftly, tensely and with a remarkable absence of overt violence. . . . The structure of *Wagon Train* is firmly grounded in the character of the wagonmaster, played by John McIntire in the Lincolnesque tradition of the strong, sensitive and somewhat melancholy hero . . . he is assisted by a hardy band of troupers. . . . The only thesping soft spots . . . were created by the two guest stars, Jane Wyman and Dan Duryea. Miss Wyman played a revenge-seeking mother in melodramatic style while Duryea's portrayal of the mutineer was equally obvious." This was one of the first sure indications that, as of the 1960s, Wyman's interest in TV work was, for the time, waning, mostly because of her disappointment with the scripts offered her.

After a hiatus, Wyman was back on TV again in 1966, age fifty-two, this time in color, on *Bob Hope Presents the Chrysler Theatre*, on NBC. The segment was called "When Hell Froze." Some of Wyman's leading men were Marty Milner, Leslie Nielsen, and Jeff Corey. It was written by Alvin Sapinsley and based on a short story of the same name by Wilbur Daniel Steele, and dealt with a farmer's wife accused unjustly by her husband of infidelity.

One reviewer called this offering "Strictly for the ladies, especially those who relish soap opera histrionics. Jane Wyman stars in a role she's played in a few films, that of a vintage 1919 hard-working farmer's wife who becomes the victim of petty gossip about an innocent interlude with a young stranger while the farmer was in town on business." There were plaudits for Wyman's handsome appearance, and for young Marty Milner's sincere portrayal (he was later to do better with such TV series as *Route 66* and *Adam 12*), but the general impression among the critics was that it was thin stuff—unworthy of Wyman.

In 1962 Wyman appeared in her first picture since the 1960 *Pollyanna*. It was called *Bon Voyage!* and in this, directed by James Neilson, she appeared for Walt Disney's Buena Vista Productions, co-starring with that other master of comedic nuance Fred MacMurray. As might be surmised from the title, Wyman and MacMurray are a solid married couple who take the kids to Europe—with all the "American in the Old Country" capers, 1962-style.

The Walt Disney film's publicity department capitalized heavily on Wyman's dancing skills in this with such P.R.-sheet headlines as "Jane Wyman Dances Again!" According to the Disney release: "For one musical sequence in the romantic-comedy, the Academy Award winning actress matches steps with a nimble-footed French sailor who invites her to join him in a street dance in celebration of Bastille Day. The dance is the French version of rock 'n roll and Jane's early hoofing experience stood her in good stead."

According to the release, after filming on the scene was completed, Wyman turned to director Neilson and said, laughing, "Now that I've mastered that one, I think I'll try the Twist."

The film, as was the trend then, was shot on the actual locales—aboard the SS *United States*, the fastest luxury liner of the time; in Paris; and on the French Riviera—all covered in the best-selling novel by Marrijane and Joseph Hayes. Seventy-five taxis, limousines, and cars, were rented by Disney for the opening Pier 86 scenes in New York, with props including five hundred pieces of luggage and one hundred cameras. Three separate camera crews were kept busy on the ship. Authentic Paris locales were used, with the Billancourt Studios outside Paris employed for some of the interiors.

The story was a slight affair with familiar shipboard excitement and mishap, including playful (and silly) implications of extra-marital dalliance by papa MacMurray and mama Wyman while in Paris and on the Riviera. As one reviewer put it: "Paris looks beautiful in the Spring—and papa gets lost in a sewer tour and never makes it to the famous Louvre. Mama has an unwilling romantic adventure with a Hungarian ladykiller and papa socks the goulash gigolo in the jaw. Daughter (Deborah Walley) gets involved in a tearful affair with a spoiled playboy and straightens him out. Son (Tommy Kirk) flirts with girls and papa is accosted in a cafe by a *demimondaine*."

Another reviewer summed up the proceedings: "It's all antiseptic and amusing, but far too long, obvious, cornball and comic-strippy. Papa Fred MacMurray works hard and is the backbone of the comicalities." The review added, "The color photography is lovely. For prospective tourists (and stay-at-homes) a Technicolor tour of Paris is included, with a stopover at Cannes."

*Bon Voyage* (1962), with Tommy Kirk, Deborah Walley, Fred MacMurray, and Kevin Corcoran.

*Bon Voyage* (1962), with Fred MacMurray.

Wyman in subsequent years indicated to me and to other interviewers that she had taken the film because she admired MacMurray's talents, respected the Disney studio for trying to keep its entertainment clean and sensible—and also because it was the best thing offered to her in 1962. In this period she was determined to avoid heavy, morbid, or grotesque roles. "I wanted to keep things light and entertaining; I wanted to bring people a little happy escapism," she added. "God knows I'd done my share of heavy dramatics; now I wanted to relax and have fun."

Archer Winsten in *The New York Post* wrote of *Bon Voyage:* "Everything is standard, competent, super-clean and efficient. Performances are all ingratiating." In fact *ingratiating* propped up several times concerning Wyman in reviews.

In November 1965, Wyman told writer Vernon Scott: "I won't lower myself to act in the type of films that are selling these days. I simply refuse to play a

prostitute, a dope addict or a murderess. I wouldn't believe myself in those roles," the then fifty-one-year-old actress said, "so I'd be doing the producers an injustice. Furthermore, I don't like all the sick pictures being made. There is so much of it going on. Why should we put the seamy side of life up there on the screen when we're supposed to be entertainers?"

After three years of retirement, Wyman, who according to an affectionately bemused Vernon Scott "still looked the part of a wide-eyed ingenue" was starring in a segment of the Bob Hope-Chrysler Theatre, playing, in Scott's facile description, "a farm girl circa 1919 in a gingham and apron."

Of this she said, "I accepted the role because I liked the sort of woman I'm playing. I have no desire to play a part I can't be proud of. Sometimes nonexposure is better than appearing."

With a cynically adaptable sanctimoniousness, Scott proceeded to declare in the same article: "Such other Oscar winners as Bette Davis, Joan Crawford,

*How to Commit Marriage* (1969), with Tina Louise, Jackie Gleason, Tim Matheson, Joanna Cameron, and Bob Hope.

and Olivia De Havilland have extended their careers in horror movies loaded with insanity, homicide, and worse. Miss Wyman says this route is definitely not for her." Scott then added smugly: "Fortunately Jane is economically independent and can afford to sit on the sidelines rather than accept distasteful pictures."

Wyman admitted to Scott that she had been somewhat anxious when she first reported to Universal for the TV appearance: "You ask yourself if you've become rusty after three years away from the cameras. And that five A.M. call comes awfully early. But once I was down on the set and the first scene was shot, everything went beautifully."

She went on to tell Scott that she felt a limited enthusiasm for work and was "not rarin!" to jump into a frenzy of activity again.

"I'll take my time about picking my next role," she said in this 1966 interview. "If a movie or a television show comes along that appeals to me I'll buckle down to work. If not, I'm in no hurry to play a wrong part."

Her good friend Aggie Moorehead said of the Wyman of the mid-sixties, "In some ways I think it was the most contented period of her life. The intense careerism had mellowed and lessened; she had her good friendships, her rewarding sessions with paintbrush and canvas, her pleasure in her developing teenage children. I think she had given up her illusions about men, and the kind of life she hoped to live with one. She had come to realize, in a sense, that she was her own best company—and understood herself better than any other human being ever would.

"She was into various worthy causes; she had enough money and her own style of 'the good life'—and moreover she had her deep inner resources of intellect *and* esthetics. Some women just aren't the marrying kind, and it isn't because they don't like men; it is because they have a kind of *positive* self-

wife Wyman, at a social event, to his big-bosomed girlfriend, Maureen Arthur, remarking, "I think you know Lois." Wyman checks the lady's cleavage, raises her eyebrows, and rejoinders: "If I didn't, I certainly do now."

Wyman made no bones about the picture's being no world-beater, but said it was the only halfway acceptable thing that was being offered her in 1968. She told an interviewer: "The studios are afraid to hire the old stars because they're afraid we might bomb. Then they bring in people who bomb anyway because they have no experience. On this thing they figure the combination of three old pros like us plus the kids and the music of today gives them something to sell."

She then said, "I haven't worked in so many years [she was then fifty-four] that I just wanted to get back in front of the cameras and see if I could do it. It's not a return. What do you call it? A re-entrance?"

She told me and other reporters that year that she had found the film a lot of fun. "How could it help but be, working with two fun-guys like Bob and Jackie?" Later, when the film was released and she found herself in third billing (Gleason had what was essentially a supporting role but was billed above Wyman anyway), she was a good sport about it, claiming that the important thing was that the film make money, and Hope's and Gleason's name—circa 1969, carried more marquee clout than hers.

Norman Panama, an old Hope standby, directed *How To Commit Marriage*. The production was slick, replete with Technicolor photography; the screenwriters tried hard, but the net result was dismal. *The New York Times*, however, was kind to the three stars, with the reviewer remarking: "I don't know what kind of magic camera filters were used, but Miss Wyman, whose first movie this is in seven years; Gleason, who loves the good life, and particularly Hope, who is on the far side of sixty-five all look remarkably fit for people who could be in physical ruins." *The Fort Lauderdale* (Fla.) critic remarked: "Miss Wyman looks trim and still glamorous," while Herb Kelly of *The Miami News* said: "[Miss Wyman] has lost none of her charm." "It's nice to have Jane Wyman back on the screen and looking lovely," Wanda Hale of *The New York Daily News* wrote, and *Variety* said Wyman looked "wonderful."

During interviews she gave in 1968 and 1969, the talk of a Broadway show kept surfacing again and again. "It would have to be the right thing—on that, I

would have to be most careful," she told me. An offer had come to do *Mame* on Broadway, but she complained that they insisted on only one week's rehearsal, and she felt that was literally impossible. She recalled singing a few songs during the audition ("Yes, they insisted on an audition!") but when her terms weren't met, she ankled it.

Also at this time she thought about writing. First on the list was to have been a book of anecdotes called *Whatever's Fair*. At the time she didn't specify either what the title meant or whether the anecdotes were to be personal or general. This project was apparently put on hold.

When asked, in 1969, if she ever contemplated an autobiography she said no, no, a thousand times no, or words to that effect, and added that she couldn't write, spelled cat *kat*—and couldn't be bothered with ghostwriters. She felt a ghost put more of him or herself into the book than the star whose story they were ostensibly telling.

In any event, she went out of movies pleasantly, if uneventfully, enough, with *How To Commit Marriage*, her last theatrical film to date.

In December 1969, Wyman appeared as a special guest star on CBS-TV's color program, *The Jim Nabors Hour*. Nabors was a longtime admirer of the star, and while original plans had called for their doing a light comedy sketch followed by a musical number, he had a brainstorm: why not take advantage of Wyman's proven dramatic skills?

They were going over songs for the show, when Nabors suddenly said, "Listen, Jane, I want to do a religious song to close the show. Why don't I sing *The Lord's Prayer*, and you do it in sign language the way you did in *Johnny Belinda*?" Wyman liked the idea but reminded Nabors that over twenty years had passed, and while she appreciated his kind thought in wanting to revive memories of her Oscar-winning performance, she doubted that there would be time for her to learn to do it letter-perfect.

Wyman in the 1948 film had done that very prayer in sign language as she knelt by the murdered body of her father, Charles Bickford. Could she learn it all over again in time for the show? For a short while she was at a loss as to what to do.

Luckily, a co-worker on the Nabors show, Karen Morrow, had a friend, Kevin Carlisle, who had worked with mute children on a volunteer basis. Carlisle said he'd be glad to work with Wyman on the prayer. It took four days, and to Wyman's glad relief, the sign language for the prayer came back to

With Fred MacMurray on set of his TV series, *My Three Sons*, 1970.

her quickly and easily. Taped before a live audience, the prayer went famously, and many eyes were wet with tears. Later Nabors was quoted as saying: "It was a highlight not only of that show, but of our entire season to date. Jane was just great and we all consider ourselves very lucky to have had her as a guest on our show." Wyman said that she was delighted Nabors had suggested it, and called the experience "richly rewarding."

In September 1970, Wyman served for a few days as co-hostess on *The Mike Douglas Show*. Wyman told Mike before the audience that she had wanted to join him because, "I love the way your audience is so close. I'm a people watcher. I adore people." She discussed her film career and advocated that more big stars show up on television. She said, "I think it's about time. I mean, how many old movies can you look at?"

On another day with Mike Douglas, Wyman said: "I don't go to see many motion pictures today because the subject matter doesn't interest me," adding that one picture she did admire was *Patton* with George C. Scott, whom she hailed as an excellent performer. (Scott later won the Oscar for that picture, but refused it, running true to his usual eccentric form.)

Going on to other matters, Wyman told Douglas' audience: "There are many potential stars among the young performers today [1970]. However, television has kind of upset the usual routine of training. It's a negative training ground because television moves so much faster than film."

As of that time she expressed an undiminished enthusiasm for appearing in films, adding, "I've never gotten bored with motion pictures. It's an exciting business, and there's always something new and different going on."

On her third day out with Douglas, she told some amusing stories about her inveterate supermarket shopping, saying she liked to do things for herself and that she'd actually rather go shopping than go to the movies. She reminisced about co-stars and said of Rock Hudson: "There was a boy who really wanted to learn. I said to him, 'Just play it for real,' and he took it from there." Adding that she liked a positive aggressiveness in young performers, she noted: "I look for sincerity and an intense willingness to learn."

On this as on other occasions late in life, Wyman went out of her way to pay tribute to Alfred Hitchcock, with whom she had done *Stage Fright* in 1950. She credited him with giving her some valuable tips on film acting. Associates recalled that he actually had paid her hardly any attention while devoting all his time to Dietrich and other personalities on the picture. Reportedly, he had not wanted her, and had taken her only because Warners executives had persuaded him that with her fresh Oscar laurels for *Belinda*, accorded only a few months before, she would perk-up a box office to which Dietrich could be expected to make but a weak contribution.

Knowing all this, as she must have, Wyman's generosity to Hitchcock is all the more striking. Asked about this once, she said, "I learn from everyone I work with, even if they don't realize it. I note and absorb."

On one of her last days on *The Mike Douglas Show*, Wyman said, "I don't think the heads of the motion picture industry would have had the nerve to ask me to do a nude scene," adding, with undisguised contempt, "You can't learn anything that way."

On that occasion (1970) she said that her two all-time favorite roles were in *Johnny Belinda* and *The Blue Veil*. She added that she loved character parts (implying, though, that she did not cherish them as an exclusive diet) and said that as of that time she had no plans to do a Broadway play or a movie.

Wyman said that Douglas was "charming" to work with, and she enjoyed such guests as comedian Bobby Wick, singer Bill Anderson, Mrs. Winthrop Rockefeller, actress Ann Blyth, opera singer Jan Peerce, her recent film co-star Bob Hope, and actress-producer Bonita Granville Wrather. More than one guest stated later that Wyman could have functioned excellently as sole hostess on a show of this type.

Wyman had a unique item on TV in *The Failing of Raymond* (1971). It was presented as an ABC-TV *Movie of the Weekend* from 8:30 to 10 P.M. In this, she co-starred with Dean Stockwell, who by then had tended to specialize increasingly in characters who were off the wall, in one way or the other.

*The Failing of Raymond* (TV Movie), 1971, with Dean Stockwell.

The screenplay was somewhat contrived, and the proceedings walked a tightrope between soap opera and melodramatics, functioning easily and naturally in neither category. The plot had to do with a pathological young man who returns ten years later to a school with the intention of compelling a teacher who had failed him in an exam to do it all over with him—conduct the exam, that is—or face the consequences.

Wyman and Stockwell tried to give the proceedings some depth via sharply drawn characterization, but it just didn't go over. *Daily Variety* called Wyman's performance in it "Highly credible," adding, "Her final moments in the film are even touching."

Among Wyman's TV appearances in the early 1970s was one for *Insight*, in which she and Gene Raymond played married thespians who, facing retirement, reminisced about their many years together. In the 1972 period she twice attempted to get a regular TV series as *Dr. Amanda Fallon* (also known as *Amanda Fallon*) and filmed two separate pilots for it, but it didn't take.

By 1974 she was telling a TV talk show host that she had decided, definitely, that her all time worst film was the 1941 *Bad Men of Missouri*. That year also found her in a telling segment on TV's *Owen Marshall*, in which she was the tippling mother of an army deserter. The segment was titled "The Desertion of Keith Ryder," and Wyman's son was played by Randolph Mantooth. She let her hair go white for this role. Also on hand was a Wyman romantic lead from thirty years before, a now grizzled and frail Regis Toomey.

With her career winding down as of 1975, Wyman gave an interview in which she stated: "I'm just not that ambitious anymore. I'm through clawing after parts. I've got other things going." Among these she mentioned her painting for an art gallery in Carmel, California, and "Of course, my entertaining. I have a new home in Pebble Beach, and I love to show it off and putter around in it to make it ever more beautiful and functional." Her children, of course, have been a constant, consuming passion.

Daughter Maureen, who has had, in her forty-five years, a haphazard career at best, told Tom Snyder

With fellow guest star Ronny Howard on NBC-TV's *The Bold Ones*, 1972.

With Shirley MacLaine and Dinah Shore on a TV talk show, 1978.

and a television audience in 1974 that when it came to adult career choices she had decided first on singing because "that was a field neither of my parents had done too much in." (This was a surprising remark, considering Wyman's many singing records and appearances in musical films.) Maureen held various other jobs until she decided to act, something she said she "had wanted to do since childhood, when I had a tiny role in a film with my mother [*It's a Great Feeling* (1949)]."

Of her younger years Maureen volunteered: "I went to school in New York and came home three times a year." She sounded on that occasion faintly bitter, albeit smilingly. Maureen then went on to try politics, without any special blessing from her father, the President, and got badly beaten in a Senate race in California. After that she worked with the White House staff. Among her duties was reaching women across the country disaffected by her father's opposition to ERA. She does not yet seem to have hit upon a career that would totally satisfy and fulfill her.

Her marital record has been every bit as bleak as her mother's—so far. At twenty (1961) she married a policeman, John Filippone. The marriage lasted a year. In 1964 she married David Sills. That marriage also ended in divorce. In 1981, at forty, she got involved, again like her mother had, with a younger man, Dennis Revell, twenty-eight, and married him. Law-clerk Revell had met Maureen at the Young Republican Club years before while her father was still governor of California. This seems to be her happiest union.

If Maureen has run an unsteady course, the emotional turmoil of her early life, when at age eight she found herself a child of divorce, and the pressures of being the daughter of two famous people, hence never knowing if she were valued for herself alone, may have been somewhat responsible.

Maureen's brother, the adopted Michael, now forty-one, tried a number of careers, starting as a sportsman, then going into business, then driving high-speed boats up and down the Pacific Coast. He claimed at times that he was used for his father's name in various business deals that didn't work out. Married and a father, he is the only one of the

With Dorothy McGuire in
*The Incredible Journey of
Dr. Meg Laurel* (TV, 1980).

President's children to give him grandchildren, at least so far.

Michael, according to Maureen, tended to feel somewhat estranged from his father because of the lack of blood ties, but his sister insisted that he had never been treated any differently because of it. The President and the First Lady countered rumors in 1984 that there was a rift with Michael by entertaining him and his family during the holidays. The President has recently gone out of his way to emphasize that Michael and his wife and children are very much a part of the Reagan family.

Wyman has said of her relations with her two children: "I was never a clinging mother. I like to believe my children are my friends; I think they are—all the more so because I leave them alone." Adding that they live their own lives, she said, "Self-sufficiency is as important in parents as in children."

Of Michael she has commented: "He's blood—that's how I think of him and that's how I treat him—as my very own."

The children of the first Reagan marriage have never been close to the children of his second, Patti and Ron. They live separate lives all down the line and are reported to feel indifference toward each other.

On TV's *Dinah!* in 1978, Wyman, on an Oscar-themed show, talked about the night in 1949 when she won the Academy Award. She said she hadn't expected to win "against so many heavyweights." When her name was called and she strode down the aisle, she remembered she was thinking: "Good Heavens, I haven't got a girdle on!"

In 1979 Wyman was seen on TV with Lindsay Wagner in *The Incredible Journey of Dr. Meg Laurel*, described by *The New York Times* as about "a young woman physician (Wagner) who goes to practice in darkest Appalachia in the 1920s." After putting down the histrionic efforts of Wagner, also known as *The Bionic Woman, The Times'* Tom Buckley wrote of Wyman: "Her gray hair beautifully coiffed, wearing stylish calicos and ginghams, and trying to hold tight to a hillbilly accent, [Wyman] plays the local healer with whom Miss Wagner comes in conflict."

On *The Love Boat* in early 1980, Wyman made a well praised TV appearance as a nun who meets a former flame (old Warner Brothers co-star Dennis Morgan) on a cruise, and is briefly tempted to relinquish the veil. Of her appearance here one reviewer commented, "Jane Wyman is now sixty-six years old, but there seems to be not the slightest diminishment of her formidable acting talents. True, one gets the feeling that if a role interests her sufficiently, and if she can empathize with it to her

satisfaction, she gives it more juice. She is pleasant enough as the nun in this, but one has the feeling that, despite her winningly professional rendition of the character, she didn't really think it amounted to much."

In November 1980 writers were commenting that the Wyman flag was going down the staff, and largely by her own choice. Some felt that since she would soon be sixty-seven, she had every right to put up her feet and take it easy—which no one, of course, really felt she would.

That same month, with 1981 only a few weeks away, Wyman was seen on a three-hour opening segment of the fifth season of *Charlie's Angels*. She appeared in the final hour as a psychic assigned to hunt kidnapped angel Cheryl Ladd.

*Daily Variety* carped: "The basic appeal of the show is that familiar old hypocritical formula, in the

On a *Loveboat* segment with Dennis Morgan, 1980.

best tradition of American Puritanism: give 'em plenty of titillation but keep it 'innocent' and do a little preaching from time to time. The show is a nonstop tease, both visually and dramatically. Lotsa flesh on view, but no actual nudity; lotsa horrible things are intimated, but not much is shown."

Another reviewer wrote of Wyman's performance as the psychic: "That a first-class actress such as this should have to bother not only with ludicrous plot situations but with ludicrously untalented, however pretty, people around her seems a desecration in artistic terms. It is time that this fine veteran with proven abilities of purest gold were given the material eminently due her."

Shortly Wyman would obtain the material that would assure fresh stardom.

# 9

## Falcon Crest: A New Beginning
## 1981–1986

The television series that was to bring Jane Wyman a career renaissance that was as unexpected as it was welcome debuted on CBS on December 4, 1981. It was originally called *The Vintage Years*, until somebody decided that the viewers would think it was about old people. Everyone involved was invited to think up new names. One production man joked about the names that came up—such as *Planet of the Grapes* and *Days of Wine and Roses* (a quickly rejected steal from an old Jack Lemmon film). Finally someone came up with the title *Falcon Crest*—and so it has remained through five successful TV seasons. Some of the readjustments prior to that December 4 debut were painful ones. Samantha Eggar, one of the originals on the pilot, was let go because her English accent sounded ridiculous in the California wine country setting—the Napa Valley, near San Francisco—where the show was set. Clu Gulager was next given the heave-ho for a similar reason—*his* accent sounded too crude and "southern." Then they hired a young actor to play a Mexican—and he turned out to be Puerto Rican. He, too, was shown the gate.

Wyman spent much of 1981 fretting over her lines—and her appearance. For the costly two-hour pilot show she sported a gray wig. That turned out to be a mistake—preview audiences laughed at it. Wyman proceeded to lay down the law: she was going back to her own dyed brown hair, like it or lump it.

Next, Jane began arguing about her character, Angela Channing. "After I told them I was plenty old enough [she was then sixty-seven] and had enough gray hair without putting on that dreadful wig," she told an interviewer, "I decided to do something about Angela. Not only was she too mean and vicious, but she was just plain boring. I wanted Angie to be an interesting character. She's a tough-as-nails businesswoman in every sense of the word—but the trouble with the pilot was that she was just too nasty. And the name of the show was so awful that we were desperate for ideas."

Wyman and writer Earl Hamner, who had done the successful TV series *The Waltons*, kept the midnight oil burning thinking up new lines, situations, and general ideas. "Jane was tough—but she was also creative, and vastly experienced," Hamner said later. "We didn't always agree on everything, but I respected her intelligent insights, and I understood where she was coming from."

While making the pilot Wyman told an interviewer: "Technically, TV is a million years ahead of what we had to deal with in the fifties. We sure have it better now. In the old days we had to do everything, including sweep out the place. And we didn't have dressing rooms like we do today. Everyone was crowded together. And in those early days we thought TV was the end of the world. And for some of us it was. But it was very good for me."

She added that she had no intention of letting Angela Channing become a sort of J. R. Ewing of the wine business: "I feel I'm representing all women in business. I may come off as a hard, tough character at first, but I want Angie to show she's also capable of love."

By the time the show debuted, Wyman and company had all the hatches battened down. The basic setting and situation was presented with precision and economy the first time out. Wyman as a Napa Valley wine tycoon, is determined to maintain her territory against all comers, including relatives. When her brother, who shares her acreage under an ancient familial legacy, is accidentally killed, she schemes with her Oriental servant to push the body into a car and send it hurtling over a cliff so it will look like he died while drunk-driving. This is to assure her surviving-sibling dominance under the rather complex terms of the will.

She primes the family for a proper but hasty burial. Her handsome, willful grandson, Lorenzo Lamas, is the heir on whom she dotes; her two daughters are respectively a vague-minded romantic and an alcoholic. To Falcon Crest come the dead man's heir, Robert Foxworth and his wife, Susan Sullivan, who, under the will, are entitled to the original property, which is only a small percentage of Angela's domain. Angela doesn't want them to move in on her (which they proceed to do) and she counters them at every turn. When Foxworth and Sullivan refuse to be bought out, it's covert and overt war on the property of Falcon Crest—a war that has been going on in various forms for five long years now, varying in intensity, in assorted strategies, but unrelenting in its overall purposes—Sullivan and Foxworth's purpose being to hang on, Wyman's to get them out.

The 1985/1986 season has seen numerous plot ramifications—violent deaths, the comings-and-goings of long-lost relatives, schemers of all persuasions, who have had their day. Celeste Holm almost burns Wyman out of her mansion; David Selby keeps trying to get the newspaper she controls in San Francisco; and meanwhile Wyman keeps trying to frustrate grandson Lance's romance with singer Apollonia (whom Wyman likes to dub *Babylonia*). Billy Moses finds himself caught between his wife, Ana Alicia, and the young lady who is bearing his child. Meanwhile Alicia is out to seduce a young priest, Ken Olin, who happens to be Angela's illegitimate grandson. And so on and so on. Though Angela uses all manner of mean tricks—influencing local politicians, telling Susan Sullivan, who has lost her memory, about her husband's previous infidelities— she has her own peculiar brand of integrity. She may be an unscrupulous businesswoman, but she fundamentally respects people who stand up to her.

In his original review of December 4, 1981, John

O'Connor in *The New York Times* wrote: "And so it goes, the standard stuff of soaps, with a crisis bubble bursting at least three times between commercial breaks . . . and at fadeout [Wyman] is meaningfully stroking a live falcon on the grounds of her estate. The stage is set for anything. Miss Wyman seems to be in remarkable control."

Meanwhile Wyman was dictating all aspects of the show. She selected her own wardrobe, telling an interviewer: "I like very sexy and very female clothes." She added, "I'm not a stranger in this business. I really don't want to get involved in all the production junk, but I do. I think everyone should. To get a good show, everything you've got must go into it, [but] you can't spread yourself too thin or everything suffers."

That first season Lorenzo Lamas's late father Fernando, a well-known film actor in his heyday, directed Wyman frequently. "Janie is a joy to direct," he told all comers. "She brings a positive approach to everything."

Some of the younger actors found disconcerting her attempts to tell them how to act. "Fun on the set takes a little finding," Billy Moses grouched that first year. "If Jane doesn't like what you're doing, she'll tell you right away. I rehearsed a scene with her one night and she directed me through the whole rehearsal—it's a little upsetting at first—you don't often have the other actor directing you."

Asked about her tendency to take over the younger performers' scenes and show them how it's done, Wyman in 1981 commented, "Poor dears. They never got the training and the discipline that we did in the old days. So someone has to fill in the gaps and help them. Also it's a practical matter; naturally I look better in a scene when the other performer is holding up his or her end."

One of her defenders said, "Jane has always wanted anything she acted in to be of top quality, and that's why she goes overboard to push the actors on *Falcon Crest*. When she comes on the set, everybody tries to keep her happy because she can really read the riot act. And she hates to go on location up north to the Napa Valley because she doesn't have the comforts she has at the studio. She calls it the wind country." The source added, "She's just not like the soft characters she used to play on the screen. She's become a strong, dominant personality."

Producer Aaron Spelling, who has closely monitored the progress of *Falcon Crest*, has said: "I had

With the *Falcon Crest* gang, 1984.

been wooing Jane back to full-scale television ever since she did *The Love Boat* for me. It was lucky for us that she sparked up when she first read the pilot script. I honestly believe that the lady has willed *Falcon Crest* into its long-run success. She watches everything; she is a perfectionist—about her own work and the work of others—but that perfectionism has kept that show bright as a new penny, and sharp as a tack."

Others felt that Wyman was so desperately anxious to succeed as a major TV star in a long-running major show because she was annoyed and frustrated with the spectacle of Ronnie and Nancy in the White House, with all the accompanying attention blitz they were getting. While having no regrets about originally short-circuiting a life with him she had found boring and enervating, she still wanted some

part of the spotlight for herself—and in *Falcon Crest*, for five years, she has found it.

With each season her pay per episode has gone up—from $25,000 to $50,000 to $100,000. The latest estimate has her making three million dollars a year. "And she was never poor to begin with," a friend has said. "She was already worth millions from all her lucrative film and television deals over the decades. It's not really more money she wants—though she realizes that good pay is linked with prestige—it's her share of the limelight, a share she feels she has earned through fifty years of hard work." Cheering her on has been daughter Maureen, who told one interviewer that she felt it was good for her mother to be engaged in stimulating work, and at seventy-two yet, that has also brought her the rewards of major public notice.

Relaxing between scenes on *Falcon Crest*, 1984.

Many have had cause to wonder what President Ronald Reagan and First Lady Nancy Reagan have thought, over the past five years, about Wyman's wide-flung media fame. They tend to keep one-hundred-percent mum on the subject, but one observer has commented: "I think Ron is glad for her—he knows it keeps her busy and that the renewed fame brings her satisfaction. As for Nancy, she would be less than human if she didn't find the shadow of that first wife a little disconcertingly competitive—especially when that shadow is flickering brightly on Friday nights on telescreens all over the nation."

One element in Wife Number One that Ronald Reagan undoubtedly does respect is her often reiterated: "Mr. Reagan and I remain good friends. I wish him all the best; I just do not discuss our marriage because I think it is poor taste to talk about former husbands and wives. After all, it was so long ago—thirty-eight years."

Wyman is known to transfix with a glare any brash reporter who dares to bring up the Reagan marriage, and she, more often than not, will simply turn on her heel and walk straight away. Or, if she fundamentally likes the interviewer and does not wish to be too abrasive when such questions come up, she will simply switch the subject. She will discuss her painting, which became a passion with her in the years when she was not so active as a player.

"I'd first taken up painting," she said, "when we were doing *Johnny Belinda* on up the coast of Mendocino. I signed up with a gallery, and that takes a lot of work, and it's lonely work. I've always painted, still do when I find any spare time, which is little enough, but I really did it for my own amusement. When you get into gallery work, it becomes very demanding and it's just as tedious as making a good movie or TV show. It's absolute concentration. I sold my paintings for 350 or 400 dollars each, which paid for my equipment and supplies. I am very realistic in my style. I love colors, so I do a lot of reflective things. The barns, the farms, the trees reflected in pools. And I only do small paintings because I use a double-aught brush, so you can imagine how long that takes to do. They're not miniatures but small, comfortable paintings that you can group on a wall. There's always room for one more small painting."

The last time she was asked the eternal question about acquiring another husband, she got fiercely impatient. "I haven't got the time to get married," she snapped. "When you come right down to it, I'm just not interested in marrying, not at my state in life!" She added: "I've tried to rid myself of everything that would take my attention away from the show."

Though she lives alone in a Santa Monica condominium (with top security and duly sensible secretiveness about the exact address), she even gave away her only companion a while back—a little dog—to her veterinarian. Her reason? "I couldn't give him the time he needed, and I knew I'd worry more about him than my job. And that job's a very fast business, honey. It's ticker tape. Once it's gone, it's gone."

Wyman gets mad when a reporter dares mention the convention stickers and other democratic media badges and whatnot displayed during the 1984 convention that stated: "Jane Wyman Was Right!" "That's utter, tasteless distortion, and moreover disrespectful to the leader of our country!" she is said to have rejoindered. Nor did she relish such items as Jack O'Brian's in his *Voice of Broadway*: "Jane Wyman's TV series, *Falcon Crest*, pays Miss Pertnose per year more than three times ex-hubby Ron Reagan's most important job in the world." (As of 1986, Wyman is getting *ten* times what Reagan is paid.)

There have been numerous comings and goings on the *Falcon Crest* casting roster over the past five years. Wyman got along well with Mel Ferrer, who played her lawyer for a while, but a year or two ago he was let go, right after playing groom to her bride in an elaborately staged wedding—followed by a "plane crash" in which Ferrer's character and Cliff Robertson's were killed off. "Mel and Cliff were felt to be too old for the image the producers wanted to convey on the show" went the party line on this. Ferrer was promptly replaced as Wyman's lawyer by the much younger Simon McCorkindale—who did *not*, however, succeed as romancer to Wyman's Angela. "After all, there are limits!" Wyman is reported to have snorted. Since Ferrer's departure her character has remained largely romanceless.

If reports are to be believed, Wyman has never gotten on well with such guest stars as Celeste Holm, Gina Lollobrigida—and especially Lana Turner. The tabloids a while back had a field day whipping up a nasty feud between Wyman and Turner for the short time the latter worked on the show. "While some of it might have been silly hype, the 'where there's smoke there's fire' saying does apply," one associate remarked.

According to one crew member: "You could cut the tension with a knife on that set. Lana had been

Jane Wyman, 1984.

hired because they felt the show's super ratings would go through the roof due to her legendary movie fame. But Jane got mad when Lana was tendered flowers the first day. 'I didn't get flowers my first day,' [Wyman is said to have fumed.] 'Why should *she*?'" Wyman also had reservations about Turner's acting skills, which she considered rusty at best. Turner was chronically late, and muffed her lines so often that she drove Wyman up the wall.

Turner also arrived with full entourage, including a secretary, hairdresser, and wardrobe person. She kept aloof in her dressing room, while Wyman enjoyed playing quick poker games with the crew. Terrified by her unaccustomed television exposure, Turner demanded a closed set; in her dressing room she worried over her looks (she was then sixty-two) and fussed endlessly with her makeup, hair, and costumes.

As one crew member recalled: "Jane was embarrassed, then infuriated by all this amateurish prima donnaism. The bad blood showed when the actresses had a scene together. The episode demanded a confrontational spat. Everyone could see that they weren't acting." The episode was two days over schedule because of Turner's inexperience with TV and fussy nervousness. The production staff and Wyman expressed obvious relief when Turner departed after completing her stint.

Through 1986 Wyman's Angela has survived attempted traffic murders, kidnappings, even an attempted eviction from her cherished mansion due to the machinations of a malicious rival, and numerous other vicissitudes. Clearly she is a survivor, on camera and off. She has been the recipient of numerous honors for her work on the series. When she goes on a talk show, as she does from time to time, she refuses to talk of her personal life past or present and spends all her time talking about the show—and only the show.

Publishers into 1986 are still pestering Wyman to write an autobiography, stressing (of course) her memories of Ronald Reagan, but her answer is always a firm, icy *no*.

She goes home to her condominium each night "and I close the door and put my feet up and relax." She claims, at seventy-two, that she is not lonely,

that there are always good friends like Barbara Stanwyck and Loretta Young to gab with on the phone. Her philosophy, as of 1986, seems to be essentially that it is better to be alone, with peace of mind, with the freedom to do what one wants without accounting to anyone, than to put up with the stresses and strains of the much vaunted "togetherness" that the romantics tout. "*That's* for younger people," is her terse comment.

Still she sees to it that she has some onscreen romancing of a kind. Cesar Romero, now white-haired and in his late seventies, gave Wyman quite a whirl for a while on *Falcon Crest* during the current season. He plays a fabulously rich titan who helps her save Falcon Crest from Celeste Holm, but at a price. He won't give her the shares he took from her rival until she agrees to marry him. The independent-minded Angela fends him off again and again, leading him a pretty chase while her sardonic lawyer, Simon McCorkindale, looks on in amusement.

Romero used to be one of Wyman's dates between marital bouts, back thirty-odd years ago. He represents a sentimental icon out of her past, and she expressly asked for him to be one of her leading men—for a time. Romero is a lifelong confirmed bachelor who lives with his sister, but his footloose and fancy-free status had always appealed to such "grasswidows" as the late Joan Crawford, who found him an ever-ready escort for numerous social events.

Wyman and Romero make a kinetic team, but of course nothing will really happen between them—onscreen or off. Wyman won't allow it—and Angela won't allow it. Wyman and/or Angela has had all that. She's been to hell and back. She's seen them all come and go. It's been fifty-four long years since the shy little chorine was edged into a lineup by brotherly LeRoy Prinz. Now she's a superstar who doesn't have to take any nonsense from anybody—and she doesn't. Jane Wyman started off alone in that grim Victorian house in Saint Joseph, Missouri, and she's used to aloneness by now. For her, even into her eighth decade, aloneness has its uses. She can be her own woman, first, last, and always. And who has earned the right more than she?

# Jane Wyman's Films

1. *The Kid From Spain.* 1932. Samuel Goldwyn–United Artists. Cast: Eddie Cantor, Lyda Roberti, Robert Young, John Miljan, Ruth Hall, Noah Beery, J. Carrol Naish, Betty Grable, Paulette Goddard, Toby Wing, Jane Wyman (in the chorus). Directed by Leo McCarey. Screenplay by William Anthony McGuire, Bert Kalmar, and Harry Ruby. Based on their story.
2. *Elmer the Great.* 1933. Warners. Cast: Joe E. Brown, Patricia Ellis, Claire Dodd, Sterling Holloway, Emma Dunn, Jessie Ralph, J. Carrol Naish, Douglas Dumbrille, Jane Wyman (in a bit role). Directed by Mervyn LeRoy. Screenplay by Tom Geraghty. Based on the play by Ring Lardner and George M. Cohan.
3. *College Rhythm.* 1934. Paramount. Cast: Lanny Ross, Joe Penner, Jack Oakie, Lyda Roberti, Helen Mack, Mary Brian, Franklin Pangborn, Jane Wyman (in the chorus). Directed by Norman Taurog. Screenplay by Walter DeLeon, John McDermott, and Francis Martin. Music and lyrics by Mack Gordon and Harry Revel.
4. *Rumba.* 1935. Paramount. Cast: Carole Lombard, George Raft, Margo, Gail Patrick, Lynn Overman, Iris Adrian, Akim Tamiroff, Samuel S. Hinds, Jane Wyman (in the chorus). Directed by Marion Gering. Screenplay by Howard J. Green. Adapted from a story by Guy Endore and Seena Owen.
5. *All the King's Horses.* 1935. Paramount. Cast: Carl Brisson, Mary Ellis, Edward Everett Horton, Katherine DeMille, Eugene Pallette, Jane Wyman (in the chorus). Directed by Frank Tuttle. Screenplay and adaptation by Frank Tuttle and Frederick Stephani from a play by Lawrence Clark and Max Giersberg, and a musical comedy by Frederick Herendeen and Edward Horan.
6. *Stolen Harmony.* 1935. Paramount. Cast: George Raft, Ben Bernie, Grace Bradley, Iris Adrian, Lloyd Nolan, Gooddee Montgomery, Leslie Fenton, William Cagney, Jane Wyman. Directed by Alfred Werker. Screenplay by Leon Gordon, Harry Ruskin, Claude Binyon, and Lewis Foster. Based on a story by Gordon.
7. *King of Burlesque.* 1935. Twentieth Century-Fox. Cast: Warner Baxter, Alice Faye, Jack Oakie, Gregory Ratoff, Mona Barrie, Fats Waller, Dixie Dunbar, Nick Long, Jr., Keye Luke, Jane Wyman. Directed by Sidney Lanfield. Screenplay by Gene Markey and Harry Tugend. Adapted by James Seymour from a story by Vina Delmar.
8. *My Man Godfrey.* 1936. Universal. Cast: William Powell, Carole Lombard, Alice Brady, Gail Patrick, Jean Dixon, Eugene Pallette, Alan Mowbray, Mischa Auer, Grady Sutton, Jane Wyman (in a bit later cut). Directed by Gregory LaCava. Screenplay by Eric Hatch and Morrie Ryskind. Based on Hatch's novel.
9. *Stage Struck.* 1936. Warners. Cast: Dick Powell, Joan Blondell, Warren William, Frank McHugh, Craig Reynolds, Carol Hughes, Jeanne Madden, Spring Byington, Jane Wyman (in the chorus). Directed by Busby Berkeley. Screenplay by Tom Buckingham and Pat C. Flick. Based on a story by Robert Lord.
10. *Cain and Mabel.* 1936. Warners. Cast: Marion Davies, Clark Gable, Ruth Donnelly, Allen Jenkins, David Carlyle, Walter Catlett, Hobart Cavanaugh, Pert Kelton, E. E. Clive, Joseph Crehan, William Collier, Jane Wyman. Directed by Lloyd Bacon. Screenplay by Laird Doyle. From a story by H. C. Witwer.
11. *Polo Joe.* 1936. Warners. Cast: Joe E. Brown, Richard (Skeets) Gallagher, Gordon Elliott, Fay Holden, Joseph King, George E. Stone, Jane Wyman. Directed by William McGann. Original screenplay by Hugh Cummings and Peter Milne.
12. *Smart Blonde.* 1936. Warners. Cast: Glenda Farrell, Barton MacLane, Craig Reynolds, Winifred Shaw,

Addison Richards, Jane Wyman, Charlotte Winters. Directed by Frank McDonald. Screenplay by Don Ryan and Kenneth Gamet. From a story by Frederick Nebel.

13. *Gold Diggers of 1937*. 1936. Warners. Cast: Dick Powell, Joan Blondell, Glenda Farrell, Victor Moore, Osgood Perkins, Lee Dixon, Irene Ware, Charles D. Brown, Rosalind Marquis, Jane Wyman. Directed by Lloyd Bacon. Screenplay by Warren Duff. Based on the play by Richard Maibaum, George Haight, and Michael Wallach.

14. *The King and the Chorus Girl*. 1937. Warners. Cast: Fernand Gravet, Joan Blondell, Edward Everett Horton, Alan Mowbray, Jane Wyman, Mary Nash, Kenny Baker, Luis Alberni, Ben Welden, Lionel Pape. Directed by Mervyn LeRoy. Screenplay by Norman Krasna and Groucho Marx, based on their story.

15. *Ready, Willing and Able*. 1937. Warners. Cast: Ruby Keeler, Allen Jenkins, Lee Dixon, Louise Fazenda, Ross Alexander, Carol Hughes, Winifred Shaw, Teddy Holt, Jane Wyman. Directed by Ray Enright. Screenplay by Jerry Wald, Sig Herzig, and Warren Duff. From a story by Richard Macaulay.

16. *Slim*. 1937. Warners. Cast: Pat O'Brien, Henry Fonda, Margaret Lindsay, Stuart Erwin, J. Farrell MacDonald, Dick Purcell, John Litel, Joseph Sawyer, Jane Wyman. Directed by Ray Enright. Screenplay by William Wister Haines, from his original story.

17. *The Singing Marine*. 1937. Warners. Cast: Dick Powell, Doris Weston, Lee Dixon, Hugh Herbert, Allen Jenkins, Jane Darwell, Guinn Williams, Jane Wyman, Veda Ann Borg, Berton Churchill. Directed by Ray Enright. Screenplay by Delmer Daves.

18. *Mr. Dodd Takes the Air*. 1937. Warners. Cast: Kenny Baker, Jane Wyman, Alice Brady, Henry O'Neill, Frank McHugh, Ferris Taylor, Gertrude Michael, Harry Davenport, John Eldridge. Directed by Alfred E. Green. Screenplay by William Wister Haines and Elaine Ryan. Based on a story by Clarence Budington Kelland.

19. *Public Wedding*. 1937. Warners. Cast: Jane Wyman, William Hopper, Marie Wilson, Dick Purcell, Raymond Hatton, Veda Ann Borg, James Robbins, Berton Churchill. Directed by Nick Grinde. Original screenplay by Ray Chanslor and Houston Branch.

20. *The Spy Ring*. 1938. Universal. Cast: Jane Wyman, William Hall, Leon Ames, Jane Carleton, Ben Alexander, Don Barclay, Robert Warwick, Paul Sutton, Jack Mulhall. Directed by Joseph H. Lewis.

21. *Fools for Scandal*. 1938. Warners. Cast: Carole Lombard, Fernand Gravet, Ralph Bellamy, Allen Jenkins, Isabel Jeans, Tempe Piggott, Marie Wilson, Jane Wyman. Directed by Mervyn LeRoy. Screenplay by Herbert and Joseph Fields. Based on a play by Nancy Hamilton.

22. *He Couldn't Say No*. 1938. Warners. Cast: Frank McHugh, Jane Wyman, Diana Lewis, Cora Witherspoon, Berton Churchill. Directed by Lewis Seiler. Screenplay by Robertson White, Joseph Schrank, and Ben Grauman Kohn. Based on a story by Norman Matson.

23. *Wide Open Faces*. 1938. Columbia. Cast: Joe E. Brown, Jane Wyman, Lyda Roberti, Alison Skipworth, Lucien Littlefield, Alan Baxter, Sidney Toler, Berton Churchill, Barbara Pepper. Directed by Kurt Neumann.

24. *The Crowd Roars*. 1938. MGM. Cast: Robert Taylor, Maureen O'Sullivan, Edward Arnold, Frank Morgan, Jane Wyman, William Gargan, Nat Pendleton, Lionel Stander, Isabel Jewell, Gene Reynolds. Directed by Richard Thorpe. Screenplay by Thomas Lernon, George Bruce, and George Oppenheimer. From an original story by George Bruce.

25. *Brother Rat*. 1938. Warners. Cast: Wayne Morris, Priscilla Lane, Jane Bryan, Eddie Albert, Ronald Reagan, Jane Wyman, Johnnie Davis, Henry O'Neill, Louise Beavers, Gordon Oliver. Directed by William Keighley. Screenplay by Richard Macaulay and Jerry Wald. Based on a play by John Monks, Jr., and Fred Finklehoffe.

26. *Tailspin*. 1939. Twentieth Century-Fox. Cast: Constance Bennett, Nancy Kelly, Alice Faye, Jane Wyman, Joan Davis, Charlies Farrell, Kane Richmond, Wally Vernon, Irving Bacon, Joan Valerie. Directed by Roy Del Ruth. Original screenplay by Frank Wead.

27. *The Kid From Kokomo*. 1939. Warners. Cast: Pat O'Brien, Wayne Morris, Joan Blondell, Jane Wyman, May Robson, Maxie Rosenbloom, Stanley Fields, Ward Bond, Sidney Toler, Paul Hurst. Directed by Lewis Seiler. Screenplay by Jerry Wald and Richard Macaulay. From a story by Dalton Trumbo.

28. *Torchy Plays With Dynamite*. 1939. Warners. Cast: Jane Wyman, Allen Jenkins, Tom Kennedy, Shelia Bromley, Joe Cunningham, Edgar Dearing, Eddie Marr, Frank Shannon. Directed by Noel Smith. Screenplay by Earle Snell and Charles Belden. From a story by Scott Littleton. Based on characters originally created by Frederick Nebel.

29. *Private Detective*. 1939. Warners. Cast: Jane Wyman, Dick Foran, Gloria Dickson, Maxie Rosenbloom, John Ridgely, Morgan Conway. Directed by Noel Smith. Based on a story by Kay Krausse. Screenplay by Earl Snell and Raymond Schrock.

30. *Kid Nightingale*. 1939. Warners. Cast: John Payne, Jane Wyman, Walter Catlett, Edward Brophy, Charles H. Brown, Max Hoffman, Helen Troy. Screenplay by Charles Belden and Raymond Schrock. Based on a story by Lee Katz.

31. *Brother Rat and a Baby*. 1940. Warners. Cast: Priscilla Lane, Wayne Morris, Eddie Albert, Jane Wyman, Ronald Reagan, Jane Bryan, Moroni Olsen, Nana

Bryant, Arthur Treacher. Directed by Ray Enright. Original screenplay by John Monks, Jr., and Fred Finklehoffe.

32. *An Angel From Texas.* 1940. Warners. Cast: Eddie Albert, Rosemary Lane, Wayne Morris, Ronald Reagan, Jane Wyman, Ruth Terry, John Litel, Ann Shoemaker. Directed by Ray Enright. Screenplay by Fred Niblo, Jr., and Bertram Millhauser. Based on a play by George S. Kaufman.

33. *Flight Angels.* 1940. Warners. Cast: Virginia Bruce, Jane Wyman, Dennis Morgan, Wayne Morris, Ralph Bellamy, John Litel, Margot Stephenson, Jan Clayton, De Wolf Hopper, Dorothea Kent. Directed by Lewis Seiler. Screenplay by Maurice Leo. Based on a story by Richard Macaulay and Jerry Wald.

34. *My Love Came Back.* 1940. Warners. Cast: Olivia De Havilland, Eddie Albert, Jane Wyman, Jeffrey Lynn, Charles Winninger, William Orr, Spring Byington, S. Z. Sakall, Ann Gillis. Directed by Curtis Bernhardt. Screenplay by Ivan Goff, Robert H. Buckner, and Earl Baldwin. From a story by Walter Reisch.

35. *Gambling on the High Seas.* 1940. Warners. Cast: Wayne Morris, Jane Wyman, Roger Pryor, Gilbert Roland, John Litel. Directed by George Amy. Screenplay by Robert E. Kent. Based on a story by Martin Mooney.

36. *Tugboat Annie Sails Again.* 1940. Warners. Cast: Marjorie Rambeau, Ronald Reagan, Jane Wyman, Paul Hurst, Charles Hatton, Chill Wills. Directed by Lewis Seiler. Screenplay by Walter De Leon. Based on characters created by Norman Reilly Raine.

37. *Honeymoon for Three.* 1941. Warners. Cast: Ann Sheridan, George Brent, Jane Wyman, Charles Ruggles, Osa Massen, William Orr, Johnny Downs, Walter Catlett, Lee Patrick. Directed by Lloyd Bacon. Screenplay by Julius and Philip Epstein. Based on a play by Allan Scott and George Haight.

38. *Bad Men of Missouri.* 1941. Warners. Cast: Dennis Morgan, Jane Wyman, Wayne Morris, Arthur Kennedy, Victor Jory, Alan Baxter, Walter Catlett, Howard da Silva, Virginia Brissac, Faye Emerson. Directed by Ray Enright. Screenplay by Charles Grayson. Based on a story by Robert E. Kent.

39. *The Body Disappears.* 1941. Warners. Cast: Jane Wyman, Jeffrey Lynn, Edward Everett Horton, Marguerite Chapman, David Bruce, Willie Best, Ivan Simpson. Directed by Ross Lederman. Original screenplay by Erna Lazarus and Scott Darling.

40. *You're in the Army Now.* 1941. Warners. Cast: Jimmy Durante, Phil Silvers, Jane Wyman, Regis Toomey, Donald MacBride, George Meeker, William Haade, Joseph Sawyer. Directed by Lewis Seiler. Screenplay by Paul Gerard Smith and George Beatty.

41. *Larceny, Inc.* 1942. Warners. Cast: Edward G. Robin-
son, Jane Wyman, Jack Carson, Broderick Crawford, Edward Brophy, Anthony Quinn, John Qualen, Harry Davenport, Grant Mitchell, Jackie Gleason. Directed by Lloyd Bacon. Screenplay by Everett Freeman and Edwin Gilbert. Based on a play by S. J. Perelman.

42. *My Favorite Spy.* 1942. RKO. Cast: Kay Kyser, Jane Wyman, Ellen Drew, Robert Armstrong, Helen Westley, William Demarest, Moroni Olsen, Una O'Connor, Hobart Cavanaugh, George Cleveland. Directed by Tay Garnett. Screenplay by Sig Herzig and William Bowers. Based on a story by M. Coates Webster.

43. *Footlight Serenade.* 1942. Twentieth Century-Fox. Cast: John Payne, Betty Grable, Victor Mature, Jane Wyman, Phil Silvers, James Gleason, June Lang, Cobina Wright, Jr., Manton Moreland. Directed by Gregory Ratoff. Screenplay by Robert Ellis, Helen Logan, and Lynn Starling. Based on a story by Fidel LaBarba and Kenneth Earl.

44. *Princess O'Rourke.* 1943. Warners. Cast: Olivia De Havilland, Robert Cummings, Jack Carson, Jane Wyman, Charles Coburn, Gladys Cooper, Minor Watson, Harry Davenport. Directed by Norman Krasna, from his original screenplay.

45. *Make Your Own Bed.* 1944. Warners. Cast: Jane Wyman, Jack Carson, Irene Manning, Alan Hale, Tala Birell, George Tobias, Ricardo Cortez, Robert Shayne. Directed by Peter Godfrey. Original screenplay by Francis Swann and Edmund Joseph.

46. *Crime by Night.* 1944. Warners. Cast: Jane Wyman, Jerome Cowan, Eleanor Parker, Faye Emerson, Stuart Crawford, Charles Lang, Cy Kendall. Directed by William Clemens. Screenplay by Joel Malone and Richard Weil. From a story by Geoffrey Homes.

47. *The Doughgirls.* 1944. Warners. Cast: Ann Sheridan, Alexis Smith, Jack Carson, Jane Wyman, Irene Manning, Charles Ruggles, Eve Arden, Alan Mowbray, Regis Toomey, Craig Stevens. Directed by James V. Kern. Screenplay by James V. Kern and Sam Hellman, with additional material by Wilkie Mahoney.

48. *Hollywood Canteen.* 1944. Warners. Cast: All-Star, including Bette Davis, Joan Crawford, Barbara Stanwyck, Jane Wyman, Ida Lupino, John Garfield, Joe E. Brown, Dennis Morgan, Eddie Cantor, Jack Benny, and Jack Carson. Directed by Delmer Daves. Screenplay (interspersed with songs and skits) by Delmer Daves.

49. *The Lost Weekend.* 1945. Paramount. Cast: Ray Milland, Jane Wyman, Phillip Terry, Howard da Silva, Doris Dowling, Frank Faylen, Mary Young, Lillian Fontaine. Directed by Billy Wilder. Screenplay by Charles Brackett and Billy Wilder. From the Charles Jackson novel.

50. *One More Tomorrow.* 1946. Warners. Cast: Dennis Morgan, Ann Sheridan, Jane Wyman, Alexis Smith, Jack Green, John Loder, Reginald Gardiner, Sig Arno,

Thurston Hall. Directed by Peter Godfrey. Screenplay by Catherine Turney and Charles Hoffman. From the play by Philip Barry.

51. *Night and Day.* 1946. Warners. Cast: Cary Grant, Alexis Smith, Jane Wyman, Monty Woolley, Eve Arden, Victor Francen, Dorothy Malone, Alan Hale, Mary Martin, Ginny Simms. Directed by Michael Curtiz. Original screenplay by Jack Moffitt, Leo Townsend, William Bowers, and Charles Hoffman.

52. *The Yearling.* 1946. MGM. Cast: Gregory Peck, Jane Wyman, Claude Jarman, Jr., Chill Wills, Margaret Wycherly, Clem Bevans, Henry Travers, Forrest Tucker, Don Gift. Directed by Clarence Brown. Screenplay by Paul Osborn. Based on the novel by Marjorie Kinnan Rawlings.

53. *Cheyenne.* 1947. Warners. Cast: Jane Wyman, Dennis Morgan, Bruce Bennett, Janis Paige, Arthur Kennedy, Alan Hale, Barton MacLane, John Ridgely, Tom Tyler. Directed by Raoul Walsh. Screenplay by Alan Le May and Thames Williamson. From a story by Paul I. Wellman.

54. *Magic Town.* 1947. RKO. Cast: James Stewart, Jane Wyman, Kent Smith, Regis Toomey, Ned Sparks, Ann Doran, Wallace Ford, Ann Shoemaker, Donald Meek. Directed by William A. Wellman. Original screenplay by Robert Riskin and Joseph Krumgold.

55. *Johnny Belinda.* 1948. Warners. Cast: Jane Wyman, Lew Ayres, Charles Bickford, Agnes Moorehead, Stephen McNally, Jan Sterling, Rosalind Ivan, Barbara Bates, Creighton Hale, Holmes Herbert. Directed by Jean Negulesco. Screenplay by Irmgard Von Cube and Allen Vincent. Based on the play by Elmer Harris.

56. *A Kiss in the Dark.* 1949. Warners. Cast: Jane Wyman, David Niven, Wayne Morris, Victor Moore, Broderick Crawford, Maria Ouspenskaya. Directed by Delmer Daves. Original screenplay by Harry Kurnitz.

57. *The Lady Takes a Sailor.* 1949. Warners. Cast: Jane Wyman, Dennis Morgan, Eve Arden, Allyn Joslyn, Robert Douglas, Fred Clark, Tom Tully, Craig Stevens, William Frawley. Directed by Michael Curtiz. Screenplay by Everett Freeman. From a story by Jerry Gruskin.

58. *It's a Great Feeling.* 1949. Warners. Cast: Dennis Morgan, Jane Wyman, Joan Crawford, Gary Cooper, Doris Day, Jack Carson, Edward G. Robinson, Patricia Neal. Directed by David Butler. Screenplay by Jack Rose and Melville Shavelson. From an original story by I.A.L. Diamond.

59. *Stage Fright.* 1950. Warners. Cast: Jane Wyman, Marlene Dietrich, Michael Wilding, Richard Todd, Alastair Sim, Kay Walsh, Sybil Thorndike, Joyce Grenfell. Directed by Alfred Hitchcock. Screenplay by Whitfield Cook. Adapted by Alma Reville with additional dialogue by James Bridie.

60. *The Glass Menagerie.* 1950. Warners. Cast: Jane Wyman, Kirk Douglas, Gertrude Lawrence, Arthur Kennedy, Louise Lorrimer, Ann Tyrell, Ralph Sanford. Directed by Irving Rapper. Screenplay by Tennessee Williams and Peter Berneis. From the play by Tennessee Williams.

61. *Three Guys Named Mike.* 1951. MGM. Cast: Jane Wyman, Van Johnson, Barry Sullivan, Howard Keel, Phyllis Kirk, Anne Sargent, Robert Sherwood, Jeff Donnell, Barbara Billingsley. Directed by Charles Walters. Screenplay by Sidney Sheldon. From a story by Ruth Brooks Flippen.

62. *Here Comes the Groom.* 1951. Paramount. Cast: Bing Crosby, Jane Wyman, Franchot Tone, Alexis Smith, James Barton, Connie Gilchrist, Robert Keith, Anna Maria Alberghetti. Directed by Frank Capra. Screenplay by Virginia Van Upp, Liam O'Brien, and Myles Connolly. From a story by Robert Riskin and Liam O'Brien.

63. *The Blue Veil.* 1951. RKO. Cast: Jane Wyman, Charles Laughton, Richard Carlson, Joan Blondell, Don Taylor, Cyril Cusack, Audrey Totter, Henry Morgan, Everett Sloane, Vivian Vance, Natalie Wood. Directed by Curtis Bernhardt. Screenplay by Norman Corwin. From a story by Francois Campaux.

64. *Starlift.* 1951. Warners. Cast: Jane Wyman, James Cagney, Gary Cooper, Janice Rule, Dick Wesson, Frank Lovejoy, Virginia Mayo, Randolph Scott, Doris Day, Ruth Roman. Directed by Ron Del Ruth. Orginal screenplay by John Klorer and Karl Kamb.

65. *The Will Rogers Story.* 1952. Warners. Cast: Will Rogers, Jr., Jane Wyman, James Gleason, Carl Benton Reid, Eve Miller, Slim Pickens, Noah Beery, Jr. Directed by Michael Curtiz. Screenplay by Frank Davis and Stanley Roberts. Based on the life of Will Rogers.

66. *Just for You.* 1952. Paramount. Cast: Bing Crosby, Jane Wyman, Ethel Barrymore, Robert Arthur, Natalie Wood, Regis Toomey, Cora Witherspoon, Leon Tyler. Directed by Elliott Nugent. Screenplay by Robert Carson. Based on Stephen Vincent Benet's story *Famous.*

67. *Let's Do It Again.* 1953. Columbia. Cast: Jane Wyman, Ray Milland, Aldo Ray, Valerie Bettis, Mary Treen, Tom Helmore. Directed by Alexander Hall. Screenplay by Mary Anita Loos and Richard Sale. Based on a play by Arthur Richman.

68. *So Big.* 1953. Warners. Cast: Jane Wyman, Sterling Hayden, Nancy Olsen, Steve Forrest, Martha Hyer, Elizabeth Fraser, Walter Coy, Richard Blymer, Roland Winters. Directed by Robert Wise. Screenplay by John Twist. Based on the novel by Edna Ferber.

69. *Magnificent Obsession.* 1954. Universal. Cast: Jane Wyman, Rock Hudson, Agnes Moorehead, Otto Kruger, Barbara Rush, Gregg Palmer, Paul Cavanaugh, Mae Clarke. Directed by Douglas Sirk. Screenplay by Robert Blees. From the novel by Lloyd C. Douglas.

70. *Lucy Gallant.* 1955. Paramount. Cast: Jane Wyman, Charlton Heston, Claire Trevor, Thelma Ritter, Wallace Ford, William Demarest, Tom Helmore, Gloria Talbot. Directed by Robert Parrish. Screenplay by John Lee Mahin. Based on the novel by Margaret Cousins.

71. *All That Heaven Allows.* 1955. Universal. Cast: Jane Wyman, Rock Hudson, Agnes Moorehead, Virginia Grey, Charles Drake, Conrad Nagel, William Reynolds, Gloria Talbot, Merry Anders. Directed by Douglas Sirk. Screenplay by Peg Fenwick. From a story by Edna Lee and Harry Lee.

72. *Miracle in the Rain.* 1956. Warners. Cast: Jane Wyman, Van Johnson, Eileen Heckart, William Gargan, Josephine Hutchinson, Peggie Castle, Fred Clark, Barbara Nichols, Minerva Urecal. Directed by Rudolph Maté. Screenplay by Ben Hecht from his original story.

73. *Holiday for Lovers.* 1959. Twentieth Century-Fox. Cast: Clifton Webb, Jane Wyman, Jill St. John, Carol Lynley, Paul Henreid, Gary Crosby, Jose Greco. Directed by Henry Levin. Screenplay by Luther Davis. Based on the play by Ronald Alexander.

74. *Pollyanna.* 1960. Buena Vista. Cast: Jane Wyman, Hayley Mills, Richard Egan, Karl Malden, Nancy Olsen, James Drury, Donald Crisp, Adolphe Menjou. Directed by David Swift. Screenplay by David Swift. Based on the novel by Eleanor H. Porter.

75. *Bon Voyage.* 1962. Buena Vista. Cast: Fred MacMurray, Jane Wyman, Deborah Walley, Mickey Callan, Kevin Corcoran, Tommy Kirk, Jessie Royce Landis. Directed by James Neilson. Screenplay by Bill Walsh. Based on the book by Marrijane and Joseph Hayes.

76. *How To Commit Marriage.* 1969. Cinerama. Cast: Bob Hope, Jane Wyman, Jackie Gleason, Tina Louise, Maureen Arthur, Leslie Nielsen, Paul Stewart, Tim Matheson. Directed by Norman Panama. Story and screenplay by Ben Starr and Michael Kanin.

# Index

**Numbers in italics refer to illustrations. Jane Wyman is pictured in every photograph in the book.**

213